Dunsfold

Surrey's Most Secret Airfield

1942 - 1992

by

Paul McCue

Air Research Publications

First published 1992 by
Air Research Publications
34 Elm Road, New Malden,
Surrey, KT3 3HD,
England.

Printed in Great Britain by
MBA Ltd, London N17

ISBN 1 871187 12 5

Contents

Bibliography

'A BRIDGE TOO FAR' by Cornelius Ryan (Hamish Hamilton Ltd. 1974).

'ACTION STATIONS 9' by R. C. B. Ashworth (Patrick Stephens Ltd. 1985).

'BAe HAWK' by Arthur Reed (Ian Allan Ltd. 1985).

'BODYGUARD OF LIES' by Anthony Cave Brown (W. H. Allen & Co. Ltd. 1976).

'BRIDGE ACROSS THE SKY' by Richard Collier (MacMillan London Ltd. 1978).

'BRITAINS MILITARY AIRFIELDS 1939 - 45' by David J. Smith (Patrick Stephens Ltd. 1989).

'BRITISH AEROSPACE HARRIER AND SEA HARRIER' by Roy Braybrook (Osprey Publishing Ltd. 1984).

'DIEPPE 1942 - THE JUBILEE DISASTER' by Ronald Atkin (MacMillan London Ltd. 1980).

'ERNEST HEMINGWAY: A LIFE STORY' by Carlos Baker (Avon Books 1968).

'FALKLANDS - THE AIR WAR' by Burden, Draper, Rough, Smith & Wilton. (Arms and Armour Press Ltd. 1986).

'HAWK' by Roy Braybrook (Osprey Publishing Ltd. 1984).

'HAWKER HUNTER' by Francis K. Mason (Patrick Stephens Ltd. 1985).

'HAWKER HUNTER - THE OPERATIONAL RECORD' by Robert Jackson (Airlife Publishing Ltd. 1989).

'HARRIER' by Francis K. Mason (Patrick Stephens Ltd. 1986).

'JUMP JET' by Bruce Miles (Presidio Press 1978).

'RAF AIRCRAFT' (Air Britain series).

'SEA HARRIER AND AV-8B' by Robert Jackson (Blandford Press 1989).

'TEST PILOT' by Neville Duke (Allan Wingate Ltd. 1953).

'TEST PILOTS' by Don Middleton (Willow Books 1985).

'THE BERLIN AIRLIFT' by Robert Jackson (Patrick Stephens Ltd. 1988).

'THE BLUE ARENA' by Sqn. Ldr. Bob Spurdle DFC and bar (William Kimber & Co. Ltd. 1986).

'THE FLYING DUTCHMAN' by H. J. E. van der Kop (Patrick Stephens Ltd. 1985).

'THE SQUADRONS OF THE ROYAL AIR FORCE' by James J. Halley (Air Britain 1980).

"WINGLESS VICTORY" by Anthony Richardson (Odhams Press Ltd. 1950).

'WRECKS & RELICS' by Ken Ellis (Midland Counties Publications 1986 - tenth edition).

'2nd. TACTICAL AIR FORCE' by Christopher F. Shores (Osprey Publications Ltd. 1970).

'320 SQUADRON R.A.F. MEMORIAL 1940 - 1945' by J. P. Kloos (privately published by the author).

Introduction

During the 1970s I first became familiar with Dunsfold by having friends who lived on the aerodrome. I was thus able to make frequent visits despite the Official Secrets Act which normally limits the public's access to the site.

Gradually, I became aware that the aerodrome had a history still to be told. The old dispersal points hinted at former military use and thus encouraged, I began some research at the Public Records Office, then in Chancery Lane, London.

After gathering the basic facts, purely for my own interest, I left the matter there until a house move in 1987 threw up my old notes. Re-reading them, I felt there was yet more to be told. In the intervening years there had been a little more publicity about Dunsfold but still nothing to reveal its past. My old research gave the bones: a unique Canadian contribution to the aerodrome's construction; the first Mustangs and Tomahawks, followed by Mitchell bombers, Spitfires, Typhoons and Tempests and a part in some of the European war's most crucial operations: Dieppe, D-Day and Arnhem. Not to mention post-war contributions to the Berlin Airlift and the Falklands campaign.

I therefore set about putting flesh on the bones, by contact around the world with those who have served and worked at Dunsfold. This book tells the long overdue story of their efforts.

Paul McCue
Godalming Surrey
December 1991

Acknowledgments

One of the most rewarding aspects of this undertaking has been the opportunity to meet and correspond with so many people. I have found it extremely satisfying to link incidents with the characters involved and, occasionally, to have been able to put in touch with one another, people from the same events of years gone by. My grateful thanks must therefore go to the following, many of whom not only helped me with my research, but also convinced me that Dunsfold's history should be written.

L. Acres; J. Adams; The Aircrew Association; Air Britain; Airwork Ltd.; P. Amos; C. Andreou; I. Anstruther; Australian High Commission; B. Baker; M. C. Balcom; S. J. Ball; D. S. Barden; F. Barclay; M. & L. Barnes; K. A. Bartley; J. Bateman; Squadron Leader A. E. Bedford OBE, AFC, FRAeS; S. B. Beevers; Belgian Air Force; Belgian Embassy; J. F. Biden; P. Bissky DFC, RCAF (retd); G. R. Blake; F. H. Bowler; R. Bolton BEM; Observer Lieutenant M. J. Brady; Roy Britain; British Aerospace PLC; British Aerospace News; Air Chief Marshal Sir Harry Broadhurst GCB, KBE, DSO and bar, DFC and bar, AFC; C. Brown; E. Burn (decd); G. W. Burroughs DFC; G. Caesar; M. Callaghan; A. Calvert; Canadian Forces Photographic Unit; Canadian Government Photo Centre Group; Canadian Veterans Association of the U. K.; G. Chappell; J. Charette; S. Clay; E. E. Colman; W. G. Cooper; S. Cooper-Grundy;Wing Commander B. Coopman; G. Cotterman; J. D. Cressman; K. Cudlipp DFC; G. Dare; W. Darnley; R. H. Davies; Flt. Lt. W. E. R. Day RAFVR (retd); J. W. de Bruyn Kops; Mme. J. de Norman et d'Audenhove; J. Dixon; R. R. Down; B. J. Doyle; N. G. H. Draffan; H. Drane; Air Marshal C. R. Dunlap CBE, CD, RCAF (retd); R. H. Durnin; J. F. Farley OBE, AFC, CEng, MRAeS; G. Ferguson; E. Fitton; Flight International; N. Franks; Air Commodore J. Frost; K. Ganderton; K. Goldby; GQ Parachutes Ltd.; P. Griffiths; O. R. Griggs; L. Groombridge; T. T. Hall DFC; Wing Commander H. J. L. Hallowes DFC, DFM (decd); Wing Commander L. G. Hamer; A. A. Handscombe; D. Hannah; T. Harbottle; Mrs M. Harbun; J. A. Harley (decd); Dr L. E. Hastings; D. Hayler; L. W. J. Hearsey; W. Hemingway; Group Captain N. Henderson RCAF (retd); A. E. Hermitage; R. Herring; P. J. Hewett; B. Hewson; C. Heywood; B. & J. Hilderly; A. L. A. Hissink; G. B. Hodgson; D. J. Howe; J.

Howe; R. F. Johnstone; M. Jones ALA; D. G. Kilvington; D. Kinsella OBE; J. P. Kloos; F. Kreuger; A. Lawson; J. F. Lazzara; F. Lohr; Mrs L. Longman; L. Macfarlane; E. MacGowan; N. MacLeod; Mrs G. Mann; S. J. Marks; A. Martin-Bird;Flt. Lt. P. J. D. Mason, 16 Sqn. R.A.F.; D. Maughan; R. & C. McCue; The Medium Bomber Association; W. Minter; Wing Commander E. H. Moncrieff AFC; W. D. Moody; J. Moore; R. C. Moore; U. Morgan BA ALA; Rev. J. D. Morris; C. Motheral (decd); Lt. Colonel G. S. Moyser, Canadian High Commission; J. Moore; Sqn. Ldr. F. Murphy DFC, AFRAeS; H. Murray; J. & S. Neale; K. & R. Neale; Netherlands Embassy; New Zealand High Commission; R. Nicholls; Norwegian Embassy; G. Nugent; Ordnance Survey; J. Ot; J. Page; E. Palmer; J. Palmer; Squadron Leader R. A. Parfitt RAF (retd); H. F. Patten; Air Commodore G. J. C. Paul CB, DFC, MA, FRAeS; W. A. Pethick DFC; D. H. Porter; J. H. Poulsom; W. Poyser; Public Archives of Canada; Public Record Office, Kew; J. H. Pugh; Quadrant Picture Library; W. W. Ransome; D. & J. Ralphs; N. Richens; K. Rimell; E. Rock; D. Rose; Royal Air Force Museum; Royal Air Force News; Royal Australian Air Force; Royal Dutch Navy; Royal New Zealand Air Force;A. Sadler; D. W. Sexton; W. J. Sharp; J. M. Sheddan DFC; D. Sherk; M. Shimkoff; S. G. Simmons (decd); K. Sleeman; Wing Commander J. H. Smith-Carington; R. Soldiuk; S. E. Spearman; Sqn. Ldr. R. L. Spurdle DFC and bar, MID; R. Standing; J. C. Standing; K. Stanton; W. Starkie; K. Stewart; R. F. Stigant; J. Stone; C. H. Stover DFC; J. C. Streeter; P. Stribling; Surrey County Council; Surrey Constabulary; B. G. Thacker; C. Thomas; Mrs G. Thropp; Colonel P. Triest; Commodore H. J. E. van der Kop DFC; Mrs E. Vink; Captain H. Voorspuy; Rev. Dr. T. E. Warner; Waverley Borough Council; Dr. F. E. Webb; R. A. Winstanley; J. Wiskar (decd); K. Wright; H. Wynn; The 137/139 Wings (All Ranks) Association.

In particular, I would wish to single out Frank Morgan DFC, formerly of 180 Squadron. From his home in Canada, Frank provided me with numerous letters detailing his recollections and came over to visit Dunsfold twice during the preparation of this project. Sadly, he died in December 1990 before he was able to see the finished book.

If I have somehow omitted any contributors, my apologies and my thanks nevertheless.

Finally, my gratitude to Marion Simmons for her word processing and patience and to Simon Parry, my publisher, for his interest and commitment to producing this book.

Chapter One

The Search for an Airfield

Early 1942, the third year of the Second World War, saw Britain consolidating her strength at home while the Allies enjoyed mixed fortunes in the far flung theatres of war.

In North Africa and the Soviet Union triumphant German armies were still very much on the offensive while in the Far East British, Dutch, Australian and American forces appeared powerless to stop the advances of Japan. In Britain, the danger of invasion had passed but the country's lifelines across the Atlantic were under continuing pressure from the Germans' U-boat attacks.

In the air war over Europe, the Luftwaffe had reverted to nuisance attacks against England after the *Baedeker* raids of March and April, provoked by the RAF's own bombing of Lubeck and Rostock. Bomber Command had a new leader in Air Marshal Arthur Harris and a new directive, approved by the Air Minisry, to henceforth strike at Germany with area bombing. Still to reach operational readiness and partner Bomber Command was the United States Army Air Force, for the moment building up the strength of its bomber and fighter groups stationed in England. American troops had also reached Britain in January 1942 and likewise began training with forces from around the world, preparing themselves for the ultimate aim of freeing continental Europe from German domination.

Long before the Americans reached Britain, another country's forces had crossed the Atlantic to stand against the German threat. By 1941 the 1st Canadian Army of Lieutenant General A. G. L. McNaughton had been in Britain for over a year and was straining at the leash through inactivity. Camped and billeted throughout south-east England, the Canadian boys were apt to be boisterous when they had nothing much to do and this soon led to friction between troops and the local population. Canadian officers had already commenced a series of local lectures on why their men tended to be high-spirited and somewhat less reserved than their English cousins, but more than words was clearly needed.

Against this backcloth of potential unrest, General McNaughton was voicing concern over the provision of air support which would be necessary for his forces when they eventually went into action. Plans called for a Royal Canadian Air Force strength of six squadrons in the army co-operation rôle but to date, only two such units were in existence. Not least of the difficulties to be overcome was the shortage of airfields on which to base additional squadrons and McNaughton therefore had this in mind when he approached the British Chief of Air Staff, Sir Charles Portal, in April 1941. After a positive meeting, the two commanders agreed that 'one or two' new airfields should be built for the Canadians.

Twelve months later no progress had been made and McNaughton then met Air Ministry officials to hurry along his request. Once again the General's need was accepted but the Air Ministry pointed out that civilian construction contractors were currently engaged with as much work as they could handle. Subject to a suitable site being located and purchased, and even if the workforce could be found quickly, it would then take a further eighteen months to build a single aerodrome.

To the energetic Canadian such a timescale was not acceptable and McNaughton therefore suggested that, if the land and materials were provided, his own army would do the work. In particular the task would provide valuable experience for the 2nd. Battalion of the Royal Canadian Engineers, currently training in south east England, and consequently McNaughton ordered that a representative be sent to discuss the proposition with the RAF's Army Co-operation Command at Bracknell.

Lieutenant K. R. Ford of the Royal Canadian Army travelled to Bracknell on 18th April 1942. In discussions with Wing Commander McIntyre, also an engineering officer, Ford confirmed the Canadian Army's proposals to supply men and equipment for the construction of one or two airfields, for the use of Royal Canadian Air Force squadrons in RAF Army Co-operation Command. The Canadians, Ford suggested, should be responsible for building runways, perimeter road and possibly dispersals. It was expected that civilian contractors would construct any other roads and accommodation. In return, McIntyre held good and bad news for Lieutenant Ford. The bad news was that the RAF could only identify one site that was suitably located, the good news was that it could be very quickly made available for work to commence.

The reason for the latter was that 1942 represented a year of great expansion for all the air forces in Great Britain and, in order to accommodate this growth, scores of new aerodromes had already been planned. In southern England a number of areas had been earmarked for use as Advanced Landing Grounds by Fighter Command of the Royal Air Force. Eventually some thirty six such sites were submitted for final approval and it was one of the first fifteen reconnoitered, between 16th and 24th April 1942, that McIntyre now had in mind. All but hidden among rolling hills south of Guildford in Surrey, the site was reputedly only discovered when an aerial survey noted that an area of level tree tops suggested level ground below. Equally important, the site was close to the 1st Canadian Army then predominantly based in Surrey, Sussex and Kent. The area was described as pasture and woodland which, with clearing and by cutting across two roads, could provide a runway of at least two thousand yards. The name of the site was Dunsfold.

In his report the same day to Major General Hertzberg, Chief Engineer of the Canadian Army, Ford detailed his intention to visit Dunsfold the next day, the 19th, in order to inspect soil and drainage conditions. He was also able to report the basic characteristics of the site, as supplied by Wing Commander McIntyre. These were that:

"The contours are fairly level except for a short fall to the north in the north-east corner, and a cross fall to the west in the western portion.....The approaches will require clearing. Drainage is now in open ditches flowing to the east and north-west. Similar sites require in the neighbourhood of 17 miles of pipe, laid an average depth of 2 to 6 feet. Grading will be very slight in soil which consists of a heavy loam overlying medium heavy clay. There is one wet area which could be drained by clearing the existing ditches and slightly regrading them. There will be demolitions at Robbins Farm and Hall Place Cottages. One road will need to be obliterated but alternative accesses are available."

On 22nd April 1942, McNaughton again met Air Chief Marshal Sir Charles Portal, expressed his satisfaction with the report on Dunsfold and pressed the Chief of Air Staff to grant his final approval to the plan for the Canadians to build the aerodrome. Three days later, Portal's approval was confirmed in a letter to McNaughton from Air Marshal Sir Christopher Courtney, Air Member for Supply and Organisation at the Air Ministry. With this level of support the future of the new aerodrome was firmly secured. The Permanent Airfields Board gave the go-ahead to construct a full-scale army co-operation aerodrome and Fighter Command therefore had no option but to relinquish its interest in the site.*

*Neither the RAF nor the RCAF were in fact the first air force to show an interest in the area. On 9th March 1941 a nocturnal Luftwaffe raider had dropped seven bombs on the area, for no apparrent reason. Causing little immediate damage, the incident nevertheless had repercussions as late as 31st January 1946 when one of the bombs, unexploded, was discovered on adjoining Barnfield Farm and had to be made safe.

Chapter Two

Of Chickens, Women and Other Removals

Sapper Harold Murray of St. John, New Brunswick had enlisted in the Canadian Army in May 1940 and September of the same year saw him aboard the troopship *Georgie* steaming into the Clyde in company with the rest of the 2nd Battalion, Royal Canadian Engineers. For eighteen months his battalion had then moved from camp to camp in southern England, impatient to get to grips with a real job. Their lot seemed to go from bad to worse when in February and March of 1942 a series of exercises, designed by an equally frustrated High Command, had them scurrying about the South Downs with only one blanket each for comfort at night. But then, in April, the sappers' lines began to agitate with rumours of a new job, a real job, no less than the building of an aerodrome.

Preparations were made to move and sure enough confirmation soon came from the officers. The destination was to be Dunsfold. Advance units arrived on site in late April, followed by the remainder in early May. A tented camp was quickly set up close to the Wey and Arun Junction Canal which skirted the eastern edge of the site and the troops marvelled at the rich crops, grazing fields and dense woodland which stood in their way. To many it appeared the finest pastoral scene in England, to destroy it seemed almost a criminal act.

There was little time for such thoughts however. On 30th April, General McNaughton had himself visited the site. He had noted a somewhat optimistic estimate from Lieutenant Ford that work could be completed in as little as four and a half months. To the General, this completion date of just eighteen weeks would be one in the eye for the Air Ministry and their cautious estimate of eighteen months. Thus the order was issued, the aerodrome was to built in eighteen weeks and the reputation of the Royal Canadian Engineers was at stake.

The Canadians met with Air Ministry representatives on 8th May in a Public House at Alfold, close to the site. The Ministry officials came with the news that runway length and the width of the perimeter track should be increased, in case of possible

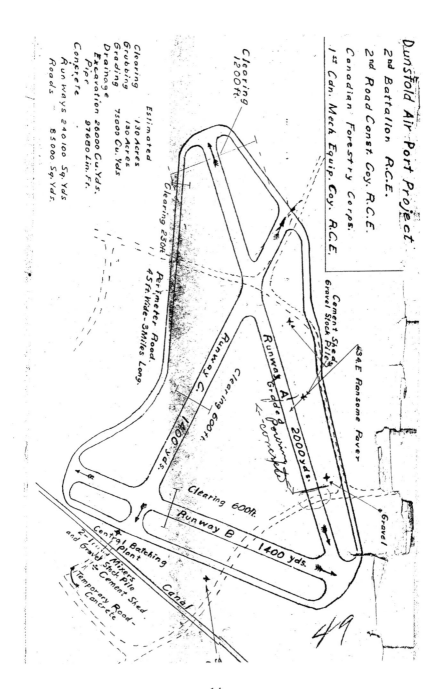

Dunsfold Air Port Project.

2ⁿᵈ Battalion R.C.E.

2ⁿᵈ Road Const. Coy. R.C.E.

Canadian Forestry Corps.

1ˢᵗ Can. Mech. Equip. Coy. R.C.E.

Estimated

Clearing   130 Acres
Grubbing   130 Acres
Grading   75000 Cu. Yds.
Drainage
Excavation 26000 Cu. Yds.
Pipe   97680 Lin. Ft.
Concrete
Runways 240100 Sq. Yds
Roads — 85000 Sq. Yds.

Clearing 1200 ft.

Clearing 230 ft.

Perimeter Road.
45 ft. Wide - 3 Miles Long.

Runway C · 1400 yds.

Clearing 600 ft.

Clearing 600 ft.

Runway A · 2000 yds.

Runway grade poured concrete

3-E Ransome Paver

Cement Shed.
Gravel Stock Piles

Gravel

Clearing 600 ft.

Runway B · 1400 yds.

Central Batching Plant
2-1 yd Mixers
and Gravel Stock Pile
Cement Shed
Temporary Road -
Concrete

Canal

49

An aerial photograph of the completed airfield taken on October 1st, 1942. (RAF Museum W13/6/5)

future use by larger aircraft. This stipulation, the officials conceded, would not help the Canadians in meeting McNaughton's timescale but they were startled when Major General Hertzberg revealed that his advance units had already started clearing ground for the main runway. Neither had Hertzberg lost any time in appointing some of his most experienced officers to the task. Construction superintendent was Major H. D. Duff MC, assigned to the project from No. 6 Construction Company, while Lieutenant Colonel D. H. Storms acted as consulting engineer. The 2nd Battalion was quickly joined by units of the Canadian Forestry Corps, the Royal Canadian Army Service Corps, the 2nd (and elements of the 1st) Road Construction Company and the 1st Mechanical Equipment Company.

Officially, work commenced on 11th May 1942. In general, the 2nd Battalion was to be responsible for runways, drainage and clearing while the 2nd Road Construction Company would lay the perimeter track and dispersal areas. Little heed was paid to the fact that the Air Ministry in London was still finalising the necessary land purchases. In one instance, a local dairy farmer never quite recovered from the shock of finally shutting the door on his home and then seeing it bulldozed into an adjacent pond before he had even reached the bottom of his garden path. At the same time, Major Rowcliffe of neighbouring Hall Place was dismayed when one of his favourite views disappeared. His custom was to stand in his bath and admire a row of ten magnificent ancient oak trees. He was doing exactly that when the Canadians bulldozed all ten to the ground within minutes.

While the aerodrome was planned to be able to accommodate a fighter wing, the Air Ministry's additional requirements meant that runways, perimeter track and hard-standings were to meet the standards of an 'A' class bomber airfield. It was also to be a *dispersed* airfield, that is with hangars, accommodation, workshops and aircraft hard-standings set out over a wide area. The first two and a half years' experience of war had shown that by such dispersal, airfields and their aircraft made a more difficult target to the enemy in the air. As far as the Canadian troops were concerned, this only magnified their logistical challenges.

The main concrete runway was to be six thousand feet long (over a mile) and a hundred and fifty feet wide. Two further runways were each to be of the same width and over four thousand feet long. A three mile perimeter track was to encircle the three runways which were set in an 'A' shape and there would be dispersal points for fifty aircraft with six miles of access and camp roads. One hundred thousand cubic yards of soil would have to be moved and two hundred acres of wood cleared. Not least of the daunting tasks would be the initial construction of a new section of the Guildford to Horsham road since the aerodrome was to lie directly across the existing line of the road.

The Canadians did have some advantages since, unlike the British, they were familiar with the giant earth-moving equipment which had been provided by the U.S.A. under lend-lease arrangements. Tree stumps were rapidly blasted from the earth by explosives and from 27th May concrete pouring progressed rapidly using huge double barrelled mixers and massive machines from which the concrete fell in heaps. It was then instantly spread and levelled by droves of sappers armed with shovels. An eighteen hour day was worked in two shifts and

Sappers of the 2nd Btn. RCE. settle into their tented camp in May 1942. (R. Soldiuk)

even in the remaining six hours at night, movement never ceased as maintenance crews made sure the machines were ready for the next day's work. Lorries rumbled into camp around the clock and neighbouring villages had to endure a steady stream of vehicles bringing cement from Shoreham on the south coast and sand and gravel from nearby Farnham and Ewhurst. Special trains too were used, nearby Baynards Station being transformed into a hive of activity as perspiring sappers unloaded rubble by hand and shovel.

The combination of hard work and life in the field meant normal army discipline and dress standards were temporarily forgotten. Sharp reminders were forthcoming when drivers not infrequently lost their way and had to approach the nearest British Army unit for directions. On one such occasion, driver Sheldon Spearman of Richmond, Ontario, had the misfortune to lose his way in Godalming while returning from Farnham in his Dennis dump truck. Unluckily for Spearman, his search for help led him to the local headquarters of a Royal Engineers unit where British standards were very different from those of their Canadian counterparts a few miles down the road. Seconds after entering, the mud-splattered soldier found himself back on the street with the clearest possible direction given by the immaculate English officer inside...."Get out of my sight!"

On a more sombre note, the Canadian drivers also experienced difficulties in coming to terms with the winding country lanes down which they had to drive. Cautious driving was asking a great deal of men from the open spaces of Canada and it was therefore only a matter of time before an accident occurred. This duly came when a driver of the Royal Canadian Army Service Corps ran down and killed Miss Ada Knight, a part-time postwoman, in Barhatch Lane, Cranleigh.

A novel problem to confront the Canadian sappers on the site itself proved to be the property named Broadmeads Cottage, sitting squarely astride the planned path of the perimeter track and main runway. Its lady owner had no option other than to leave but had made an impassioned plea that the structure should not be demolished and Major Duff eventually conceded that the building might provide a pleasant officers' mess. The order therefore went out not to flatten the structure, but to attempt to move it.

Sergeant Fred Kreuger of the 1st Mechanical Engineers Company had already taken on considerable responsibility for the aerodrome's construction since he had been involved with such work before. Kreuger had been put in charge of all mechanical equipment and its operation from day one, while Major Duff looked after discipline, supplies and off-site personnel. On receiving his latest order, however, the experienced Sergeant realised that specialist skills were needed and the sappers' ranks were searched for someone who might have undertaken a similar project back home in Canada. By great good fortune one such person was found, a Sergeant Whidden, and together he and Kreuger assembled the plan and men for the challenge. Fred Kreuger today still recalls every detail of the task:

"We had lots of beech logs that had been removed so we undermined the structure one log at a time, the major problem proving to be a fireplace in the middle which appeared to tie the cottage together. While the cottage was resting on the logs, we then rigged a cable, pulley and eveners. The idea was to work with three large D8 Caterpiller tractors pulling side by side and in preparation for the move we graded, or flattened, the terrain for probably half a mile or more.

"First of all the three tractor operators practiced responding to signals so that they would move their machines in unison. At the first attempt however, the three tractors would not pull it, so we then used five, again with cables and pulleys. Shortly after we started, the weight of the fireplace on the logs created so much friction that fires started squirting out on all sides of the logs. So, we then took up some of the floor and put men in the house with Carbon Tetrachloride and told them to watch the fire so that it didn't catch onto the boards of the house. Fortunately the freshly felled beech logs were very green and wouldn't support a flame. A BBC News crew did film some of the move and interviewed myself and Sergeant Whidden. I remember that only Whidden came out on the news later - I was told my name was too Germanic for the BBC's liking!"

The move was a success and the cottage found a new home close to the southern boundary of the aerodrome. A cluster of nissen huts was thrown up around it and throughout the war years it served as a squadron flight office for a group of nearby dispersal points. One such squadron to use the property in 1943 and 1944 was 98 Sqn. who re-christened it *Rose Cottage* in recognition of the blooms almost covering one external wall. Initially unaware of the cottage's history, the airmen were puzzled that despite provision of bathroom, lavatory and wash basins, these could not be used as no services were linked to the building and the winter of 1943 highlighted this deficiency in terms of heating. During the move, the walls' insulating lining had largely fallen out and despite a standard RAF issue black stove located in each room, the cottage's charms were only really appreciated in the summer. Services were eventually provided, and a cess-pit dug, but post-war the cottage stood neglected until 1952 when the Hawker Aircraft Company took over the aerodrome's lease and test pilot Frank Murphy moved in with his family. For four years the Murphys restored the cottage to the standard of a family home but since then it has remained empty and used only by the aerodrome's Fire Service for smoke and evacuation exercises. Also latterly known as *Canada House* and then *Murphy's Cottage* the building again revived memories when it featured in the correspondence columns of British Aerospace News during 1986. Wing Commander George Hamer, former 98 Sqn. commanding officer, wrote in to query the fate of the cottage and this led to two further letters, one explaining the current use by the Fire Service, and the other from Frank Murphy which asked whether the Wing Commander 'can throw some light on my discovery in the roof space of pillows and Service blankets and a tin containing old cigarette butts with and without lipstick traces...' No doubt the rafters can tell a story or two!

Even the RCAF Overseas Headquarters in London were caught unawares by the speed with which the Canadian Army units commenced their work. Air Commodore Curtis was to act as the RCAF's liaison officer with the Canadian Army and it was not until mid May that even he was informed construction was already under way. On 26th May the Ministry Of Information's official censors were provided with scant details for a news item, but no indication was given as to the location of the new aerodrome. On May 31st Air Commodore Curtis belatedly realised how rapidly General Hertzberg's sappers were speeding ahead when he was invited to lunch at McNaughton's headquarters on 3rd June, to be followed by an inspection of progress at Dunsfold. Before attending the lunch, Curtis hurriedly signalled his superior, Air Vice-Marshal Edwards, who at the time was back in Ottawa:

S I G N A L
(IN SECRET CYPHER)
OUR FILE: S.2-7-1

TO: C.A.S. A.F.H.Q. OTTAWA.
FROM: ROYCANAIRF LONDON.
0.115 ATTENTION AIR VICE-MARSHAL EDWARDS FROM CURTIS . SECRET . LIEUTENANT GENERAL McNAUGHTON HAS AERODROME UNDER CONSTRUCTION AT DUNSFOLD . AM ATTENDING LUNCHEON AT HIS HEADQUARTERS ON WEDNESDAY AND WILL INSPECT SITE AND OBSERVE CONSTRUCTION .

(W. A. Curtis) Air Commodore,
for Air Officer-in-Chief,
R.C.A.F. Overseas.

TIME OF ORIGIN: 1130 HRS. BDST.
DATE: 31-5-42.
THIS MESSAGE MUST BE SENT IN SECRET CYPHER

On 3rd June, 1942 General McNaughton proudly conducted his guests around the site. Besides Curtis, Air Vice-Marshal Stedman and Wing Commanders Smith and Waddell (from 414 and 400 Squadrons respectively) represented the RCAF. Air Chief Marshal Sir Christopher Courtney came from the Air Ministry while Mr Massey, the High Commissioner for Canada, provided a Canadian Government presence. The attendance of the two squadron commanders was clearly a portent of the aerodrome's coming use and an historic moment soon followed when, on 20th June 1942, the first aircraft landed. Alighting on a newly completed section of perimeter track to the cheers of the toiling men, this was Tiger Moth BB728 of 414 Squadron RCAF paying a brief visit on liaison duties from RAF Croydon.

Another visitor to inspect progress arrived on 2nd July when Clement Atlee, then Minister for Dominion Affairs and Deputy Prime Minister, accompanied Colonel Archibald on a tour of the sappers' efforts which were progressing smoothly. The next stage of construction was to be the erection of living sites and accommodation, the responsibility of civilian contractors. Work started in the first week of August, aiming for completion by the end of November. It was one of the contractor's employees, an Irish driver, who sadly became the aerodrome's first fatality. Due to heavy rains, large pools of water had formed in numerous muddy clay pits and the hapless driver was drowned when his tractor overturned and fell into one such pit. Local word of mouth eventually distorted this fact into a tale, surviving today, that the unfortunate man had fallen into the cement-laying machine and had subsequently been laid out somewhere in the runway foundations!

A brief interruption to the Army's work came in early August when elements of the 2nd. Battalion left camp for a 'hush-hush' operation. Returning a few days later, they told of a perilous cross-channel journey in support of the bloody raid on Dieppe. At the last moment they had been ordered away from attempting to land and sent back to England. They returned with the sobering knowledge that they had been fortunate not to join those of their countrymen left dead on the beaches or captive in German hands. Transportation units of the Royal Canadian Army Service Corps had also pulled out of camp to carry troops of the

Clement Atlee visits the construction work, seen here with Colonel Archibald, in crash helmet. (National Archives of Canada /PA163762)

Canadian Essex Scottish regiment to Portsmouth. After unloading their charges, the drivers then bivouaced in the hills around Lewes until they were called down into Newhaven to pick up the shattered survivors of the regiment who had managed to return from Dieppe's Red Beach. The waiting drivers began to comprehend the scale of the disaster when they learned that only 52 men had come ashore, out of 553 who had been taken into Portsmouth.

Chastened by their first real experience of war, Dunsfold's Canadians were glad to be back in the peaceful Surrey countryside and they set to with renewed vigour. By 15th August runways and the remainder of the perimeter track were completed and camouflage measures began. The general planned layout of the aerodrome already helped in this respect in that the dispersed sites were located in wooded areas some way off the main airfield. Somewhat unusually, two patches of woodland had also been left standing within the perimeter track close to the runways, thus helping to break up the wide open space. Under the summer sun the bleached white concrete of the runways and perimeter track could be seen from miles away in the air. The problem was solved by spraying the concrete with a mixture of tar and wood chippings. Experiments had shown that this method produced a dark textured finish which was optically non-reflective and from the air closely resembled grass. The chippings also added extra surface grip without damaging

Tiger Moth BB728, the first aircraft to land at Dunsfold. (National Archives of Canada /PA163757.)

aircraft tyres. The overall effect was somewhat spoiled however as it appears the camouflage efforts were not extended to the aircraft dispersals and hard-standings. These therefore continued to attract attention to the aerodrome throughout the war.*

Perhaps not surprisingly, the civilian construction works lagged behind the efforts of the Canadian military who were still determined to meet General McNaughton's seemingly impossible deadline. But, as in every workforce, not all took the same pride in the job and it gradually became evident that some of the sappers had different achievements in mind.

As equipment, materials and other supplies poured into camp, thoughts turned to the eternal aim of making a fast buck. The honest types had already started a trade with local people by selling carved wooden mementoes in pubs for the price of a pint. Puzzled by the British class distinction of public and lounge bars the Canadian boys nevertheless quickly settled into the neighbouring hostelries and struck up friendships. Soon the pubs became the trading place for more than wooden figures as budding Canadian entrepreneurs realised how easy it was to spirit supplies from camp. In the village of Dunsfold itself word went round 'The Sun' one night that socks were to be had if you were to join the queue outside leading to the shadows where two

---

*When the first aircraft were based at Dunsfold, the runways were still littered with wood chippings which had not adhered to the tar. A favourite trick of pilots was therefore to fly low along the length of a runway, blasting away an impressive cloud of chippings with their propeller wash.

sappers stood with a bundle. Any guilt feelings amongst the villagers were eased the next day when the local policeman cycled past. With his uniform trouser bottoms safely tucked up by cycle clips, the blissfully ignorant bobby displayed his own pair of standard issue grey Canadian Army socks. Of a more startling nature was the disappearance of a giant earth mover. Of a size and kind previously unseen in Britain, an example entered camp one evening and had vanished by the next morning. Amazingly, it was never traced. Military petrol stocks fell too, yet suddenly some of the local population found the means, despite fuel rationing, to go for Sunday drives. Determined to halt the trade, the Battalion's commanding officer, Lieutenant Colonel Sutherland, called a stock taking exercise in order to attempt to identify the culprits. The first step was to place all supplies under canvas with an armed guard but mysteriously, the night before the counting was due to begin, the canvassed stores went up in flames. To add to the fiasco the flames also spread to the ammunition tents. Awakening to the sound of explosions and crackling gunfire, one of the more imaginative Company Sergeant-Majors leapt from his bed and called out the guard. Certain that Hitler's invasion had finally come, the C.S.M. rushed about in his underwear, bawling orders as only a Sergeant-Major can do. No doubt the culprits looked on with great satisfaction.

The additional funds which came from such enterprise may have been the reason why the Canadians always seemed to have handfuls of dollars available for a quick round of dice throwing. To the British servicemen attached to the camp, it seemed that gambling was always going on in some form or another, normally accompanied by much drinking of Coca-Cola. When the Canadians threw the empty bottles over their shoulder, the wily (and poorer!) British onlookers were not slow to realise a sorce of income overlooked by their transatlantic brothers-in-arms. As the rowdy games continued, the empties would be quietly collected and returned to the NAAFI for 2d. a bottle.

Shortly after the night of the fire the Regimental Sergeant-Major did succeed in tracing some contraband, but of an entirely different nature. This was a red-haired A.T.S. girl with a notoriously generous nature who had befriended several of the

Canadians. Recognizing that distance impeded her 'friendships', the girl eventually decided to make her residence in the camp. The R.S.M. decided not and the entire camp held its breath while she defied him and spent four pleasant nights in certain tents. On the morning following the fourth night the R.S.M. went smartly into action and the girl was hauled off to jail, much to the indignation of several sappers.

It was at this time too that the notorious 'chicken incident' occurred. Close to the camp lived a widow and two daughters whose livelihood largely depended on the well-being and egg-producing capacity of their half a dozen hens. One dark night all six creatures disappeared. The local constabulary was hot on the trail next morning and followed a morbid trail of blood and feathers into the camp's perimeter. Apprised of the facts, the Colonel undertook to put matters right and soon the Battalion paraded before him. The choice was made clear to the men: either the birds were returned to their rightful owner that same night or all leave would be cancelled for a month. The next morning the perplexed widow found herself the owner of no less than 186 hens while a chicken farmer in the district discovered almost his entire stock had vanished overnight.

Fortunately, the activities of the unscrupulous few were far outweighed by traditional Canadian friendliness and the local villagers took to their hearts these boys far from home. Previously quiet and sedate village halls shook to popular dances where army lorries delivered Guildford girls to help out the beseiged local lasses. Many a lovelorn sapper tried to smuggle himself aboard a lorry for the return trip to Guildford, but few succeeded. For Harold Murray one local Cranleigh girl was to be the reason that he married, came back to the area at the end of the war and never returned to Canada. Several other sappers made similar choices but took their English brides back to Canada with them in 1945.

On 17th August 1942 came a further indication of the plans already afoot for usage of the aerodrome. This was the visit of Mustang AM151 of 400 Squadron RCAF, its pilot, Flight Lieutenant Paul Bissky being in charge of a detached flight of his squadron currently based at RAF Odiham aerodrome in Hampshire. Bissky's squadron was expected to move to Dunsfold in the near future and the young pilot was keen to see for himself how his new base was shaping up. Another, unexpected, visitor dropped in on 29th September when a B-17 Flying Fortress of the USAAF called to enquire as to its whereabouts. The aircraft proved to be at the end of its transit flight from the United States so at least its navigator had succeeded in finding the British Isles!

By now, Air Vice-Marshal Edwards had returned to Britain from Ottawa and, promoted to Air Marshal, became the officer responsible for dealing with the British Air Ministry now that the Canadian Army's rôle was coming to an end. Consequently, Edwards wrote to Air Chief Marshal Sir Christopher Courtney, confirming the agreement that the aerodrome would be for the use of Canadian army co-operation squadrons. For convenience and efficient operations, he proposed that the two existing operational squadrons, 400 and 414, should move to Dunsfold on its completion and that the aerodrome should come under the headquarters of the new 39 (Army Co-operation) Wing RCAF for administrative purposes.

In his letter, Edwards also requested that Dunsfold be designated an RCAF Station, rather than an RAF Station, and this matter then proved to exercise the bureaucratic mind for many months to come. Fortunately for the future of the aerodrome, neither the Canadian Army nor the civilian contractors knew anything of the tussle which now raged in London. The problem was that no other military airfield in Britain carried a foreign title yet, from its construction alone, Dunsfold held the best claim to now do so. RCAF correspondence referred to RCAF Station Dunsfold, possession being nine tenths of the law. But the Air Ministry was not to be trapped. Courtney readily agreed to the Canadian's proposals for unit dispositions, but avoided Edwards' request concerning the title. Despite the fraternity of the air, there was no doubt as to which side the RAF supported. From the start, RAF letters and signals mentioned only 'RAF Station Dunsfold', although one message did acknowledge 'the Canadian-manned RAF Station Dunsfold'. On 15th October 1942, the RAF's Army Co-operation Command issued an 'Opening-Up Order' for the aerodrome which was in no doubt. The new base was 'RAF Station Dunsfold, Nr. Guildford,

Surrey' and its initial commissioning, commencing on 2nd November 1942, would be undertaken by RAF personnel. Canadian staffing would only later be gradually introduced. The Order did note however that Dunsfold was special to a certain extent. It acknowledged that the aerodrome would soon become a 'Dominion Home Station'. This title came from the Empire Air Training Scheme Agreement of May, 1942 in which the Canadian government had agreed to the creation of training bases in Canada for allied aircrews. In return, the British government had promised Canada a number of 'Dominion Home Stations' in Britain for the use of Canadian forces, and the RCAF was determined that these should be RCAF Stations in their own right. The first chink in the Air Ministry's armour came via their ally, the RAF. In October 1942 the RAF Record Office at Gloucester wrote to the RCAF, referring to 'RCAF Station Dunsfold'. But if the Air Ministry was aghast at this slip, they themselves let the side down with two letters the following month. Both communications, addressed to RCAF Overseas Headquarters, confirmed flying control postings to 'RCAF Station Dunsfold' - the game was all but won by Canada.

On 15th December 1942 RAF Army Co-operation Command issued a marvellous self-contradictory order. Headed 'RAF Station Dunsfold', the text stated that 'the postal address of RAF Station Dunsfold is.....RCAF Station, Dunsfold, Horsham, Surrey.' So, Dunsfold was still an RAF Station, but was to be addressed as an RCAF Station - simple! Neither was Dunsfold now near to Guildford, but instead was near Horsham....and the RAF had also cleverly moved Horsham from Sussex into Surrey. In February, 1943, the RAF proposed: 'to treat RAF Station Dunsfold as a Dominion 'Home' Station of the Royal Canadian Air Force w.e.f. 15.3.43. The Station to be known as RCAF Station Dunsfold as from the above mentioned date'. On 4th March, 1943 the Air Ministry issued what seemed to be the definitive ruling: '....DOMINION 'HOME' STATIONS. Under the Empire Air Training Scheme Agreement we are committed to the gradual formation of a limited number of Dominion 'Home' Stations. Certain of these stations have already been formed. It has now been agreed that RAF Station DUNSFOLD will become a Dominion 'Home' Station of the Royal Canadian Air Force with effect from 15th March 1943, and will be known as RCAF Station DUNSFOLD with effect from that date....' That should have been the end of the matter, but one further note went on Ottawa's file before it was closed in December 1945. Wing Commander Crozier of the RCAF reported that the Legal Branch of the Air Ministry had recently asserted 'in point of fact no Stations....have ever been declared RCAF Stations'!

Meanwhile, back on the aerodrome, two large T2 hangars and a technical site were erected on the northern edge of the perimeter track either side of a control tower, while squadron offices and other workshops were spread around the dispersal areas on the eastern and southern boundaries. Beyond the northern boundary of the immediate airfield a number of other building sites were commenced over Stovold's Hill and stretching as far as the Cranleigh to Godalming road. These areas included the administrative and main communal sites, WAAF and general accommodation sites, sick quarters and sewage disposal works.

On 16th October 1942, just twenty weeks from the official start of work, the aerodrome was considered complete enough to be handed over to the RCAF. Many local civilian guests were invited to join the formidable array of senior army and air force officers and, diplomatically, the simple title of 'Dunsfold Aerodrome' was used throughout the day rather than further complicate the arguments still simmering.

The focal point of the ceremony was to be the unveiling of a commemorative plinth outside the control tower. This had been skillfully sculpted by Sapper Trenka of the Royal Canadian Engineers and recorded the unique achievement of the units involved. Somehow, a guard of honour was conjured up using some of the sappers, miraculously transformed from mud-caked navvies into a semblance of military order. Little did the General know that his arrival had been preceeded by a delivery of new uniforms, solely for the use of the honour guard! The speeches followed the precise programme of events, General McNaughton formally handing the aerodrome over to Air Marshal Edwards for the use of the RCAF Overseas. As McNaughton admired the fine commemorative stone which he had unveiled, he was

Left to right - AM Edwards, Gen. Crerar, Gen, NcNaughton, ACM. Courtney and Spr. Trenka inspect the plinth. (National Archives of Canada /PA163751)

presented with a miniature replica of it, likewise crafted by Sapper Trenka.

Meanwhile, the control tower was opened up and Flying Officer Nolan Henderson, of 400 Squadron RCAF at Odiham, arrived to act as Dunsfold's very first 'duty pilot' for the day. The initially cloudy skies had cleared by the time twelve Mustang aircraft swept low over the field and peeled off to land, lining up on one of the runways. But again, the spectacle was not all that it seemed.

Six aircraft, from 414 Squadron RCAF based at Croydon, had first flown to Odiham to join up with an equal number from 400 Squadron RCAF. The idea was to put up a joint formation from the two squadrons to fly to Dunsfold, but someone had overlooked the fact that the Canadian army co-operation pilots were only accustomed to flying in pairs. Pilot Officer George Burroughs of 414 clearly remembers the aerial mêlée which ensued in trying to get the formation right and eventually the two formations made their own separate ways to Dunsfold. Burroughs' log book shows a flight from Odiham to Dunsfold lasting one hour and ten minutes instead of the normal fifteen to twenty minutes and he keenly felt his embarrassment as they presented what he felt to be a 'pretty ragged spectacle' in the sky above General McNaughton, Air Marshal Edwards and, perhaps worst of all, his own commanding officer, Wing Commander Begg. To add to the young pilot's unease, matters worsened after landing. One machine from 414 Squadron had to be hauled out of a mud pool bordering the perimeter track while another later bent its propeller blades when its brakes locked on the new surface. Only five of 414 Squadron's aircraft were in a fit state to make the return journey and the next day Burroughs and Flying Officer Steeves flew down from Croydon in a Miles Master to collect the Mustang left behind.*

To complete the impression of theatre on the day, as soon as the General had departed, the uniforms of the honour guard were reclaimed and followed the top brass out of the camp gates!

---

*400 Squadron's flight was led by S/L Woods, that of 414 by S/L Greenwood. The commanding officers of both squadrons, Wing Commanders Waddell and Begg respectively, were present on the ground for the opening ceremony.

The Opening Of
DUNSFOLD AERODROME
16th October 1942

1440 hrs.   Guests arrive, are met by Chief Engineer and
            are shown to enclosure.

1445 hrs.   Guard of Honour mounts. (Guard of Honour
            consists of 50 ORs from 1Cdn Rd Const Coy R.C.E.
            & 2 Bn R.C.E. and 50ORs from400 Sqn R.C.A.F.)

            Bands of R.C.A.S.C. & R.C.A.F. will play.

1500 hrs.   Army Cmdr., A.O.C. in C., R.C.A.F., and Air
            Ministry rep. arrive and are met by ChiefEngineer.

            Received by Guard of Honour.

            Inspect Guard of Honour.

1512 hrs.   C.E. introduces C.R.E., First Cdn Army Troops
            who in turn, introduces Superintendent of
            Construction & O.C.s 2 Bn R.C.E. and 2 Cdn
            Rd Const Coy R.C.E.

1514 hrs.   Chief Engineer speaks, welcoming guests, and
            asks Officiating Clergy to dedicate the
            Aerodrome.

1522 hrs.   Chaplain 2 Bn R.C.E. assisted by Chaplain
            R.C.A.F. dedicates the Aerodrome.

1524 hrs.   Lt. General A. G. L. McNaughton speaks on
            behalf of Canadian Army.

1527 hrs.   Air Chief Marshal Sir C. L. Courtney speaks on
            behalf of the Air Ministry.

1530 hrs.   General McNaughton unveils the
            Commemoration Stone.

1531 hrs.   Air Marshal H. Edwards replies on behalf ofthe
            Royal Canadian Air Force.

1535 hrs.   R.C.A.F. planes land on the Aerodrome.

National Anthem.

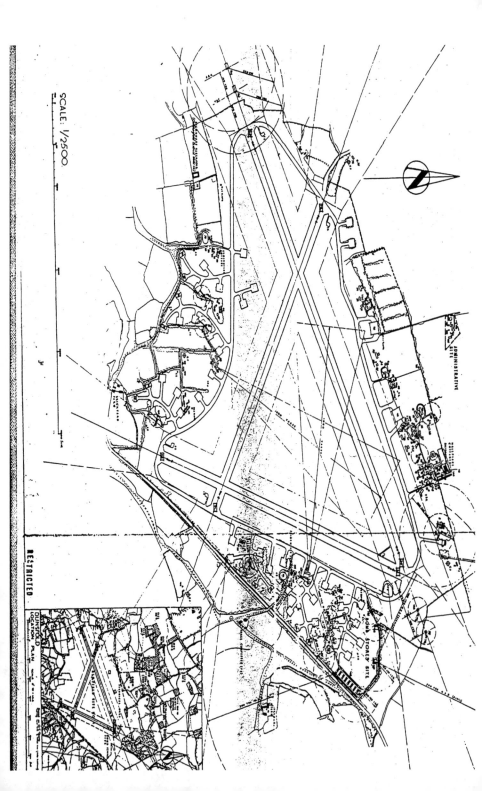

SCALE: 1/2500.

RESTRICTED

ADMINISTRATIVE SITE

BOMB STORES SITE

DUNSFOLD
LOCATION PLAN

Chapter Three

Enter The Squadrons

Despite the official opening of the aerodrome, Dunsfold was far
from ready for operational use and the only aircraft remaining
on the airfield were plywood dummy examples, dispersed around
the site. No official record remains to explain for certain the
purpose of the dummies but it is likely that they were serving to
attract Luftwaffe attention to Dunsfold. While this might at first
sight appear unwise, one of the first units to be posted in was
4153 Squadron of the RAF Regiment, designated to provide the
airfield's anti-aircraft defences. Without any real aircraft on the
aerodrome the dummies could therefore have acted as bait,
luring sneak raiders into range of the Regiment's guns. Such a
scheme is documented for at least one other new aerodrome in
the south east during the same period and it is also a fact that
lone Luftwaffe aircraft were still proving a nuisance in the area
with surprise low-level attacks. In late September a German
aircraft had bombed a school in Petworth, 15 miles away, killing
many pupils and the headmaster. Much closer to home, a
Dornier Do 217 bombed and machine-gunned a train at nearby
Bramley, killing seven people.

The RAF Regiment's personnel had in fact arrived in the area
as early as July, camping in the wooded areas which had not yet
been converted into accommodation sites. Leading Aircraftsman
Norman MacLeod had been bemused to have to defend an
airfield which did not yet exist and for which no gun posts had
yet been built. As winter brought the first snow the gunners
were therefore much relieved when the Canadian sappers
quickly erected their permanent billets and cookhouse rather
than waiting for contractors to finish the job. One newly found
luxury was the ability to shave in relative comfort - previously it
had been necessary to hang a shaving mirror on a bush!

Gradually the Canadian Army finished its allotted tasks and
began to move out, leaving only a few liaison staff and the
civilian contractors working on the accommodation sites. Delays
were met as these contractors suffered from slow supplies, but
by early December the main communal site, just over Stovold's
Hill, was completed. This site included an officers' mess,

sergeants' mess, airmens' dining hall and kitchens and the Station Institute. Other buildings on the same site, but still to be finished, were the gymnasium, squash court, NAAFI, grocery store and ablutions.

Despite the delays, the influx of Royal Canadian Air Force personnel soon began. Station Headquarters staff arrived in November and were housed on number two site close by the Godalming to Cranleigh road, even though the contractors had not yet either handed over or completed the facilities. Among these first airmen to arrive was Corporal Joe Cressman.

Cressman had only arrived in England in November and prior to the war had worked as a morse operator with the Canadian Pacific Railway Company. He was therefore posted to Dunsfold, from the Personnel Depot in Blackpool, to take up duties as a teleprinter operator. The first indication that his posting was to a new establishment came to the Canadian when, on his journey south via London and Guildford, no-one seemed to know of an aerodrome at Dunsfold. On his eventual arrival matters proved even more uncertain when he discovered the aerodrome did not yet possess any teleprinters and he consequently took up general duties with the headquarters staff. One advantage of this was that Cressman quickly became acquainted with the airmen signallers who manned the camp's switchboard. With no women on camp, these telephone operators quickly set up a network of links with English girls at various army bases, chattering away and frequently succeeding in obtaining invitations to their parties and dances. The comparative isolation of Dunsfold could not deter the young Canadians from reaching these social events and the problems caused by the lack of public transport after midnight certainly encouraged a reluctance to return to camp. Many a cold winter's night was spent in a draughty bus shelter before an eventual dawn return to Dunsfold. Fortunately the geographical spread of the camp, and particularly of the living sites, made such returns easy as there was no difficulty in slipping in or out of the camp's perimeter without bothering the guardhouse!

Before long all staff were instructed to stand by to receive the first squadron aircraft and it seemed these would come from 414 Squadron RCAF after a visit on 1st December 1942 from their

Tiger Moth communications aircraft. The pilot of this aircraft was Flying Officer Don Sherk who brought with him, from RAF Croydon, Major MacDonald of the Canadian Army. The two officers spent some time discussing the imminent move of 414 to Dunsfold and consequently set off for home later than intended. The flight back was memorable in that Sherk wandered into London's barrage balloon corridor at dusk and only just managed to locate Croydon with the help of flares fired from the airfield. By the time the two relieved officers stepped from their aircraft, Sherk had logged thirty minutes of night flying and the Major threw a big party in the Officers' Mess to celebrate his survival.

On 3rd December 1942 squadron aircraft duly landed at Dunsfold but 414 Squadron were beaten to their new base when the new arrivals proved to be the Mustang aircraft of Flight Lieutenant Bissky's detachment of 400 Squadron RCAF from RAF Odiham. While the aircraft were dispersed on the airfield, all personnel were billeted on number one site, albeit without the benefit of electricity. It was to be five days later that the aircraft* of 414 Squadron RCAF arrived from Croydon and their Commanding Officer, Wing Commander R.F. Begg RCAF, took up the dual rôle of Dunsfold's first station commanding officer, albeit in a temporary capacity. The squadron's aircraft followed a small advance party of ground personnel who had moved into numbers three and four sites on 2nd December. The main ground party arrived on 5th December and looked aghast at their half finished living sites. Heavy rains added to the sea of mud and curtailed flying to local flights only.

Both squadrons' pilots had already gained considerable experience of operational flying, 400 having been in Britain since 1940 (originally designated as 110 Squadron RCAF). 414 had then been formed in 1941, partly from personnel of 400 Squadron RCAF, so that strong ties were forged between the two units. Firstly equipped with Curtiss Tomahawks, the squadrons' task as army co-operation units should primarily have been tactical reconnaissance on behalf of ground forces. Until the invasion of Europe, however, this rôle could only be practised and in the meantime the squadrons had to be kept at as high an

*These were: 14 Mustang Mk I, 1 Fairey Battle, 2 Tiger Moths and 1 Master.

operational level as possible. Consequently, low-level photographic reconnaissance missions along the French Channel coast were flown, together with standing patrols over the Isle of Wight and English south coast in order to deter enemy sneak raiders. Earlier in the year, 400 and 414 had re-equipped with Mustang Mk I aircraft and with such had participated in *Operation Jubilee*, the raid on Dieppe. A total of 37 sorties had been flown over Dieppe by the two squadrons, 400 losing one Mustang with its pilot killed while 414 suffered one aircraft ditched and three others damaged, fortunately without fatalities. For these experienced and tested pilots, the poor weather on arrival at Dunsfold therefore provided a welcome respite during which they could settle in and try to improve the comforts of their living quarters.

Sadly, on 10th December, the routine daily inspection of a Mustang led to the aerodrome's first fatality. As cockpit checks were made, the aircraft's gun-firing mechanism was accidentally activated with the result that Leading Aircraftsman Colbourne, of 414 Squadron, was killed while standing in front of the aircraft.

Flying soon re-commenced and by Christmas personnel began to appreciate that Dunsfold would eventually prove an attractive posting. Organisation improved too, as the previously inexperienced staff came to grips with the logistical and administrative problems of setting up a new airfield.

One such difficulty concerned the strict standards of discipline which were laid down by the aerodrome's administrators who were largely fresh from Canada. To the experienced types of 400 and 414 Squadrons, Dunsfold's regulations appeared petty, a typical reaction being that of Flight Sergeant 'Chiefy' Stewart, a crew chief with 400. In Stewart's opinion, aircraft servicability was the only real consideration for ground crews of an operational squadron. Dunsfold's set meal times and overdose of 'Bull' therefore came as something of a shock and the men of 400 Squadron came to appreciate their comparative isolation on the opposite side of the aerodrome to Station Headquarters. Just over the perimeter fence behind their dispersals lay 'The Three Compasses' pub where Bert and Billie Evans were happy for the Canadians to use their establishment as an unofficial mess hall.

Above, The Gibbs Hatch Family Restaurant as it was.

Right, the daughter of The Gibbs Hatch's owner, with two Canadian sappers. (Mrs Harwood)

Also quickly popular was 'The Gibbs Hatch Family Restaurant' and 'The Sundial Café' just a little further up the road where real eggs were to be had, something akin to a miracle at the time.* Many a Canadian today still recalls the meals of egg and chips savoured at these venues, but it was not too long before authority discovered and frowned upon the practice. 'Chiefy' Stewart also met with difficulties over the question of authority for the beaten up Crosley which he had acquired and drove about the airfield. Naturally, he had no such authority.

A major source of administrative assistance was still lacking since Dunsfold's WAAF personnel had yet to arrive. Their

---

*'The Three Compasses' remains little altered and under the same name. 'The Gibbs Hatch Family Restaurant' is now the 'Alfold Barn' pub and restaurant, while 'The Sundial Café' is re-named the 'Chez Jean' restaurant.

37

accommodation site was not completed until late December and from then on the male population eagerly anticipated female company. For the men of 400 Squadron's detached flight, the wait seemed to have been in vain. On 28th December, with still not a WAAF in sight, they left Dunsfold for their parent base at RAF Middle Wallop.

1943 arrived with improving fortunes for the Allies. In the Far East the Japanese had suffered a series of naval defeats which shattered the myth of their invincibility and Australian troops had commenced their bitter fight back up New Guinea. In North Africa, Rommel was in flight from El Alamein while Allied forces under Eisenhower had landed in Morocco and Algeria. The German 6th Army was close to surrender at Stalingrad and in the skies above Europe the Allies' superiority was growing. Bomber Command was now able to unleash awesome raids of over 1,000 aircraft against German and at the same time had begun, in conjunction with the USAAF, to attack targets in Italy. While Dieppe had been a salutary lesson against acting too soon, planning for an all-out assault on occupied Europe was clearly about to commence in earnest.

The new year also brought Wing Commander E. H. G. Moncrieff AFC RCAF, posted in as station commanding officer and then aircraft strength rose once more when 430 Squadron RCAF started to arrive on 2nd January 1943. This was a new squadron which had only just formed on 1st January 1943 at RAF Hartfordbridge (later Blackbushe aerodrome). Moving to Dunsfold, it was initially equipped with Tomahawk aircraft for training purposes and in order to speed the training of the new squadron, a nucleus of experienced pilots was moved across from other squadrons, including Flight Lieutenant Paul Bissky from 400 and Flying Officer Don Sherk of 414 Squadron. This not only helped the raw recruits, but extended the bond among the three squadrons (400, 414 and 430) who together now formed 39 (Army Co-operation) Wing RCAF. On 4th January, the officers of 430 Squadron moved into Stovoldshill Farm, requisitioned for use by the aerodrome. At the same time, work began on renovating nearby Hall Place for the use of the officers of 400 Squadron RCAF, already under orders to move in its entirety to Dunsfold in February.

F/O Duff's Tomahawk AK189 after the crash on January 18th, 1943. Nat. Archives of Canada /PMR76-720

The tempo of flying increased considerably as 430 Squadron in particular seized every chance to gain experience for its fresh pilots. A spate of incidents marred the squadron's initiation however. On 18th January, Pilot Officer Duff chalked up Dunsfold's first aircraft crash when his Tomahawk (AK189) blew a tyre on take-off. Crash-landing on the aerodrome boundary, Duff was fortunate to walk away uninjured while the aircraft sustained moderate damage. Three days later, fellow 430 pilot Pilot Officer Lowndes underwent a harrowing first Tomahawk flight when AH905 suffered a mid-air engine failure. Managing a difficult forced landing, Lowndes climbed from the wreckage just in time before the cockpit burst into flames, destroying the aircraft.

On the arrival of 430 Squadron, Wing Commander Moncrieff had become that unit's first commanding officer as well as continuing as Dunsfold's station commanding officer, but it was soon clear that the demands of the inexperienced squadron

Sgt. Eve Palmer, Dunsfold's first WAAF. (Eve Palmer)

would be considerable. It was therefore a great help to Moncrieff when command of the station was formally passed to newcomer Wing Commander H. J. Burden DSC DFC RCAF on 19th January, 1943, the event being celebrated by a dinner hosted by Moncrieff at the 'Hogs Back Hotel'.*

Another reason to celebrate was the arrival of Dunsfold's first WAAF, Sergeant Eve Palmer. Still relatively fresh from boarding school, Eve was thrown into a totally unknown world amongst a breed of men of which she had, as yet, no experience. Her own immediate commanding officer, Section Officer Clapham, arrived a week after her but, with the background of a doctor's daughter from sedate Brighton, was similarly ill-prepared. The hard-gambling, hard-fighting initial impressions of camp life were however soon replaced with an appreciation for the way in which the Canadians cut through, or simply ignored, red-tape. It also quickly became obvious that a considerable number of the airmen were homesick and the WAAFs spent many an hour listening to tales of back home and looking at snapshots of family life left behind in Canada. One immediate result of this was that firstly Eve, and then Section Officer Clapham, fell prey to the measles virus which swept through the camp. Soon after their arrival, both women found themselves

---

*Wing Commander Burden was the brother-in-law of Canada's famous World War One fighter ace, Air Marshal Billy Bishop VC.

*Above, the burnt out wreck of P/O
Lowndes' Tomahawk (PMR76-259)*

*Right, P/O J. A. 'Butch' Lowndes.
(National Archives of Canada /
PL29195)*

hospitalised and their administrative talents were sorely missed
until they returned from hospital in Guildford some weeks later.

As more WAAFs arrived, the aerodrome's headquarters were
determined that no more of these valuable helpers would fall
foul of the ailments currently prevalent amongst the airmen. A
round of innoculations was arranged for all the men and in the
interim the newly-arrived WAAFs were strictly off limits. On the
day of their shots a group of 430 Squadron pilots decided to
undertake an excursion after receiving the jabs. Renting bicycles
in Alfold, they pedalled off on a pub crawl to drown their
disappointment at not yet being able to fraternise with the
WAAFs. Contrary to all their medic's advice, pint followed pint
to mix with the cocktail already injected and the ride back to

camp became an obstacle course of crashes and falls. Collapsing back in their quarters, the young pilots then suffered an unforgettable lesson as they spent a night wracked with the worst nightmares any of them had ever experienced.

Meanwhile, the local population was cautiously assessing whether the new blue uniformed Canadians were any less boisterous than their green uniformed predecessors. From the gusto with which the airmen threw themselves into local dances and pubs, the immediate answer was in the negative. A favourite for the pilots on a Saturday night was 'The Cranley Hotel' and, subject to the operational demands of the next day, this would be followed by a late Sunday brunch at 'The Crown' in nearby Chiddingfold. One local custom there which amused Paul Bissky and the other pilots of 430 Squadron was that no drinks orders would be taken on a Sunday until the arrival of the vicar from the church opposite the pub. Thirsty after the late morning service, the vicar would first be served his 'half and half' before the demands of the Canadians were met.

The airmen's behaviour in the locality was generally good, albeit boisterous, but as is often the case, a minority threatened the reputation of the majority. By the end of January, two airmen of 430 Squadron were already languishing in Godalming's jail for a burglary in Dunsfold village. On the aerodrome itself, a Sergeant of 414 Squadron was arrested and charged with breaking into the Sergeant's Mess.

On 1st February 1943, the entire strength of 400 Squadron RCAF, commanded by Wing Commander R. C. A. 'Bunt' Waddell, moved into Dunsfold from RAF Middle Wallop. This briefly brought the aerodrome's strength to all three squadrons of 39 (Army Co-operation) Wing RCAF, but due to the lack of completed dispersals and accommodation it was decided in the interim to only base two of the squadrons at Dunsfold. 414 Squadron therefore moved out to replace 400 Squadron at Middle Wallop on 1st and 2nd February 1943. When they did so, 414 were obliged to leave one aircraft behind. Since their arrival at Dunsfold they had managed to add a Piper Cub light aircraft to their strength, impressed from the civil register (BV180, former G-AFWA). This versatile little aeroplane was soon lost when strong gales on 30th January blew it over, resulting in a write-off.

Hall Place had now supplemented Stovoldshill Farm as officers' quarters and this relieved some of the pressure on accommodation as personnel numbers swelled to over 1,000. The situation was not helped by the staging of *Exercise Spartan* from 1st to 12th March. This was a large army co-operation exercise held in south-east England and, in order to take part, 414 Squadron again flew in on 20th February 1943 to join its two sister units. With still not enough fully equipped dispersal points for the entire Wing (now some sixty aircraft), aircraft had to be tied down on the runways and perimeter track. *Spartan* itself enjoyed clear and warm weather and the Dunsfold squadrons took a busy part in the proceedings. In mock air combat, 414 Squadron's experiences were fairly typical, they were credited with ten 'enemy' aircraft destroyed and three damaged, for the loss of five of their Mustangs. It was later learned that *Spartan* had been the largest grouping of men and equipment in the south of England to date and many valuable lessons had been learnt.

A new experience in life at the aerodrome had occurred on 10th February when the station recorded its first 'Air Raid Red' alert. Enemy aircraft were reported in the immediate vicinity but did not find the aerodrome, bombs being dropped a few miles to the south of Dunsfold at 16.45 hours. It is doubtful that the Luftwaffe were even aware of the proximity of the still relatively new aerodrome, but the incident did lend some purpose to the training which Norman MacLeod and his fellow insructors of the RAF Regiment were now giving to the Canadians. Over the winter months 4153 Squadron had busied itself with setting up temporary sand-bagged gun posts around the airfield perimeter and instructing the Canadian soldiers and airmen in drill and small arms use. With the coming of spring, and a semblance of order to camp life, training had commenced in anti-aircraft gunnery and the first course, from 414 Squadron, left for the south coast in mid-March to practise firing at drogues towed by biplanes.

Even had the Luftwaffe raiders chanced upon Dunsfold, it is unlikely that they could have improved upon 430's continuing ability to damage or destroy aircraft. Its Tomahawks, now tired and ageing, were unforgiving mounts for relatively new pilots. Conversion and familiarisation was not helped by the fact that the aircraft were fitted with metric instrumentation, having come from a production batch originally destined for the French Air Force. Since 21st January therefore, the Air Transport Auxiliary had started to deliver replacement Mustangs and this exercise in itself brought a lesson for the Canadian boys. On one occasion, Flying Officer Nolan Henderson of 400 Squadron was returning to Dunsfold alone when he spotted another Mustang heading in the same direction. His curiosity was aroused by the fact that it carried no identification letter on its fuselage so, edging closer for a better look, Henderson tucked into close formation with the mystery aircraft. Immediately, the unknown pilot made very definite and agitated signs for the young Canadian to move away so a puzzled Henderson pulled out of formation and watched from a distance as the other aircraft turned into Dunsfold's circuit and landed. A few minutes later Henderson likewise dropped onto the runway, noticing as he did so that the unmarked Mustang had not taxied into the squadron dispersals but instead was parked in the visitors area by the control tower. Its pilot was just climbing out as Henderson rolled by on the main runway and the Canadian was startled to see that the visitor was a very blonde young lady. Realization dawned that this must be one of the lady pilots of the ATA delivering a fresh aircraft and Henderson realised he owed an apology. By the time he returned his own aircraft to its dispersal and cadged a lift to the control tower, precious minutes had been lost. As the eager young pilot arrived at Flying Control, he was just in time to see the shapely ferry pilot climbing aboard a Dragon Rapide sent to collect her. The door of the aircraft closed, its engines revved, and the exotic visitor was gone. His dash around the aerodrome wasted, Henderson could only admire from afar.

Despite 430's gradual change to new equipment, Ernie Moncrieff's training programme continued to suffer from a spate of accidents. On 14th February Mustang AM135 had to be struck off charge when it returned damaged from hitting a tree during over enthusiastic low flying and on the 28th, Pilot Officer

Left, Nolan Henderson. (Grp. Cptn. N. Henderson)

Below, P/O Forster's Tomahawk crash. (Nat. Archives of Canada PMR76-263)

Forster had written off one of the remaining Tomahawks, AH910, in yet another forced landing necessitated by engine failure. Again the pilot was able to walk away with only minor cuts and bruises, but he was not so lucky a month later when he crashed Mustang AM120 near Ockley. Although alive, Forster was immediately rushed to hospital with serious head and spine injuries. Prior to this latter incident there had also been two aircraft accidents on the ground at Dunsfold, the first on 9th March involving Pilot Officer Rose's Mustang which was badly damaged by a Master making a hurried forced landing. Rose himself was fortunately unhurt, as too was Flight Lieutenant Clarke when ten days later the tail of his Mustang AG376 was sawn off by the propeller of another aircraft. Flying Officer McQuoid in a Mustang of 414 Squadron had been behind Clarke in the circuit and on landing had unfortunately got a little too close for comfort!*

While 430 Squadron was working towards operational status, the experienced 400 and 414 Squadrons were chafing at their relative inactivity. There was still no opportunity at this stage of the war in north-western Europe for them to carry out their designated rôle of army co-operation and routine patrols over the south coast and Isle of Wight did little to relieve the tedium. 39 Wing headquarters were, however, about to give their impatient pilots other means of flexing their muscles.

*During this period, the aerodrome was also used for practice 'deck' landings by visiting Spitfires. This was almost certainly one of the trials of Prime Minister Churchill's idea of 'floating aerodromes' to be anchored just off an invasion beach.

Chapter Four

Flak Lessons

Rhubarbs and *Rangers* were to be the code-names for two types of offensive sweep over occupied territory. *Rhubarbs* normally consisted of daylight, fairly shallow penetrations of the French coast, at low-level. Any targets of opportunity were to be attacked, but with particular emphasis on disrupting communication and transportation systems. *Rangers*, usually undertaken at night, were longer-range operations and were aimed at enemy airfields or other known military targets. For the Canadians, equipped with the Allison engined Mustang,* such operations were deemed perfect. Experience over the Dieppe beaches in August had shown that their aircraft were better suited to low-level work rather than dog-fighting with German fighters and their twin cannon armament would be useful for attacking locomotives, power lines and vehicles. *Rhubarbs* and *Rangers* were also designed to be undertaken by small formations, normally pairs, and again this matched the Canadians' army co-operation experience where they had usually operated in twos. Pairs of pilots therefore commenced planning, huddling over French maps and even railway timetables, in order to pinpoint ground targets worth attacking. Poor weather returned to dampen enthusiasm for a few days but on 26th March conditions cleared sufficiently for the first sortie to take place. Flying Officers Stover and Hutchinson, of 414 Squadron, took two Mustangs on a daylight low level sweep over Northern France, destroying an electricity transformer station and two locomotives. Both safely returned to Dunsfold and news of their achievement was enthusiastically received by their colleagues.

Determined to emulate the success of this first *Rhubarb* from Dunsfold, two more pilots of 414 Squadron, Flying Officers Steeves and Mossing, planned a similar operation for the next day. The 27th March dawned dull, but with the meteorological report advising of only rain and a few mist patches, the two

---

*The Mustang came into its own as a fighter aircraft when later models were fitted with a variant of the British Merlin engine. The American Allison engine only proved adequate for low level duties but as such was suitable for the photo-reconnaissance and ground attack work undertaken by the Canadians.

pilots considered their operation still viable for the late afternoon.

Flying as number one of the pair, Steeves lifted off from Dunsfold's runway at 16.00 hours in Mustang AP185, closely followed by Mossing in AG525. Climbing steadily, Steeves set the course for France but, as the pair approached the south coast of England, they ran into dense fog. Unable to see his leader, Mossing concentrated on his instruments in the gloom and followed Steeves' immediate order over the radio to climb. Familiar with the hilly nature of the countryside below him, Mossing was only too glad to follow Steeves' advice and he was was not surprised when, approximately a minute and a half later, the still unseen Steeves again radioed, advising a return to Dunsfold.

Continuing to climb, Mossing emerged from cloud at 6,000 feet, but could not raise Steeves on the radio. Calling RAF Tangmere's flying control instead, Mossing requested a course back to Dunsfold, landing there at 16.40 hours. Of Steeves there was no sign. Fears for the worst were confirmed when, from Sussex, Hassocks Police reported that an aircraft had crashed on the side of a hill north of Brighton at 16.10 hours. The wreckage of Steeve's Mustang was subsequently found half buried into a hill-side north of Shoreham and it was obvious that the young officer had died instantly on impact. Dunsfold's first operational flying fatality, Steeves was buried on 30th March, in Brookwood Military Cemetery. His grave, still beautifully maintained today, lies alongside so many of his countrymen who never returned home.

With the death of Steeves, Dunsfold's baptism into the shooting war was complete. The pace of offensive operations had to be maintained however and again 414 Squadron was to the fore on 1st April when Flying Officer McQuoid in AG525 failed to return from a low level sweep over St. Pierre in France and was posted as missing, presumed killed.

Three days later, the aerodrome scented the distant air war over Germany when it received its first emergency landing by an aircraft returning from bombing operations over the Reich. At 15.30 hours, Dunsfold's flying control received a telephone call from 11 Group asking them to look out for a B17 Flying Fortress

Charles 'Smokey' Stover of 414 Squadron RCAF who flew the first Rhubarb from Dunsfold. (National Archives of Canada PL-22862.)

in distress. Two minutes later Dunsfold made radio contact with the aircraft and gave immediate clearance to land. Local resident Derek Porter watched fascinated as the huge bomber limped towards the airfield and, looking up at the wing markings of the United States Army Air Force, he was startled to be able to see daylight through gaping holes caused by flak. As he watched, flares were fired out from the aircraft to alert the aerodrome that wounded were on board and gradually the four engined bomber sank out of sight to make a safe landing on Dunsfold's runway. Medical teams rushed to the aircraft to carry off two injured gunners to hospital in Cranleigh while the remaining eight crew surveyed their aircraft and were happy to find her still airworthy in spite of the damage. Less than two hours later the pilots had recovered sufficiently from the strain of the incident to take off and return to their home base.

From this beginning, Dunsfold was to play a vital rôle throughout the remainder of the war as a home for aircraft lost or in distress. During the first half of 1943, a particularly warm welcome was given to a number of stragglers from the RCAF bomber squadrons based in northern England, two Wellingtons of 431 and 427 Squadrons RCAF being the first nocturnal refugees in April.

Dunsfold's strength once more dropped to two squadrons when 414 left for RAF Middle Wallop on 9th April. The departure of this aggressive unit did not, however, mean that Dunsfold was left in peace since now it was 400 Squadron that returned to the offensive with *Rhubarbs* and *Rangers* - and with immediate success.

On 11th April ten officers of the US Army Air Force arrived for temporary duties with this squadron and they soon learned the measure of 400's expertise when on the night of 13th April, Flight Lieutenant Peters and Flying Officer Duncan 'Bitsy' Grant took off at 21.30 hours for a *Ranger* to the south of Paris. Above Melun Villarouche airfield the two Canadians spotted the aircraft of a German night flying school and Grant, flying AM259 - R, quickly fastened onto a Dornier Do 217 twin-engined bomber. Carefully stalking his prey in the airfield's circuit, Grant closed to 400 yards before opening fire with a two seconds burst. Strikes were observed all over the enemy machine as Grant again opened fire from 100 yards, with a longer four seconds burst. The Dornier, witnessed by Peters, staggered and plunged to the ground while the two Mustangs sped for home and landed safely at Dunsfold at 23.30 hours.

Three nights later a similar sortie took place, only this time Dunsfold was almost on the receiving end. The aerodrome's flying control staff were still on duty at midnight as night flying was in progress by the Mustangs. Suddenly the darkness was split by a bright flash from the direction of Dunsfold village, followed moments later by the crash of an exploding bomb and a wave of concussion which was felt throughout camp. Some five minutes later the air raid warning was belatedly broadcast, but no trace was picked up of the enemy raider which had dropped a solitary bomb in open land near to the village.

While the similarity to Grant's recent operation was marked, there was no solid evidence that the German aircraft had been aiming for the airfield and certainly, in no way did it deter the Canadians. On the night of 17th April, 400's commanding officer, Wing Commander Waddell, led from the front on a night *Ranger* with Flying Officer Pepper. Heading for the Chartres region, the pair crossed the French coast near to St. Valéry, but were immediately picked up by searchlights. The ensuing flak hit AG528 flown by Pepper, who reported to Waddell that he was losing coolant fluid. Rapidly assessing the situation, Pepper then radioed that there was no chance he could make it back to England. Watched by his commanding officer, Pepper therefore baled out successfully and Waddell returned to Dunsfold with high hopes that Pepper would have landed uninjured. The squadron's log of the time reflected these hopes by recording Pepper as 'missing -believed P.O.W.' and a cryptic note added that 'his personal effects were safeguarded at once'!

As 400 Squadron continued to take the fight across the Channel, 430 Squadron looked forward to the day when they too would be able to take part. In this they were helped by the arrival in early April of Squadron Leader Dick Ellis DFC as their new second in command. Ellis had spent almost two years with a Canadian Spitfire squadron, 412, and had risen from the non-commissioned rank of Sergeant Pilot. Decorated for his success in attacking both enemy aircraft and locomotives, Ellis was to add considerable experience to 430's ranks. Yet, as intensive training was kept up, ill fortune remained with the squadron. On 19th April, Flying Officer Jackson was engaged on a practice flight over Hampshire when his Mustang AP181 collided with a Spitfire. Attempting a forced landing, Jackson was killed when his aircraft hit a hidden earth bank and broke up, the Spitfire pilot was also killed as his aircraft spun in. On 22nd April, the combination of hilly country and poor weather claimed another victim when Flying Officer Reed's Mustang AM255 flew into high ground at Hindhead while trying to return to Dunsfold. Both Jackson and Reed were Americans serving in the Royal Canadian Air Force.

A ten days air firing course in Somerset brought 430 to the culmination of their combat training and a final series of exercises was undertaken prior to the squadron becoming operationally ready. The first such exercise, in early May, involved 'B' flight being detached to Oulston, near Durham, in order to provide artillery reconnaissance for the Army on manoeuvres, while 'A' flight practiced further night flying at Dunsfold.

'B' flight's temporary move was to prove eventful in more ways than one. While six Mustangs safely took off for Oulston, Flying Officer Don Sherk was allotted the task of following them in the squadron's Tiger Moth biplane. As he lifted off from Dunsfold for the long, slow haul north, Sherk was quickly and unceremoniously returned to earth by an engine failure. Lucky to emerge unscathed, Sherk was unable to continue with the flight as the frail aircraft was extensively damaged.

For the ground crew too, an unpleasant shock was in store as they learned that they were to be taken to Oulston by glider. Sure enough a Whitley tug aircraft and Horsa glider arrived at Dunsfold for the two officers and twenty men who filed aboard with considerable trepidation. Their fears seemed only too well founded when a few minutes after take off the combination separated and had to return to the aerodrome. Several hours later a second attempt was made, tug and glider this time reaching Bicester, near Oxford, where again they were forced to land. While some of the party continued to Oulston in the Whitley, others of the group had to remain overnight at Bicester to await the arrival of a new tug aircraft for their, by now, despised glider. At the third attempt, Oulston was eventually reached.

Returning to Dunsfold on 18th May, 'B' flight joined 'A' flight in another army co-operation exercise *Saturn* which proved to be a great success, ending on the 22nd with compliments from the Army for the squadron's good work. With over 1900 flying training hours under its belt, 430 was ready for operations but overlooked one old adversary - the English weather. Throughout May only five *Rhubarbs* were mounted by 430 and all were subsequently abandoned due to poor weather conditions over the target areas in Northern France. If any further encouragement were needed, however, news arrived on 23rd May that Flight Lieutenant Peters and Flying Officer Grant of 400 Squadron were to receive the DFC in recognition of their recent successes and 400's commanding officer, Wing Commander Waddell, was likewise decorated soon after.

It was not until 1st June that 430 eventually met with success when Flight Lieutenant Clarke and Flying Officer Pethick attacked locomotives and freight cars some fifty miles inland from the French coast. Throughout the operation, which lasted over two hours, no flak was encountered and the two pilots returned much encouraged. The following day, two more *Rhubarbs* were flown, the first, by Flight Lieutenant Chesters and Flying Officer Alliston, again struck at enemy railway targets as well as boats and electricity pylons and the pair returned safely. The second operation of the day was to have a very different ending.

Tom Pethick this time teamed up with Flying Officer Sherk and together they took their Mustangs to zero height over the Channel, speeding in over occupied territory just north of Caen. They were immediately rewarded by sighting a freight locomotive, which was attacked and hit. The two pilots then swept low over Caen airfield, but streams of flak forced them away and they then picked up the main railway line westwards out of Bayeux. Following this, the junction at Airel provided a tempting target with no less than four locomotives present and once again Sherk and Pethick dived to the attack. As Don Sherk watched his cannon strike home, a storm of flak suddenly erupted and he wrenched his Mustang away in a desperate evasive manoeuvre. As he did so, he glanced towards Pethick's aircraft, AM200, and to his alarm, saw it bracketed by the enemy fire. The aircraft staggered beneath the onslaught of shells, rolled onto its back and plunged into the ground. 430 Squadron's first operational fatality, Pethick was buried with military honours by the Germans in Airel.

The beginning of June 1943 also saw the demise of Army Co-Operation Command and Dunsfold's Mustang squadrons were transferred instead to RAF Fighter Command. Their rôle then received the new description of 'Fighter Reconnaissance' and this was felt to better fit the current operations of *Rhubarbs* and *Rangers* as well as the photographic reconnaissance duties along the enemy coast - operations known as *Populars*. These latter sorties again usually involved a pair of aircraft, one taking the photographs required, while the other acted as top cover against enemy aircraft. As in the case of *Rhubarbs*, *Populars* called for precise navigation, and thorough training continued at Dunsfold in between operations. For 430 Squadron, this led to more loss of life, when on 11th June, Flying Officer Brouillette in Mustang AP171 was caught out by thick fog which closed in suddenly during a cross country exercise. In unfamiliar terrain, Brouillette was killed when he flew into a hillside near Ludlow, in Shropshire.

As the station became more established, the squadrons' social activities increased. 430 Squadron found themselves 'adopted' by an aristocratic English family, the Challiners who had an estate in Staveley, Westmoreland. As a break from operations pilots were invited for sailing week-ends on Lake Windermere and entertainment included being driven by Rolls-Royce to local dances. One young Canadian, somewhat awed by his surroundings, managed to commit a social gaffe which seemed to threaten his squadron's favours. Having been introduced to both the lady of the house and her small dog, the hapless pilot managed to confuse the names and addressed her ladyship as 'Queenie'. Her ladyship was most certainly not amused.

In the locality of Dunsfold, it was particularly through the Canadian's strong liking for all types of sport that friendships were forged. 400 Squadron's two basketball teams were already leading the Forces' Leagues, while softball was growing in popularity too. A one-sided contest took place when 400 challenged the British Army to a baseball match in Godalming. Emerging victors by a resounding 19 - 0, the Canadians also took the honours in the post-match hospitality provided by Godalming's British Legion Club!

Another means of becoming known in the locality was via the 'Wings for Victory' appeals. These were appeals for money from the population to help aircraft production, each village and town setting a financial target to be reached. As the local area's airforce representatives, Dunsfold's personnel and aircraft were frequently called upon to stage march pasts and flying formations to assist the collecting tins. Such parades were held in Dunsfold, Guildford, Godalming, Hambledon, Haslemere and Cranleigh and provided a good morale boost for the local people.

On 17th June, 1943, a meeting of Dunsfold's headquarters' personnel gave a hint of future plans for the aerodrome when Wing Commander Burden addressed his staff on plans to create a new command, a Tactical Air Force. This Air Force was designed to closely support the Army's ground forces when the time for the invasion arrived and was based upon the lessons learned in *Operation Spartan*. The plan entailed the formation of mobile airfield units with airfield, rather than squadron, support staff. This was further explained two days later when Group Captain Smith arrived from Wing headquarters to talk to the executive officers of both 400 and 430 Squadrons.

On the same day familiar faces were seen yet again, when 414 Squadron once more returned to line up alongside its two sister units. Since its move to Middle Wallop in mid April, 414 had undergone a busy and nomadic existence involving detachments to Harrowbeer and Portreath in Cornwall. The latter deployment had involved a tragic incident when the squadron had clashed head on with a group of unidentified aircraft low over the sea. Opening fire instinctively, the two formations hurtled through each other, only to belatedly recognise the opposition as allied aircraft. This recognition had come too late for Flying Officer Vaupel of 414 and a fellow Canadian in the other formation, which proved to be the Spitfires of 412 Squadron RCAF. Vaupel's Mustang and one Spitfire both fell into the sea with the loss of the two pilots. It was thus a somewhat chastened unit which returned to Dunsfold, the more so as they learned they were only to stay briefly while forming one of the new Airfield formations independent of 400 and 430.

The aerodrome was now bursting again with personnel and aircraft. In the first week of June, yet another unit had added to the crush when 403 Repair and Salvage Unit arrived on the 4th. While their workshops and vehicles were based on the site, there was no accommodation available for the unit's 160 personnel who therefore had to be billetted in nearby Alfold. With the return of 414 Squadron neither was there a lack of aircraft. Sixty or so Mustangs predominated among the three squadrons, with just some two or three Tomahawks left for training purposes. In addition, all squadrons used Miles Masters and Tiger Moths for communication duties and, although 414 Squadron had by now given up their sole Fairey Battle, other unusual aircraft included four of the new Auster Mk I light aircraft for 430 Squadron and two Hawker Typhoons allocated to 400 Squadron. The Typhoons were early Mk 1b aircraft from the second production batch and had been with 400 Squadron since

February 1943 for evaluation. While the speed of this large rugged fighter made it ideal for catching the Luftwaffe's FW 190s on low level sneak raids, its reputation for problems was still worrying in the first half of 1943. The reliability of its Napier Sabre engine was a continuing cause for concern and mid-air stoppages of this power unit were no minor matter in an aircraft reputed to have the gliding qualities of a seven ton brick. More serious still had been a series of accidents where the Typhoon's tail had broken away, invariably leading to a fatal crash. The Canadians therefore treated their two charges with healthy respect before eventually rejecting them as Mustang replacements later in the year.

22nd June, 1943 brought the operation which was to ultimately lead to Dunsfold's first recorded evader from enemy territory. In good weather, four Mustangs of 400 Squadron took off for early morning intruder operations over the French coastal region. Once over the coast the aircraft became separated and, in particular, nothing was seen of Flying Officer Jimmy Watlington in AG641 - 'B' until Flight Lieutenant Peters heard him calling over the radio. Watlington had been hit by flak and was baling out, he gave his height as 8,000 feet, ten miles north of Dieppe and as the others returned to Dunsfold, it seemed probable that Watlington stood a good chance of surviving. This was indeed so. Watlington did land safely by parachute and was picked up by the French Resistance before he could be captured. After a long walk through France and Spain, Watlington returned to Britain eleven months later.

The struggle for available space on the airfield was not helped by the return in June of an element of Royal Canadian Engineers, whose task it was to construct a new type of experimental runway alongside the existing main runway. This involved grading, draining and compacting the soil, after which two ply impregnated hessian was applied to the surface and rolled down. The idea of this surface was to enable swift provision of runways for the planned mobile airfield units of the Tactical Air Force. Consequently, on 23rd June, the new surface was given an initial trial at Dunsfold before a host of top brass. Already known to the aerodrome from its official opening were Lieutenant General McNaughton and Air Marshal Edwards

Jimmy Watlington. (Photo Grp. Cpt. Nolan Henderson)

RCAF and they were joined by Air Chief Marshal Sir Trafford Leigh-Mallory, Commander in Chief of RAF Fighter Command, Air Vice-Marshal D'Albiac, AOC Tactical Air Force, and Air Vice-Marshal Dickson, AOC 83 Group, along with representatives of the US Army Air Force, Canadian Army, US Marines, British Army and the Air Ministry. The strip was divided into several sections, each of which used one of three different methods for laying the surface. The demonstration commenced with numerous take-offs and landings by four Mustangs, four Spitfires, a Mosquito and a Wellington. When these were completed and all aircraft were back on the ground, an explosive charge was detonated to blow a sizeable crater in the surface of the new temporary runway. The Canadian sappers then immediately sprung into action, filling the crater with hardcore and earth before rolling and compacting a fresh surface. Within one hour the operation was completed and the runway ready for all aircraft to take off again. While the high command expressed general satisfaction with the scheme, it was only ever used to any great extent by the Canadians, its inclination to become waterlogged making it less popular than the Sommerfeld Tracking variety or the American pierced steel planking (PSP) design.

In the meantime, Dunsfold was gaining early involvement in preparations for the invasion of Europe. Throughout June, the demand for *Popular* sorties increased in line with the good weather conditions available and it was soon noted that these missions now concentrated on photographing the French coast-line. On 29th June, Flight Lieutenant Paul Bissky, of 430 Squadron, took sixty three photographs while watched over by Flying Officers Winiarz and Manser. The area covered, between St Aubin and Port-en-Bessin, was to prove to include the eventual invasion beaches.

The next day saw a return to *Rhubarbs* when both 400 and 430 Squadron mounted sorties, but an inauspicious start was made as Flying Officers MacLeod and Roberts of 414 Squadron approached the Channel. MacLeod reported engine trouble from his Mustang AG615 as the pair were about to leave the coast. Turning back, MacLeod headed for an emergency landing at nearby RAF Ford, only to overshoot and crash into the sea wall. While the Mustang was completely destroyed by fire, the young Canadian pilot escaped with only superficial injuries.

From 430, Paul Bissky and Butch Lowndes crossed to the Lisieux area where they attacked an electricity pylon, railway sheds, a power station, a military lorry, a tug with three barges and a locomotive. Although two Junkers Ju 88s and a Focke Wulf FW 190 were spotted in the distance, the two Canadians made good their return without interception. At the same time, Flight Lieutenant Clarke and Flying Officer McKessock under-took 430's other *Rhubarb* in an adjacent area to the south and west of Bissky and Lowndes. After a couple of inconclusive attacks on locomotives, the pair left the French coast near to Trouville in order to head back to Dunsfold. As they did so however, an enemy aircraft, probably a Junkers Ju 88, was spotted turning towards them and at the same time, Clarke picked out a Focke Wulf FW 190 coming in from the left. Even at low level, Clarke appreciated that the Focke Wulf could spell trouble for the Mustangs and he therefore ordered McKessock to speed up and head for the safety of a rain squall ahead. As he glanced back, Clarke saw disaster befall his fellow pilot when McKessock's Mustang suddenly hit the sea and shattered into pieces. Since the German fighter had not yet come within range it would seem that McKessock had misjudged his height above the waves - a mishap only too easy when flying low level at high speed. McKessock's body was subsequently recovered from the sea by the Germans and buried at Le Havre.

By July, 1943 it was known that all Dunsfold's units would soon be leaving Dunsfold in order to join the new mobile airfield commands and changes in command had therefore already commenced, Wing Commander Begg having been replaced by Squadron Leader Godfrey on 414 Squadron in June. 403 Repair and Salvage Unit then became the first lodger to leave when it departed for RAF Detling on 4th July, but compensation came via a number of interesting visits. These commenced on 1st July when four Halifax bombers began a short stay at Dunsfold for fighter affiliation training with the Mustangs. The next day saw the first of Dunsfold's many royal visits when HRH Princess Marie Louise visited the aerodrome to inspect the squadrons.

This latter visit proved just in time as on 3rd July, 430 Squadron began their farewell celebrations with a last fling in Cranleigh. They left Dunsfold with 414 Squadron for RAF Gatwick two days later, designated as 129 Airfield. This new command was to partner 128 Airfield in what was renamed 39 RCAF Sector, although it was initially unclear as to which unit would join 400 Squadron as its partner in 128 Airfield.

The puzzle was solved when, on 6th July, the advance party of 231 Squadron RAF arrived from Clifton near York. The following day brought the squadron's main party and aircraft, led by Wing Commander V. A. Pope, with Squadron Leader J. P. Lucas as his deputy. Likewise equipped with Mustang Mk Is, the unit made a suitable, albeit RAF, partner for 400 Squadron. As 231 Squadron did not have any operational experience to date, its pilots immediately began to practice formation flying and fighter tactics under the guidance of their experienced Canadian partners of 400 Squadron. A better example could not have been displayed when, on 8th July, two of the Canadians managed to slot in a *Rhubarb* amongst their training duties.

Flying Officers Robb and Hanton swept in over northern France, attacking and damaging no less than eight locomotives. Better still, five miles east of Cabourg, the pair chanced upon a Fieseler Storch aircraft of the Luftwaffe. At a height of only 200 feet, 'Hank' Hanton closed to 800 yards but the highly manoeuvrable Storch turned into him. At 300 yards Hanton opened fire head-on and the Storch's engine was immediately seen to stop, forcing the small aircraft down to a hurried crash landing in a field. No-one was seen to emerge from the German machine before first Robb and then Hanton strafed the crippled Storch. Following the second pass made by Hanton, the Storch burst into flames, still with no sign of life from the occupants. Elated at their luck, Robb and Hanton returned safely to Dunsfold where the latter was credited with a confirmed 'kill'.

Four days later, it was the turn of 'Bitsy' Grant to again display his marksmanship. Promoted to Flight Lieutenant, Grant was accompanied by Flying Officer Carlson on a *Rhubarb* which took them to the Chartres region in the late afternoon. Flying at zero feet, three locomotives had already been attacked when Grant spotted two Dornier Do 217s, flying line astern at 1,500 feet and some three miles apart. The two Mustangs swept in and passed directly below the second of the two Germans, before turning and attacking in line astern. Climbing up from ground level, Grant opened fire and his bursts quickly set the enemy's port engine on fire. As its crew baled out the Dornier fell away out of control, turning over onto its back, hitting the ground and exploding. The two Canadians, realising the second German was now too distant to catch, turned for home. When ten miles west of Le Havre, however, two FW 190s were vectored onto the Mustangs, approaching from the port side and a mile to the rear. The Mustangs opened up to full throttle, indicating just over 350 mph, and were chased for some seven minutes. Although one of the Germans was seen to open fire on Carlson at extreme range no hits were scored and the Canadians succeeded in keeping ahead until the enemy fighters broke away.

Flight Lieutenant Grant continued to become one of 400's most successful operational pilots. He possessed an unerring eye when attacking targets, even when such targets were on the move. His tally of locomotives destroyed was renowned, albeit it was appreciated his greatest value lay in his air combat skills. Determined to specialise as a fighter pilot, Grant successfully applied for a posting to a Canadian Spitfire squadron. On his last operation before leaving the squadron, Grant took a young newcomer, Bill Jessiman, on his first *Rhubarb* on 28.9.43. Attacking a train, Grant spotted a flak car which promptly

Flight Lieutenant Duncan 'Bitsy' Grant DFC. (Photo Grp. Cpt. Nolan Henderson)

opened up and chased the Canadians into the cloud cover. Never one to shirk a challenge, Grant dived back down to the attack, only to find the flak car waiting for him. Jessiman watched helplessly as his leader's Mustang exploded in a clump of trees. Grant was killed instantly.

Wing Commander Waddell was posted from 400 Squadron on 15th July, his duties being temporarily taken over by Squadron Leader Woods who quickly found there was more than the impending squadron move to keep him occupied. On the same day that Woods assumed command, a flying accident led to Pilot Officer Crites being killed when Mustang AG659 crashed four miles south of Godalming and the squadron lost another Mustang the following day when Flight Lieutenant Knight was forced to bale out from AM187. Returning from a *Rhubarb*, Knight had nursed his aircraft back over the Channel after flak had damaged his oil system. As he reached Beachy Head, Knight had to take to his parachute at 4,000 feet over RAF Friston when his engine seized.

Suitably inspired by the aggressive example of 400 Squadron, 231 Squadron had temporarily left Dunsfold for a week's air-firing course at RAF Weston Zoyland, their strength increas-

A Mustang of 400 Sqn. undergoing checks in a blister hangar. (National Archives of Canada PA19833.)

ing there when they were rejoined by a detached flight which had been serving in Northern Ireland. On 21st and 22nd July the squadron, now at full strength, returned to Dunsfold but found the aerodrome winding down fast. All operations from Dunsfold had ceased on the 19th and the Station lost its organisational independence when it came under the temporary administration of RAF Kenley. On the 27th of the month, Wing Commander Burden signalled the Air Ministry that henceforth Dunsfold should be considered unserviceable, as Flying Control had closed down with the posting out of its personnel. The next day 400 and 231 Squadrons left under their new title of 128 Airfield for Woodchurch, in Kent. On 31st July, all remaining personnel were posted away with the exception of Wing Commander Burden and his headquarters staff, the WAAF complement and the RAF Regiment unit. After the flurry of activity of the last two months, these personnel were left in relative peace as consideration continued as to the aerodrome's future use.

Chapter Five

The Bombers of Fighter Command

The reorganisation which moulded the Canadian Mustang squadrons into Airfield formations proved to be part of a wider plan to create a new command in the RAF. Experience in the North African campaign had shown the value of the Desert Air Force, dedicated to providing tactical support to the armies on the ground, and it was recognized that a similar command would be vital for the invasion of Europe. The existing structure of Army Co-operation Command was deemed inadequate and therefore preparations for the new Second Tactical Air Force commenced within the framework of Fighter Command.

On 1st June, 1943, 2 Group of RAF Bomber Command had been transferred to Fighter Command since it operated all the light-medium day bombers which would be an essential ingredient of the new Tactical Air Force. Army Co-operation Command was subsequently disbanded a couple of weeks later, all its squadrons likewise moving to Fighter Command. It was therefore these moves which provided Fighter Command with, on the one hand, the aerodrome at Dunsfold, and on the other, the 2 Group bomber squadrons which ideally now needed moving to the south-east from their existing bases in East Anglia.

First thoughts on the use of Dunsfold had involved the move of 464 Squadron RAAF and 487 Squadron RNZAF to the aerodrome from RAF Methwold in Suffolk, planned for 12th July, 1943. These units were equipped with Lockheed Ventura bombers but the move was called off at the last minute when both squadrons were told they were to be equipped with Mosquito VIs fighter/bomber intruders and they moved instead to Sculthorpe in Norfolk. The visit of two RAF officers from 2 Group headquarters on 5th August, 1943 nevertheless indicated that plans were still afoot to prevent Dunsfold from languishing.

Group Captain Kippenburger and Squadron Leader Cruikshank were at Dunsfold to assess its potential for use by the Mitchell medium bombers of 2 Group. The pair were obviously impressed, as only four days later orders were received to re-open the officers' quarters at Hall Place and Stovoldshill

Farm and word quickly spread that accommodation would shortly be required for some seven hundred personnel. An advance party from 2 Group arrived on 12th August and commenced preparations for the new arrivals.

While the aerodrome's administrative wheels and cogs again began to turn, some flying activity was still to be seen despite the temporary absence of squadrons. Bomber Command had increased its raids over the Alps to northern Italy and as a consequence southern England played host to many a straggler from these long trips. The early morning of 13th August saw Dunsfold well to the fore in this rôle when a Lancaster and two Halifax aircraft landed at 05.30 hours on returning from Milan. The aerodrome's emergency services were also called out for two more returning Lancasters which had collided in mid-air some three miles away at Plaistow. Fortunately, the crews of both aircraft, JA844 of 619 Squadron and ED361 of 207 Squadron, had managed to bale out and all were located with the exception of one gunner. For three days the search continued, using seven hundred men of the 5th and 6th Canadian Infantry Brigades then based in the area. Despite these huge manpower resources, no trace could be found of the missing gunner and the hunt was eventually called off. On the 17th a further one Stirling and three Halifax bombers dropped thankfully in at 04.00 hours. after another raid on Italy.

Local inhabitants spotted a new silhouette on 18th August when the first North American B-25 Mitchell Mk. II bomber slipped into the Dunsfold circuit. The type was easy to recognise in the air due to its twin tail rudders and only two engines (in contrast to the four engines of the larger twin-tailed Halifax and Lancaster) and the Mitchell was particularly distinctive in the course of landing and take off due to its tricycle undercarriage. Although very much the norm today, this was still a relatively new innovation in the 1940s and differed from the pre-dominantly tail wheel designs used by the RAF. As the day wore on it became clear that the Mitchell was something more than just a visitor, as it was followed by more and more examples of the type, all arriving individually. To the Southern Railways staff at Cranleigh and Witley Stations, the aicraft droning overhead came as no surprise as they had begun to receive

ammunition trains loaded with 1,000 and 500 lbs bombs bound
for Dunsfold. Another indicator was the arrival of 228 Maintenance Unit in the area. Under the command of Flight
Lieutenant Geary, 228 M.U. moved into a camp site in the
grounds of Sachel Court, a large country house just across the
road from the aerodrome's eastern perimeter, pending more
permanent quarters and underwent a change of title to reflect
its latest task. As 414 Air Stores Park it now held the
responsibility of providing a range of spare parts for the 2 Group
squadrons at Dunsfold, Hartford Bridge and Lasham aerodromes.

The Mitchells constituted the air parties of 98 and 180
Squadrons RAF which had come from Foulsham in Norfolk,
flying singly in a somewhat optimistic attempt to disguise
squadron strength movements for security purposes. Led by
Wing Commander Phillips and Wing Commander Magill respectively, 98 and 180 were the medium bomber units of 2 Group
which had been anticipated, moving south in order to be closer
to their target areas which were mainly in northern France.
Ground parties of both squadrons arrived by rail the same day
and soon expressed pleasure with their posting. Foulsham had
likewise been a new airfield and 98 and 180 Squadrons had
undergone the same difficulties there with rain and mud as the
Canadians had experienced at Dunsfold. By the August of 1943,
however, Dunsfold was a much better established station with
most problems ironed out. Nor did it suffer from Foulsham's
mind-numbing cold winds which swept in from the North Sea.
By contrast, Dunsfold was at its lush and pastoral best at the
height of summer. Rolling hills, leafy lanes and the slowly
flowing canal framed the aerodrome's site while, glory of glories,
it was discovered that girls of the Land Army were sited both in
Cranleigh and, better still, at Sachel Court on the very edge of
the airfield. The aircrews of 180 Squadron soon replaced 414
Squadron RCAF at 'The Three Compasses', while ground crews
of both squadrons preferred 'The Leathern Bottle' on the
Guildford road. A typical reaction of the new arrivals was that of
Leading Aircraftsman Reg Day, a flight mechanic (engines) with
98 Squadron. Already thrilled by his first ever flight when he
accompanied his charge from Foulsham to Dunsfold, the young

serviceman thought he had 'died and gone to heaven' in Surrey. After Norfolk's remoteness, it was also appreciated that London could be easily reached by train from Guildford. In no time at all the men were enjoying such attractions as the Crazy Gang at the Victoria Palace - this was more like it! On the debit side, it was a three mile walk to the nearest fish and chip shop! 180 Squadron also quickly established a reputation when, somehow, a goat was obtained as a mascot. Unfortunately, the beast ate anything and everything in sight, cigarette ends seemingly holding the greatest attraction. When the goat managed to gain entrance to the aircrews' locker room and started on the flying clothing, enough was enough. Wing Commander Magill banished the animal forthwith.

The title of the aerodrome now underwent a change to reflect its new users. Hitherto, Dunsfold had retained its Canadian title and this must have led to families of Dunsfold's new lodgers believing that their loved ones had been posted overseas. A typical 98 Squadron postal address read 'B Squadron, Hut 7, Site 4, RCAF Station Dunsfold'. Now the two new squadrons were part of the Royal Air Force, albeit with air crews from a number of Commonwealth air forces, including that of Canada. The aerodrome's new designation was therefore to be RAF Station Dunsfold and this was duly underlined when on 19th August, the orders of Wing Commander Burden relinquished RCAF mess customs in favour of those of the RAF. Although Burden and some of his headquarters staff were Canadian, this was expected to change in the near future.

The mode of operations for the Mitchells was at this time strictly daylight formation bombing. Strong fighter escort was usually provided for their sorties across the Channel and consequently enemy fighter attacks, although not unknown, were rare. Of much greater danger was the opposition faced in the form of the enemy's formidable flak barrage. Bombing was normally carried out at not more than 15,000 feet and frequently well below in the interests of accuracy. At such heights, the deadly German 88mm flak guns were highly effective with their proximity fused ammunition - and unfortunately there was plenty of this ammunition.

The preferred formation was a box of six aircraft and boxes were stepped up in height, usually from 11,000 to 14,000 feet. This meant only limited evasive action could be taken once the flak opened up and it also led to problems in poor weather, or if an aircraft were damaged and experiencing control problems. It nevertheless seemed a good omen for the future when, on 23rd August, 98 and 180 Squadrons each put up a box of six Mitchells for their first operation from Dunsfold and all returned from St. Omer without loss. A week later, it was netherthless clear that the Germans were still on target when only 23 out of 24 Mitchells returned from attacking targets in the Forêt d'Eperlecques. The missing aircraft was FL190, that of Pilot Officer 'Curly' Motheral, a Canadian of 180 Squadron. Flying number four position in the second box, Motheral's aircraft was seen to have been hit in the starboard wing by flak. As the Mitchell went down watching crews saw at least two men bale out and the fighter escort later reported seeing three parachutes open, giving hope that some of the crew might be able to put their escape and evasion training to good use.

Both at Foulsham and Dunsfold, escape and evasion exercises had been practised for the dual purpose of demonstrating valuable techniques, while at the same time hopefully keeping idle aircrews out of mischief in between operations. Without money or any means of identification, the airmen were driven several miles from the aerodrome and dropped off. The objective was then to return to Dunsfold, without being arrested by either the Police or the Home Guard. Some of those who successfully made it back to camp were followed by irate citizens, complaining bitterly of stolen bicycles. On one occasion a group of evaders returned in style by car, the owner eventually turning up at the aerodrome gates uttering every threat from prosecution to execution. His anger only subsided when it was pointed out that it was he who had broken the law by leaving his vehicle without immobilising it - a war-time requirement. Deflated, but with a generous helping of petrol coupons, the car owner quickly departed! Had the car owner thought a little more of the serious intent behind such escapades, he may have been more amenable in the first instance. Had he known of the adventures of 'Curly'

Motheral, he would surely have offered his car to the practicing escapers.

Pre-war, 'Curly' Motheral had enjoyed employment both as a hard-rock miner and then as a teacher, displaying the mixture of brain and brawn which served him well after baling out. During his parachute descent he was wounded in the leg by enemy rifle fire but successfully avoided his pursuers, shot a number of German soldiers and made contact with the French underground. Guided through occupied France, Motheral was chased through the sewers of Paris and sat drinking in the same Lyons café as a Gestapo officer. By 30th November, 1943 he arrived back at Dunsfold via Spain, Gibraltar and rumours of trouble with the officers of H.M. Customs! Returning to Canada for some well-earned leave 'Curly' helped open up and instruct at a new training unit. In July 1944 he was posted back to Britain and rejoined 180 Squadron at Dunsfold on 6th August, flying on operations again on the 18th.

The day of Dunsfold's first Mitchell loss was also memorable in terms of the RAF Regiment's exercise which was held on the 30th. 2847 Squadron had not been idle during the lull in the aerodrome's flying activities since Squadron Leader Frogley had appreciated that there was still one side of the airfield not covered by his Bofors and Hispano gun posts. Consequently, the gunners had laboured in July to set up a new post due south of the airfield and actually beyond the base's perimeter. This had entailed building a small bridge over the canal for access but with this completed, Frogley was confident he now had all the air angles covered. At the end of August he felt it was time to test the aerodrome's ability to withstand a ground raiding force. Just 35 of his enthusiastic men were detailed to attack the airfield and in next to no time they had overwhelmed a Bofors post, the underground battle headquarters and even flying control in the tower. Their determination was amply illustrated by the fact that two men had to be packed off to hospital in Horsham for treatment of injuries received!

As organisation of the new 2nd Tactical Air Force continued, it was appreciated that 2 Group operated a variety of types, namely the Mitchell, Boston and Mosquito. Each of these designs had differing operating requirements and it was therefore frequently attempted to concentrate the same types of aircraft on sorties, even if from different aerodromes. As a result, in the autumn of 1943, Dunsfold's two Mitchell squadrons often joined up with the other Mitchells of 2 Group, usually 226 Squadron, based at nearby Hartford Bridge. There, 226 shared the aerodrome with two squadrons of Bostons due to the fact that the Mitchells, with their GEE navigational aids, could when required lead their colleagues who possessed no such equipment. When 226 did join up with Dunsfold's Mitchells, a fine spectacle would be provided. As the Dunsfold aircraft taxied out to the perimeter track and runways the 226 boys arrived overhead, usually in two boxes of six, and circled while the 98 and 180 formations climbed to join them. To those watching from below, the sky seemed full of bombers jockeying for position.

Another 2 Group squadron to use the Mitchell was 320 Squadron of the Royal Dutch Naval Air Service. This unit was in a similar position to 226 Squadron as it was the only Mitchell squadron on its aerodrome at Lasham, shared with 107 and 613 Squadrons who were both equipped with Mosquitos. The Dutchmen therefore also began to join 98 and 180 on operations and it was then decided to evaluate whether Dunsfold might be able to accommodate an additional squadron on the ground as well as in its air operations.

Consequently, on 8th September, 1943, fifteen Mitchells of 320 Squadron were ferried into Dunsfold by their crews from Lasham. Ground crews arrived later by bus and were given a meal before setting to work in the early hours of the 9th. Twelve aircraft of 320 were to join 98 and 180 Squadrons in bombing gunposts at Boulogne. Engines were started up still in darkness and the blue, yellow and red exhaust flames from 72 engines made a spectacular sight around the dispersal points. As dawn broke, the first aircraft roared down the runway and there was soon enough light to show the last flights climbing to join the formations circling above. The Lasham ground crews had never seen so many Mitchells together and the sense of occasion was heightened by the option given to them of flying back to Lasham when their aircraft returned.

Aircraftsman Ganderton, an RAF armourer attached to the Dutch 320 Squadron, was one of those who had jumped at the chance of the flight back to Lasham. His excitement appeared shortlived when all aircraft returned safely overhead at 07.50 hours, only to find Dunsfold covered by low cloud. As yet the Mitchells were not equipped with any suitable blind landing equipment and therefore 320 Squadron's aircraft carried on to Lasham, arriving at 08.07 hours. Frustratingly, the same weather conditions as at Dunsfold were encountered, so the twelve Mitchells were diverted again, nine landing at Greenham Common at 08.55 hours and three at Thruxton. Fortunately for the stranded ground crews back at Dunsfold, their aircraft did eventually return to fly them back the following day, but even this short trip was not to be without incident for Ganderton.* To his delight, for he loved the opportunity to fly, the short 15 to 20 minutes flight dragged on and on until the Javanese navigator admitted he was unable to identify any landmarks. After two and a half hours of flying, the Mitchell eventually landed at Oxford before it could find its way back to Lasham.

This combined operation by the Mitchells also constituted the final stage of *Operation Starkey*. Since early August the allied air forces had commenced heavy attacks on enemy airfields and other military targets in northern France while, at the same time, large troop concentrations and the gathering of ships and assault craft were meant to convince the Germans that an invasion was imminent. The aims of the operation were not only to tempt the Luftwaffe up to be destroyed, but also to bring back German army units from Italy, where the Allies were still struggling. The Luftwaffe was not ready to fall into the trap and thus declined to send up fighter formations of any real strength. A total of only 150 enemy aircraft were estimated to have joined battle throughout the entire course of *Starkey* and of these only two were shot down, despite up to six squadrons of Spitfire or Typhoon fighters accompanying each bombing raid. Instead, the brunt of defence was left to the formidable flak and many a crew wondered, as the deadly foe burst all about them, who had thought up this great scheme which in effect turned them into

---

*Aircraftsman Ganderton remained with 320 Squadron for a year before moving on to another posting. As he wryly points out, he received a fine certificate of thanks from the Dutch Government for his 12 months with 320. There was no similar formal thanks from the British Government for the remainder of his service.

180 Sqn. Mitchell EV-N photographed on September 9th, 1943. (IWM-CH11038)

live bait. On 6th September one of 98 Squadron's flak damaged Mitchells, FV921, had crashed at Ivychurch in Kent and therefore, as the Dunsfold and Lasham formations returned on the 9th from attacks on Boulogne and Bryas-sud airfield, there were few who were sorry to see the end of *Starkey.*

On 17th September, 180 Squadron received a new commanding officer when Wing Commander Magill finished his tour and was posted away. Squadron Leader John Castle DFC, already a flight commander with 180, was promoted to Wing Commander and took over from Magill, thus continuing a line of sound experience. It was John Castle who around this time suffered from a peculiar affliction, similar to that experienced by the Canadians earlier that year at Dunsfold. Like many members of 180 Squadron, Castle had been warmly welcomed to 'The Three Compasses' by Bert and Billie Evans. One day, Bert Evans had made a special gift of just one bottle of his home-produced cider to Castle, explaining that the brew involved using strong west country 'scrumpy' as a base, matured in the barrel by adding raw steak and port! After an afternoon's chestnut-gathering in the woods, Castle and a brother officer returned to their billet in Hall Place with the bottle. As the chestnuts roasted over an open fire, the cider made a delicious aperatif, adding considerably to the warmth felt from the fire. When the time came to go to the mess for dinner, the startling discovery was made that the cider had taken away all use of both officers' legs. While the two men were carried down to their meal, the reputation of 'The Three Compasses' soared.

For the remainder of September, the two Dunsfold squadrons continued their usual *Ramrod* operations, fighter escorted bombing raids directed against specific targets. On the 21st, one such operation for 98 Squadron provided a harsh reminder that, despite the results of *Starkey*, the Luftwaffe could still put in a surprise appearance. As Pilot Officer Cooke-Smith took his turn at leading a formation of six aircraft against the synthetic paint plant at Lens, some thirty German fighters attacked and Focke Wulf FW 190s broke through the strong Spitfire escort. Mitchell FL674 was first hit when cannon fire found its hydraulic system and then FV944 was crippled and forced to ditch in the sea some ten miles off Berck-sur-Mer. While the crew were eventually rescued by Air Sea Rescue launch from Dover, not so lucky was the crew of FL683 which dived straight into the ground near Hesdin, killing all on board. Escorting Spitfires of 331 Squadron managed to catch the Germans, shooting down one and damaging another, but 98 Squadron's ground crews were dismayed when only four aircraft returned, one of which was badly shot up.

Despite its losses, Dunsfold managed to improve on morale and social life throughout September, beginning on the 8th when high spirits and celebrations greeted news of the unconditional surrender of Italy. Of more immediate and practical benefit was the opening on the 11th of the camp's own cinema on the communal site, this being performed by Wing Commander Burden. Despite confirmation that Dunsfold had been officially transferred to the RAF's 2 Group, 2nd Tactical Air Force (with formal effect from 7th September 1943), there were still no moves to replace Burden and his fellow remaining Canadians amongst the headquarters' staff. This continued presence of Canadians may not have been unconnected with the title of a talk given in the WAAF Airwomens' Mess on 10th October - 'The advisability of marrying overseas personnel during wartime'.

From the tone of the lecture, there was little doubt that its title might have more truthfully advertised 'The inadvisability of marrying.........'

The month of October saw the tentative start of night flying practice for the Mitchell crews. As day bombing experts, the two squadrons looked askance at this new task and wondered at its implications, but for the time being daylight operations continued to absorb most of their attention, October bringing yet another unpopular operation where the squadrons were used as bait for the Luftwaffe. At short notice, an attack was mounted against Brest aerodrome where both heavy flak, as well as the incumbent fighters, could be expected as opposition.

Taking off, the formation headed directly for the target, but due to thick cloud was obliged to circle over the Channel Islands to establish position. This served to alert the German defences and consequently the reception over Brest was every bit as hot as had been feared. By great good fortune, all aircraft managed to return more or less intact and back at Dunsfold the intriguing news emerged that the operation had been put on solely to draw the Germans away from a V.I.P. aircraft coming up through the Bay of Biscay. Rumours abounded as to the personage involved, some speculation being centred on a famous actor or even Churchill, but later reports were received that, despite the Mitchells' efforts, the Luftwaffe had found and shot down the mystery aircraft.

The nearby village of Cranleigh suffered a worrying episode in late October when the aerodrome received a top security demonstration of a deadly weapon not used since the First World War. The first indications of this came with the solemn instruction for all staff of Cranleigh railway station to evacuate their work place as a military 'special' was soon expected in. As they left, the staff watched RAF detachments arrive and cordon off the village centre. Ominously, some of the airmen wore waterproof capes despite the clear skies and were also seen to have their gas masks ready. Fire engines pulled in to stand by as the mysterious cargo arrived and was unloaded for its journey to the aerodrome. Safe from inquisitive eyes, all the aerodrome's available personnel were called to attend the demonstration held close to the re-sited Broadmeads Cottage and the reason for secrecy was soon made clear - Mustard Gas. This weapon was banned from the battlefield by international convention but the Allied High Command were taking no chances. Intelligence planners had warned that the Germans could not be expected to stand by their agreement not to use the gas, particularly in desperate situations such as the eventual invasion of Europe. This being so, the RAF had started to stock pile a quantity of the deadly bombs just in case retaliation would be called for, and it was made clear that it could be Dunsfold's daylight bombers ordered to make precision attacks. No-one was sad to see the gruesome weapons leave the airfield immediately after the exercise.*

On a more pleasant note, Dunsfold also now began to entertain visits from boys of the local Air Training Corps units, 1015 Billingshurst Squadron being among the first to be treated to flights in late October. For the young cadets the aerodrome provided a busy and fascinating insight into RAF operational life. Up to sixty Mitchells could be found dispersed around the airfield with a sprinkling of Oxford, Proctor and Magister communications aircraft. In addition, hardly a day went by without dawn revealing drop-in visitors of the previous night - bombers still predominating and the Halifax in particular seeming prone to running out of fuel in the vicinity. Two such aircraft had landed in September while no less than five came in one night in November. Also in November, the crew of an Avro Anson training aircraft had a narrow escape when their radio and compass failed while on a flight from RAF Moreton Vallence. Eventually locating Dunsfold, the crew made a safe landing with fuel gauges reading empty and this was shown to be none too soon. As the aircraft taxied off the perimeter track, both engines stopped due to lack of fuel.

The aerodrome's emergency services continued to deal with any crashes in the general locality and this led to attendance at the crash sites of a Canadian Spitfire at Ockley, a Mosquito at Abinger, a Mustang which crash-landed just short of the airfield and a frustrating night-time search at Oakwood Hill, some seven

---

*Author's note: I have been unable to confirm that mustard gas bombs were supplied to Dunsfold shortly prior to D-Day. Official confirmation does exist that such bombs were delivered to RAF Hartford Bridge. Despite the fears of the invasion planners, no calls were made upon the weapons and they were subsequently returned to their parent bomb dump.

miles from the aerodrome. This latter task followed distress calls from Lancaster✱JB665 of 100 Squadron which ran out of fuel returning from a raid on Berlin. All the crew baled out and were soon found in the vicinity of Oakwood Hill, with the exception of the French navigator, Flying Officer Henri Foisson, who was missing. After treatment for minor injuries, the other crew members were pronounced fit by medical staff back at Dunsfold, but worries remained for the well-being of the missing Frenchman. This mystery was solved when an injured airman was found the next day - in a field outside Hall Place, one of Dunsfold's officers' mess sites. By some quirk, Foisson had come down several miles from his fellow crew members and crashed Lancaster and by pure chance had alighted on the doorstep of the medical team so anxious to locate him. After immediate treatment in Dunsfold's sick quarters, Foisson was transferred to the 6th Canadian Casualty Clearing Station in Cranleigh.

With November came changes of accommodation and command. 414 Air Stores Park moved to winter quarters in nearby Hascombe, while on the aerodrome itself, the 1st of the month saw an Airfield Headquarters created at Dunsfold. This meant that Wing Commander Burden's departure would now be hastened since a new commanding officer would be required, not just to administer the station, but also to operationally oversee the units based there. Dunsfold therefore became known as 139 Airfield and it's two squadrons henceforth operated as a wing formation under this command. Advance notice also arrived that Fighter Command would formally disband on the 15th when it would be replaced by the two new structures of Air Defence of Great Britain and the Second Tactical Air Force. It was confirmed that Dunsfold was designated as a 2 Group base under the 2nd TAF, the Group's Air Officer Commanding being the famous Air Vice-Marshal Basil Embry. Embry, one of the RAF's most able and respected senior commanders, was charged with switching 2 Group to a new type of target.

Intelligence sources had already managed to identify over one hundred sites under preparation as launch pads for the Germans' new pilotless aircraft, the V-1. The campaign to attack the secret sites was codenamed *Crossbow*, while individual operations received the designation of *Noball* targets. Attacks commenced, appropriately enough, on 5th November 1943 when extensive fireworks were planned for a huge site located near Mimoyecques, south west of Calais. At this stage of the war, the crews were only briefed that their target consisted of 'enemy excavations and installations', but it was clear that strong importance was attached to the raid.

Dunsfold contributed twelve aircraft each from 98 and 180 Squadrons and these were to be joined by a further twenty four Mitchells and twenty four Bostons from other squadrons. Due to poor weather the Bostons turned back over Guildford, but the Mitchells, with GEE navigation aids, went on to attack in two waves. No fewer than eighteen squadrons of Spitfires provided escort cover but, once again, flak proved to be the main defence. The amount of heavy flak not only showed the importance of the site, but also made bomb aiming extremely difficult and photo reconnaissance later revealed that the target had hardly been touched.

On 8th November the Mitchells therefore returned accompanied by Bostons, but already it was clear that the target's defences had been stiffened and bomb aiming was once more spoiled. The next day a further raid on the site had to be called off due to bad weather, it being a principle of 2 Group that attacks would not be undertaken in occupied territory unless weather conditions gave a good chance of precision. Crews then heaved a sigh of relief when a change of tactics led to attacks instead being aimed at the village of Audinghen, headquarters of the Todt labour organisation from where the Mimoyecques works were organised. Five strong raids were mounted over the remainder of November and, as usual, as the number of attacks increased, so the defences improved. This was clearly illustrated on 25th November when, in the last of the series of raids, every one of 98 Squadron's twelve aircraft was damaged.

On 19th November Wing Commander Burden had finally left the aerodrome, having relinquished his command on the 11th into the temporary care of Group Captain L. W. Cannon, RAF, pending a permanent replacement. Burden had been posted to RCAF Headquarters Overseas in London and his departure was expected to signal the end of Dunsfold's Canadian command influence. Events were to prove otherwise. Group Captain (now Air Marshal retired) Larry Dunlap RCAF takes up the story:

"Air Marshal Gus Edwards, the AOC in C of RCAF Headquarters Overseas, didn't make a practice of having his airfield commanders appear before him on the occasion of their reassignments, yet here I was, on November 9 1943, for the second time in less than a year, standing before the Chief. Even though, at the outset, he dwelt at some length on the achievements of 331 Wing RCAF, which I had commanded in North Africa, Sicily, and Italy and was quite complimentary, it was nevertheless apparent that the real purpose of the meeting was the matter of my next assignment. I was soon made aware, in no uncertain terms, that it was his wish that I become the commander of the new Royal Air Force 139 Airfield at Dunsfold.

"That I looked startled was hardly surprising, for up to this time, in the Second World War, no RCAF Group Captain had ever been placed in command of an operational Airfield or Wing of the RAF. Reacting to my expression, Air Marshal Edwards hastened to unfold the rather unusual circumstances. The airfield at Dunsfold had been built by Canada, which in itself was somewhat unique, as such construction within the United Kingdom was normally a British responsibility. The base had been built by the Royal Canadian Engineers expressly for 39 (Army Co-op) Wing, RCAF, then commanded by Group Captain D. M. Smith. Within a year, due to reorganisation of the British and Canadian Armies in the south of England, it had become advantageous for Canada to seek an alternative field closer to the Canadian Army, and to offer the base at Dunsfold in exchange. At a meeting at the Air Ministry, when this arrangement was being consummated, Air Marshal Edwards, as a parting shot, said to his RAF counterparts, 'It would be a nice gesture, having regard to the part which Canada has played in the construction of the base at Dunsfold, if you were to invite an RCAF Group Captain to take command of the RAF Wing which is about to be located there.'

"This caught the Air Council a bit off guard, and for a few momemts a strained silence prevailed. Then one of the Air Chief Marshals spoke up and said, 'The Wing in question, 139, is a day bomber formation and, since the RCAF does not possess any day bomber squadrons, it would hardly seem likely that Canada would be capable of making anyone available with the necessary qualifications'.

"Gus Edwards was not one to be turned aside lightly, so without a moment's hesitation he said 'I have an officer in mind who, in my opinion, would be more than equal to the task. However, I realise the difficulty of attempting to settle the issue at this meeting......why don't we leave the matter to the Air Officer Commanding 2 Group? I can arrange for my RCAF Group Captain to proceed to 2 Group HQ at any time convenient to the AOC (Air Vice-Marshal Embry)'.

"This seemed a reasonable approach and a good way out as far as the Air Ministry authorities were concerned. Indeed, they were well aware that Basil Embry was most unlikely to take anyone on who failed to meet his exacting standards. The Air Staff present knew from experience that no-one had ever been able to make Basil accept an operational commander against his will, so it seemed pretty safe to leave the matter up to him. It was finally agreed that the Air Ministry would get in touch and make the necessary arrangements with AVM Embry and then, when the date of interview was settled, RCAF Overseas Headquarters would be informed.

"Those were the events which gave rise to my presence in the office of Gus Edwards at Lincolns Inn Fields, London. He spared no effort to impress upon me what this appointment meant to him, to the RCAF and to Canada. The fact that my experience, both in No. 6 Bomber Group and the Mediterranean Air Force, had been confined entirely to night bombing, didn't bother him in the least and he didn't hesitate to state that it wasn't to bother me either. I can remember his parting words as clearly as if they had been said yesterday: 'Don't leave a stone unturned when relating your past accomplishments, don't limit the account of your experience to the events of the past year. Give chapter and verse on your years of flying in the Canadian north, on the three years spent with the RAF during the mid thirties, on your experience in command of the Air Armament School and the Bombing and Gunnery School, to say nothing of your spell as Director of Armament in Ottawa at the outbreak of war. Make it clear that you feel capable of handling the assignment in spite of the fact that some aspects may be a bit different'.

"Nothing was left in doubt on either issue, neither on the objective of Air Marshal Edwards, nor on the part I was to play. This was accomplished in a forceful, yet persuasive manner. As soon as he felt that he had properly set the stage, he told me I was to proceed to Bylaugh Hall, in Norfolk. Not only would AVM Embry be expecting me, he had even suggested that I stay for the weekend so that he and his Senior Air Staff Officer, David Atcherley, could become thoroughly acquainted with me.

"The net result was that I took over Dunsfold and 139 Airfield RAF in late November 1943."

Dunlap subsequently arrived at Dunsfold on 22nd November. Bad weather greeted his arrival and flying was curtailed for the next few days, the only point of note in the station diary being the showing of a film on venereal disease on the 24th!

One result of the poor weather over south-east England was to provide Group Captain Dunlap with a glimpse of another, little-known, use of Dunsfold. When other aerodromes were fogged in, Dunsfold sometimes escaped the worst of the conditions and thus played host to visits of black-painted Lysander aircraft engaged in clandestine operations to the continent. Often flying from RAF Tangmere, where sea mist could suddenly roll in off the Channel, the Lysanders would continue inland to diversion airfields such as Dunsfold. They would park close by the control tower and not even Larry Dunlap was permitted to ask questions of the crews or shadowy passengers.

On 25th November the weather cleared and Dunlap lost no time in joining the squadrons on a sortie to Audinghen and again, the next day, against construction works at Martinvast, near Cherbourg. These works were also identified as being for the Germans' pilotless missiles and strong flak defences were therefore anticipated.

Dunlap joined 180 Squadron for the operation, flying in Mitchell FZ188 captained by Flying Officer Fooks. In anticipation of stiff defences, the formation attacked simultaneously in four individual boxes, running in on a variety of headings in order to split up the flak barrage. Unfortunately, this plan did not prevent the Germans from concentrating their fire against one box in particular - the one in which Dunlap was flying. In a split second the Group Captain saw a Mitchell drop from either side of Fooks' aircraft, followed by the aircraft immediately behind them (FL205, FL707 and FV912). The entire sky seemed black with shell bursts and the experienced Canadian was sobered by the all too apparent dangers of daylight bombing. It seemed a mystery to him how the remaining three aircraft of the box managed to get through. For 180 Squadron, the three Mitchells shot down represented 25% losses.

Following this daylight baptism of fire, Dunlap's expertise in night flying was put into practice when, on 29th November, the squadrons commenced a programme of intensified night flying training, following the unpopular beginnings in October. The purpose behind this was the aim of Air Vice-Marshal Embry to enable 139 Airfield to operate 'round the clock' when the time came for the invasion of Europe. Initially, there was some resentment at this extension of rôle, but Embry was a man to lead by example. On numerous occasions he would arrive unannounced at Dunsfold and pick a crew at random to join for an operation. He took pains to remind the crews that necessity had to outweigh any personal preferences and he reminded them that he, too, had been a day bombing expert. At a briefing designed to end all argument against night operations, Embry stressed that night bombing could be just as rewarding as daylight operations -"Believe me, gentlemen" he told the crews, "there are no greater thrills without taking your clothes off!"*

Poor weather heralded the commencement of December 1943 and although this hampered the Mitchells' operations, it also served the aerodrome well in an incident on the 1st.

The day dawned cold and damp, a heavy mist blotting out any features beyond a few yards. All crews were stood down as weather reports confirmed little likelihood of a break in the conditions, and only the gunners of the RAF Regiment were expected to maintain any standard of operational readiness.

In the tower, the duty controller maintained a radio watch and stared out into the gloom, unable even to see the squadrons' Mitchells in their dispersal bays on the opposite side of the airfield. In their ill-heated hut, the gunners of the Bofors post close to the threshold of runway 13 tried hard to keep up a semblance of alertness. The Luftwaffe had yet to show any inclination to test Dunsfold's defences and only a fool would be flying on a day like this - or so they thought. The muffled snarl of an approaching aero engine brought the gunners to their feet and suddenly, out of the fog, appeared the unmistakeable shape of a Focke Wulf FW 190, skimming over the woods at the eastern edge of the airfield. Before any gun could be brought to bear, the German fighter-bomber was swallowed up in the mist as quickly as it had appeared. Only the sound, receding in the distance, convinced the startled gunners that they had not imagined the whole affair, and it was estimated that the raider had only been visible for three seconds. What might have been dismissed as a tall story was nevertheless corroborated by the control tower. From their vantage point on the same side of the airfield, flying control staff had also struggled to their feet just in time to

*Embry, as a Wing Commander, had been shot down over France in May 1940 while flying a Blenheim bomber. In an amazing series of adventures, (see 'Wingless Victory' by A. Richardson), Embry managed to get back to Britain, killing three German soldiers on the way and at one point convincing the Germans that he was a pro-I.R.A. Irishman. Despite the Germans having put a price on his head, Embry continued, even as an Air Vice-Marshal, to fly with his squadrons when the opportunity arose. He was to win the DSO and three bars, and the DFC for his exploits.

snatch a glimpse of the shadowy intruder as it streaked by. An alert was rapidly flashed to Group headquarters but despite Dunsfold's warning, the German was not seen or heard of again and was never plotted on radar.

Three days prior to Christmas, old friends were welcomed back when aircraft of 400 Squadron RCAF returned to Dunsfold. Based at Redhill, 400 were in the process of converting from fighter reconnaissance to a purely photo reconnaissance rôle. In terms of equipment this also meant giving up their Mustangs, 'A' Flight receiving Spitfire XIs while 'B' Flight changed to Mosquito PR XVI aircraft. Although Redhill was suitable for training on the new Spitfires, it was not ideal for Mosquito operations and the problem was compounded by work then underway to improve the aerodrome's grass runways. Ultimately, a permanent move from Redhill would be needed but, in the interim, 'B' Flight needed a temporary home to commence their training. As Dunsfold was both local and already familiar to several of the crews, it was a natural choice. 'B' Flight commander Paul Bissky led the conversion duties having himself undergone a quick conversion course onto twin-engined aircraft. The Mosquitos were ferried in from Benson and Hartford Bridge, surviving records suggesting that just four Mk XVIs were based at and flown from Dunsfold (MM274, MM275, MM278 and MM279), along with a Mk III dual control trainer Mosquito (HJ993) and an Airspeed Oxford for the initial conversions to twin-engined flying. Due to the continuing pressures on available living space, the 400 Squadron pilots and navigators drove back and forth from Redhill each day for conversion training.

While the Canadians began to familiarise themselves with their Mosquitos, the two Mitchell squadrons of 139 Airfield had concentrated throughout December on refining their techniques for locating and attacking the small, well camouflaged, *Noball* targets. Dunsfold's sister formations of 2 Group; 140 at Sculthorpe, 138 at Lasham, and 137 at Hartford Bridge likewise stepped up their respective parts in this offensive, one straggler from the latter being a Boston of 342 Free French Squadron which failed to make its home airfield when returning from a raid on Mesnil Allard on 23rd December. Attempting instead to put down at Dunsfold, the Boston did not quite make it and crashed into woods near to the aerodrome. Depite such losses, a new strength of purpose was felt throughout the squadrons of 2 Group as all personnel were aware that 1944 would bring with it great demands. Pressure for the second front was becoming intense and it was clear that Dunsfold would claim an important share in the preparations. Notwithstanding this sombre realisation the end of the year did, however, bring some light relief.

On 31st December a breach was discovered in the aerodrome's admittedly scant security measures.....an enemy soldier was reported to have been picked up on the airfield. Dramatic as the news sounded, this was no downed Nazi flyer determined to steal an aeroplane and return to the Fatherland. Instead, it proved to be an Italian PoW from a nearby work gang who had lost his way in the woods. These PoWs were perfectly content to labour in the Surrey countryside frequently with minimal, or even no, guard and the startled Italian was more than happy to be returned to his unit from the reminder of distant war upon which he had stumbled. Even the description as an 'enemy' was arguable at this stage of the war, Italy having surrendered back in September.

The incoming year of 1944 saw the Axis powers clearly in retreat world-wide. Driven from North Africa, the Germans were now conducting a fighting retreat up the Italian peninsula while on their eastern front they faced the Red Army's latest onslaught in the Ukraine. In the Far East theatre, U.S. forces were rapidly 'island hopping' towards the Japanese home islands and in Burma, British and Indian troops were back on the offensive. In the air, the RAF's heavy bombers were at the height of the Battle of Berlin, a series of punishing attacks on the German capital lasting from November 1943 to March 1944.

At Dunsfold, 1944 began inauspiciously when, on 7th January, a tragic accident occurred as aircraft of both 98 and 180 Squadrons returned from a sortie in bad weather. As the formations circled and awaited their turn to land, Mitchell FR396 of 180 Squadron collided with FL682 of 98 Squadron. FR396 dived straight into the ground and detonated in a huge explosion as it had returned without dropping its bombs. The other machine spiralled down and smashed into open land at

Flight Lieutenant Paul Bissky (left) with his navigator and Mosquito PRXVI of 400 Sqn. RCAF. (Paul Bissky.)

Alfold, just a couple of miles from the aerodrome. There were no survivors from either aircraft.

This tragic incident provided a grim welcome for an officer newly-posted to Dunsfold, Squadron Leader Tom Warner. A regular RAF officer and chaplain, Warner had already served as a Sergeant air gunner on Blenheims in 1941/2 before someone had belatedly noted his ordination. He had therefore been obliged to remuster as a commissioned chaplain and had subsequently been appointed as 139 Wing's Padre. It was Warner's duty to preside over the burials from the mid-air collision but the colourful Irishman nevertheless looked forward to the flying he would be able to do at his new base. Warner was somewhat unique as a Padre in that he was also a qualified air gunner, sporting the gunners' brevet on his uniform. He spent much of his time around the crew rooms with the air crew and, as a result of this, built up a special relationship with the flyers. Because of his air crew qualification, he often sneaked aboard an aircraft going on an operation, particularly making a habit of this when a crew needed a little re-assurance. One immediate task found for him was to fly with a number of USAAF crews who were attached to the Mitchell squadrons for operational experience. It soon became clear to the Padre that the training of his American comrades had been nowhere near as thorough as that of their British counterparts, particularly in the area of navigation. On one night flying exercise with Warner, the American navigator eventually confessed "Gee Skip, I haven't a clue where we are," and much embarrassment was only saved when the experienced Irishman was able to make out the flashing code signal below them for Western Zoyland airfield, in Somerset.

On 21st January, 98 Squadron lost Mitchell FL674 when it crash-landed at Lympne in Kent returning from France and the same day Dunsfold's medical team had casualties to deal with - but of an unusual kind. A night call-out came when a Heinkel He 177 bomber crashed at Hindhead, this being the first of four such aircraft shot down that night and the first occasion that the Luftwaffe had sent the new heavy bomber over Britain. Two of the crew were killed outright and later buried in Haslemere, while the two surviving air gunners were taken to Godalming Police Station. For Senior Medical Officer Squadron Leader Williams and his staff there could be no discrimination between friend and foe, the two Germans were quickly and efficiently given treatment for their wounds by the medical team summoned from Dunsfold.

Another Mitchell crash in Kent occurred on 25th January when FL218 EV-W of 180 Squadron could not make it back to Dunsfold. While the remainder of his crew baled out, Australian pilot Warrant Officer Rodger stayed with the aircraft and was killed in the resultant crash-landing near Hawkinge. In a similarly stricken Mitchell on 9th February, all the crew remained aboard as Flying Officer Struthers nursed FL689 of 180 Squadron back over the Sussex coast after an attack on construction works at Livossart. Lining up for a landing at cliff-top RAF Friston, Struthers was unable to maintain altitude and the aircraft crash-landed short of the airfield, killing air gunner Warrant Officer Hammond.

As losses mounted, a verbal exchange broke the tension before one particular operation. Dunsfold's Dental Officer was a popular South African Flight Lieutenant named Rex Fane. Fane had watched as the medics and the Chaplain had taken the opportunity to join sorties and he eventually determined to put his name forward too, in order to share the experiences and

Squadron Leader, the Reverend Tom Walker, snatches a cuppa between ops. (Rev. Dr. T. E. Warner.)

dangers of those he treated. At that time, one of the most unpopular targets for the Mitchell crews was the Abbeville region of northern France, where the flak defences were particularly heavy and accurate. To Fane's horror, the target for the operation he was permitted to join was announced as Abbeville and the poor dentist was convinced his hour had come. Determined nevertheless to maintain a stiff upper lip, Fane drove up to the dispersal of his designated aircraft and stepped out. As he donned his Mae West prior to boarding the Mitchell, Fane noticed Flight Lieutenant Stewart watching him from the doorway of a nearby nissen hut. Stewart, a laconic fighter pilot from New Zealand, was currently attached to Dunsfold on fighter affiliation duties. Cigarette dangling from his lips, the experienced pilot guessed at the emotions beneath the surface of the dentist's studied air of nonchalance. "Rex!" came the call in a strong antipodean accent. The dentist halted in his preparations, anticipating a word of encouragement or advice. "Rex, can I have your car if you don't come back?" Fortunately, Rex came back.

Chapter Six

A Darker Shade of Blue

The second week of February 1944 saw the culmination of a fortnight's mad scramble to find additional accommodation on the already crowded airfield. On the 4th, 'B' flight of 400 Squadron had left with its Mosquitos for RAF Odiham, leaving just enough space for the move on the 10th of an additional squadron into 139 Airfield. With the arrival of this new unit, the local population could have been excused for believing that the aerodrome was being transformed into a naval base. This was due to the fact that the newcomers were 320 Squadron of the Royal Dutch Naval Air Service from RAF Lasham, its personnel dressed in typical dark blue naval uniform despite their flying duties. In addition to its naval airmen, the squadron also boasted a contingent of Dutch Marines who served to enforce discipline, thereby fulfilling the same function as RAF Police. To add to the novelty of the newcomers, a fair proportion of 320's personnel had come to England from the Dutch East Indies and dark skinned Javanese were thus a common sight among the Dutchmen's ranks. Sadly, one such young airmen was tragically killed soon after arrival at Dunsfold. While paying a return visit to Lasham he ran into a propeller blade running at high speed.

The addition of this squadron proved a major headache to Dunsfold's headquarters staff as the aerodrome had originally been given accommodation to house only a fighter wing. In aircrew alone there were now four times as many personnel, let alone double the ground crew. The only spare short-term accommodation was in the WAAF compound, but the senior WAAF officer, the 'Queen Bee,' was horrified when told that some of the buildings would have to be allocated to Dutch officers. Aghast, she immediately complained "It wouldn't be quite so bad if they were British RAF officers." When asked why, she gave the very logical female response, "because the Dutchmen are all too good looking."

Along with 320 Squadron's arrival came Wing Commander Alan Lynn DSO DFC who was posted to 139 Airfield headquarters to fill the position of Wing Commander (Flying). South African Lynn, supposedly on a rest tour, immediately went

Wing Commander Lynn's crew and ground crew in the summer of 1944. Cees Waardenburg, killed with Harry Payne on August 31st, 1944, is in the centre of the back row. (Photo K. Cudilpp)

about assembling a crew in the hope of commencing a fourth tour. This he quickly managed, notably including a Dutchman, Lieutenant Cees Waardenburg, from 320 Squadron, as his navigator. Waardenburg, a popular and intelligent young man, was in fact a qualified pilot but, in accordance with practice in the Royal Dutch Naval Air Service, was obliged to complete a number of operations as a navigator before he could be given command as a pilot of his own aircraft. Alan Lynn, somewhat in jest, promised he would ensure the Dutchman received the captaincy of an aircraft, but only after completing 100 operations as his navigator.

139 Airfield operated all three squadrons together for the first time on 12th February in *Operation Savvy*. Despite the grouping of the three Dunsfold units, operations still continued in conjunction with 226 Squadron from RAF Hartford Bridge and one such occasion took place on 24th February when 320 Squadron joined 226 for an attack on a *Noball* target. The attack

was to prove memorable for one young Dutch navigator on his first sortie over enemy territory.

Hans van der Kop had reached 320 Squadron after evacuation from the Dutch East Indies, via South Africa. For the attack on the 24th, he joined the crew of Jan Maas and was shaken by the barrage of vicious flak which greeted the formation over the target. Shortly after bombing, Maas suggested that van der Kop leave the exposed nose of the aircraft and return to his navigation compartment, as it was obvious that the German gunners were making a determined effort. Hans van der Kop takes up his own story:

"In a trice I was back in the navigation compartment, my bundle of maps clenched in my hand. Another loud bang. Involuntarily I closed my eyes and, when I opened them again, I saw a jet of hydraulic fluid gushing out of one of the pipes. Rather nervously I reported to Jan Maas, while turning the cock to try to stem the flow; it was no use, oil kept streaming out. "How bad is it?" Maas asked. I replied "It's not getting less but thank God we have the emergency system".

"The air outside was grey with the clouds from exploding shells and as I looked, there was an ear splitting clap which shook the Mitchell to the core. I looked down, and there was a large hole in the floor. I looked up, and there was a hole in the roof too. In a flash, I realised a piece of shrapnel had passed from below and up through the ceiling at the very moment I had turned my head. "We've been hit" I called. "There are holes here, rather big ones". Without answering, Jan Maas indicated that I should sit down next to him. Only as I fastened my seat belt did he calmly tell me that there was something wrong with the port engine. Maas called Henk Voorspuy on the radio "Silver Leader, this is Silver 4, I am damaged. Cannot stay in formation." Vicious little clouds of flak still burst around us, but it was a great relief when our gunner, Sergeant Harsevoort, reported "Flak now behind us."

"We were crossing the French coast again with the returning formations and flanked by two groups of Typhoons. Meanwhile, Jan Maas was busy consulting his instruments and finally he concluded, "We won't make it to Dunsfold. We'll have to land somewhere as quickly as possible". He radioed this message using the emergency frequency and the prompt reply gave us a course for RAF Friston, on the cliffs near Beachy Head.

"There was a final call of "Good Luck" from Voorspuy and we were on our own. Our port engine was still running unevenly and the starboard engine began a high pitched whine as we slowly lost height. Our altitude was only 4,000 feet and, according to the radar station, there was still fifteen miles to go. Then I saw the outline of the English coast looming out of the mist. "The coast, the white cliffs!" I almost shouted. Jan Maas remained unperturbed and asked "Can you see Friston?" At the same moment the port engine began to splutter and the starboard was opened up even more. As our altitude continued to decrease, I read out that Friston was situated behind Beachy Head, a grass field with a runway about 1,600 yards long. Jan Maas nodded and told us, "I'm going to put this kite down at Friston. The port engine is packing up and I haven't been able to feather it. Stand by in case of an emergency and stay on the intercom." I stuck my thumb up to indicate that I had understood and the gunners replied with a brief "Roger." From the airfield, we heard, "Silver 4, this is Friston, we are ready for you and have cleared the runway as much as possible of snow. There is practically no wind, so I advise you to land landwards. That'll also give you more room for braking." Jan Maas smiled and said, "What he really means is that if we land from the other direction, and don't manage to brake in time, we stand a good chance of dropping a few hundred feet to the bottom of the cliffs."

"However hard we looked, the airfield remained hidden in the white and grey mass below and Friston offered to send up flares. Harsevoort saw them first and reported, "Friston at four o'clock." We went into a right turn and spotted the airfield, which was not much more than a meadow, down the centre of which a runway was outlined in the snow. "Right," called Maas, "prepare for landing, it might be a hard one. Harsevoort, stand by in case I need the emergency system to lock the wheels". He then called the airfield, "Friston, I see you now. I'm coming in to land". Friston's reasssuring reply was "The field is yours. Take all the time you need".

"Jan Maas seemed to be preparing for an ordinary landing as we made a slow turn towards the runway with our starboard engine now screaming at full power. The cliffs seemed to come dangerously close, but the runway was straight ahead and the undercarriage came down okay. Now the cliffs came rushing up to meet us and, at the same time, the whine of the starboard engine stopped. We were floating above the runway at an alarming speed and already I could see the end of it. Then the wheels touched the grass and we braked once and then a second time. We still seemed to be moving too fast and Jan Maas braked a third time, the nose pitching down as the aircraft swerved to the right in the direction of the aerodrome buildings. Less than twenty yards from a wooden shed, we came to a halt.

"My main concern was to get out of the aircraft as quickly as possible. When I released the hatch, a stream of hydraulic fluid gushed out onto the ground. I stepped down and slipped, landing on the grass stained red from the oil. Some RAF people were staring at me, but their looks hardly registered. All I was aware of was a shaky feeling in my knees and the rattling of my teeth."

Van der Kop was unlucky to face such an unnerving ordeal on his very first operation but he soon came to appreciate that similar dramas were all too commonplace. Many crews experienced close calls but were nevertheless expected to 'press on' and treat the dangers as part of the normal working day.

In order to balance the stress and tension of operations it was important to maintain morale and provide entertainment on camp. One effort made by a young pilot of 180 Squadron came when Flying Officer Dicky Leven discovered an art class at a Guildford night school which used nude female models. Leven worked hard to organise attendance, even being allowed transport in the cause of education and self improvement. Unhappily, his efforts came to nought when ulterior motives were suspected and the project withered on the vine.*

Entertainment was more successfully arranged through the services of 180 Squadron's Catering Officer who proved to have links with the West End due to working in the theatre pre-war. Consequently, several acts were invited down from London, and were accommodated at the Bramley Grange Hotel just a few miles from the airfield. Group Captain Dunlap and his staff also made every effort to book popular acts, their best success perhaps being at the end of February when a camp concert in the cinema included Arthur Askey and Patricia Burke.

An equally spectacular performance was presented on 21st February, when yet another wandering Halifax, this time of 78 Squadron, made a dramatically heavy landing on runway 21. The subsequent bounce was so pronounced that the aircraft literally took off again and flew out of the aerodrome, crashing just outside 'The Three Compasses' pub beyond the perimeter. The pilot claimed that a frostbitten foot had led him to the misjudged landing, but the Senior Medical Officer, Squadron Leader Williams, could find no trace of this condition. By some miracle there were no crew casualties other than the observer's sprained ankle.

The gunners of the RAF Regiment could have been excused itchy fingers when in early March another visitor dropped into the airfield's circuit and lined up to approach the runway in use. Sharp-eyed observers on the ground were startled to pick out the silhouette of a Focke Wulf FW 190 but fortunately, the airfield

---

*Well-liked Dicky Leven was another of Dunsfold's 'characters'. He completed a tour with 180 at Foulsham and Dunsfold and then later returned to Dunsfold for a second tour, this time as a flight commander with 98 Squadron in the rank of Squadron Leader. Post-war, Leven pursued an acting career and is reputed to have played the part of a RAF fighter pilot in the film 'Angels One Five.'

Aircrew of 320 Squadron RDNAS at Dunsfold. Extreme right is Hans van der Kop. (Royal Dutch Navy 2214)

defence posts had been warned of its impending arrival. Painted yellow overall and sporting RAF colours, the German aircraft was at Dunsfold to give the Mitchells experience of Luftwaffe fighter performance and tactics - a rôle known as Fighter Affiliation. Occasional visits by Spitfires had already helped to train the Mitchell crews in evasive manoeuvres but the arrival of the Focke Wulf certainly added realism. Subsequently, a Messerschmitt Me 109 fighter also spent a few days at Dunsfold for the same purpose.

March 1944 saw a change of commanding officer for 98 Squadron when Wing Commander Phillips was posted away and his place was taken by Wing Commander Bell-Irving, formerly a flight commander on 180 Squadron. Bell-Irving was a Canadian and with Group Captain Dunlap in charge of the station, the RCAF command influence continued. Dunlap and his staff generally enjoyed high esteem from the operational squadrons in their care, and although some misdemeanours continued, discipline on the station had improved. This may have been the reason that relatively severe punishment was meted out for what would seem to be trifling incidents. The enthusiasm of 320 Squadron for all forms of speedy transport had already been noted when they introduced cycle races around the perimeter track, but their antics soon spread around the district. A stiff rebuke on 11th March reminded the Dutchmen that. "All personnel must comply with Civil Law when riding cycles" and two official warnings were also delivered on the mis-use of government petrol and service transport. Despite the Dutch being under the greatest suspicion, it was a luckless 'erk' of 98 Squadron who finally ran foul of the local Constabulary. Aircraftsman Streeter, an armourer with 'A' flight, received the steep fine of ten shillings when he was charged with a most serious offence - cycling from Dunsfold to Cranleigh without lights.

On 14th March a seven month old mystery was solved when Dunsfold's sick quarters were notified of the grim discovery of a body in Kingspark Wood, Plaistow, a few miles to the south. Clearly an airman, the body was found by a forester who assumed there was a connection with Dunsfold. This proved to be true, albeit the connection was not with units based at the aerodrome. Instead, the body proved to be that of Sergeant Goedsall, an air gunner of 207 Squadron, which operated Lancasters. It was one of 207's Lancasters, ED361, from which all the crew had baled out on the night of 13th August 1943, an occasion when Dunsfold's emergency team had located all the crew safely, with the exception of one gunner - Sergeant Goedsall.

One of 320 Squadron's most eventful days of operations came on 18th March 1944 when several of the flying Dutchmen were called upon to use their naval training. The squadron was detailed to attack a *Noball* target at Gorenflos in the afternoon and, led by Lieutenant Commander Mulder, two boxes of six aircraft pinpointed the target and managed a good concentration of their 500lb bombs from 11,000ft. But as they swung away from the target, deadly and accurate flak bracketed the formation, hitting no less than eight aircraft. Worst damaged was aircraft 'H' FR180, with Sergeant John Ot at the controls. Ot had just started to weave with the rest of the leading box when flak ripped into his Mitchell, hitting the port engine and belly turret and wounding the wireless operator/air gunner, Corporal Posthumus, in the leg. Ot watched anxiously from the cockpit as the damaged engine began to shed metal. Almost immediately, the stricken aircraft was hit again, this time in the starboard engine and wing, and Ot was unable to keep formation as the Mitchell lost altitude, its port engine now in flames and hydraulic system useless. Quickly, Ot feathered the port engine and with great relief, saw the flames die out. Taking stock of the situation, the young Dutchman nevertheless realised that he was still in desperate straits. The last barrage of flak had wounded his navigator, Sergeant Gans, in the head and Dunsfold was still a long way off as the bomber limped towards the French coast, the wind howling through its shattered perspex nose. All instruments were out of action as were the ailerons and rudder, and Ot had to fight to control the shuddering machine with only limited elevator movement available.

At 8,000 feet, Ot gave the order for his crew to be ready to jump, but it was an order they were reluctant to follow. Clearly, their skipper would have little chance himself once he left the controls since the unstable aircraft would begin an immediate plunge earthwards. Baling out over occupied France also meant a good chance of capture by the Germans.

As the crew deliberated, the remaining starboard engine spluttered ominously, picked up for a few moments, then died into silence. The mainland of enemy-occupied France was still below, but ahead Ot could see the coast and he calculated that the powerless Mitchell might just glide to a ditching in the Channel, thereby giving some hope of avoiding capture. Ot's decision was unanimously approved by the other crew members who scrambled to their ditching positions. The pilot then turned to the radio in order to transmit his 'MAYDAY' signal, but Ot had to wait as he heard another aircraft already calling for help on the same channel and giving a commentary as it too prepared to ditch somewhere further ahead. The French coastline slid beneath with Ot's Mitchell at 3,000 feet but falling fast, and it was only at 1,000ft that the Dutchman finally had the chance to transmit a hurried 'MAYDAY'. As the grey and uninviting sea loomed ahead, Ot jettisoned the escape hatch and tried to lower flaps, only to discover these too were unserviceable. Before he could attempt any other measures, the sea rushed up to meet the bomber and Ot just had the time to heave on the control column with all his strength, pulling the nose up at the last minute so that the aircraft hit the water belly first. Due to the lack of flaps, impact speed was still dangerously high and the aircraft twice bounced viciously before settling on the surface.

With not a moment to lose, Ot deperately tried to clear his senses from a bad knock to his forehead, caused when he pitched forward on to the control column. Gans had suffered similarly but although dazed, the navigator staggered out onto the wing. The wounded Posthumus was already in the water and was soon joined by Sergeant Lub, the other air gunner. Ot managed to inflate the dinghy and quickly paddled it some twenty yards out to pick up Posthumus, returning for Lub and finally Gans who, still dazed, only jumped off the wing at the last possible moment before the Mitchell slid below the waves. Since impact, the whole drama had lasted only two minutes.

Turning to his two wounded men, Ot put his first aid kit to good use by bandaging Posthumus' leg and, more crucially, Gans' wrist which had suffered a severed artery during the crash. Within ten minutes two Spitfires arrived overhead and circled protectively since the French coast was still only some two miles away. After thirty minutes the Spitfires departed and the soaked bomber crew were left alone to open their survival kits.

Their solitude was interrupted only a few minutes later when an American B17 Flying Fortress jettisoned five bombs just a few yards from the Dutchmen. The small dinghy was lifted bodily from the water by the explosions, but remained upright and its shaken occupants were relieved when six more Spitfires then arrived to resume the protective umbrella. The Spitfires were soon followed by a Sea Otter aircraft of the Air Sea Rescue service which alighted close by and only an hour after ditching, the four airmen were taken aboard. Their adventures were far from over however. In the heavy Channel swell the rescue aircraft could not take off and so eventually began to slowly taxi back through the pitching seas. Over four hours later, and with the light almost gone, an Air Sea Rescue launch met the struggling aircraft and relieved it of the weary Dutchmen. The Sea Otter, free of its burden, succeeded in taking off and headed back towards RAF Hawkinge while the rescued men thankfully changed into dry clothes aboard the launch.

It was not to be until well after nightfall that the launch eventually reached Dover at 21.00 hours. Its crew had orders to remain on station until all daylight airborne sorties had returned and the Dutchmen therefore had no alternative but to share in the task.

For John Ot, the episode sadly had an unsavoury ending. On being landed at Dover, his telephone call back to Dunsfold failed to elicit transport for the exhausted airmen, two of whom were suffering from wounds and in no fit state to undertake the lengthy train journey as advised. Only the offer of an ambulance and two WAAFs, from a sympathetic Adjutant at RAF Manston, saved the day and Ot returned to his squadron furious at the off-hand treatment he felt his crew had received. To add insult to injury, he found he was expected to produce clothing coupons and cash for a replacement uniform and he further discovered that his English wife, living locally, had received official notification that he had drowned in the Channel. Only a personal call from another Dutch airman had later told Mrs Ot, albeit in broken and halting English, that her husband was believed to have taken to his dinghy. Ot had been with 320 Squadron since December 1941 and had served his time as a navigator on Hudsons. He felt that the actions of those in authority had been unpardonable, and he subsequently made his feelings vociferously clear. Soon after he left the squadron.

The 320 Squadron formation which returned to Dunsfold from Gorenflos was not only missing Ot's aircraft. As Ot had waited to make his MAYDAY call, the other aircraft in trouble was 'M' FR177 from the same box as Ot's Mitchell. Flying the penultimate operation of his first tour, pilot Henk Voorspuy had hoped to make England with his crippled machine but the starboard engine was practically useless after being hit by flak and progress was not helped by the undercarriage and flaps hanging down. Only some four minutes after Ot's ditching, Voorspuy carefully judged wind direction and wave swell to put the Mitchell down at a relatively safe 98mph.

As the aircraft settled into the water, Voorspuy quickly moved onto the wing in order to release the dinghy while his navigator, Jan Vink,* bravely dived back into the flooded aircraft for the emergency packs. The two gunners soon joined their pilot and navigator in the dinghy and once again, help was quickly at hand in the form of two Spitfires which remained overhead until a Walrus amphibious aircraft landed an hour later. As the drenched fliers were hauled aboard a cheery, "Good gracious, Henk!" greeted the Mitchell's pilot. The captain of the Walrus proved to be Squadron Leader Wallens of 277 Squadron, whom Voorspuy had recently met in hospital.†

The chance reunion was to lead to more problems for Voorspuy. After the Walrus had safely dropped the Dutchmen back at RAF Hawkinge, Wallens suggested to Voorspuy that the two of them should go for a quick drink in the local pub. Readily agreeing, Voorspuy first had to discard his wet battledress, revealing in the process that he was still wearing his pyjamas underneath! In the borrowed uniform of an RAF Aircraftsman (second class) Voorspuy was finally ready and the two pilots quickly repaired to the hostelry. While Wallens visited the toilets, Voorspuy found himself in deep water once again. Overhearing his native language being spoken, Voorspuy spotted two Dutch Navy sailors at the bar and approached them, introducing himself as being an officer of the same service and asking them where they were serving. The two ratings took in Voorspuy's ill fitting RAF uniform and promptly called the Military Police. As the Dutch pilot was being dragged from the bar, proclaiming loudly that he was *not* a German spy, Wallens emerged just in time to save his friend from the cells.

Despite the drama of the day, 320 Squadron had not lost a single crew member thanks to the efforts of the Air Sea Rescue

---

*Like John Ot, Jan Vink had also recently married an English girl and, post-war, remained in England to follow the profession of schoolmaster. He settled with his family in Godalming, close to his former base. In 1987, his was therefore the shortest journey to 320 Squadron's reunion at Dunsfold. During the church commemorative service at Dunsfold Church, Jan confided to his old comrades that recent poor health had left him convinced that he had little longer to live. He also expressed the wish that he would wish, if possible, to eventually be buried in the church's beautifully kept graveyard. Only weeks after the reunion, Jan died according to his premonition. In accordance with his wishes, his burial took place at Dunsfold, the only former airman from the aerodrome to be buried there.

†See Appendix B for the ditching reports submitted by the pilots.

Adje Bevelander, lost on March 20th, 1944, with only one operation to go to complete his tour. (H. J. E. van der Kop.)

Service. By way of thanks, the Dutchmen later presented 277 Squadron with six inscribed tankards.

Two days later, 320 Squadron's good fortune ran out. While 98 and 180 Squadrons attacked a *Noball* site at Gorenflos, losing FV940 of 98 Squadron in yet another Channel ditching, the Dutchmen sent their Mitchells to a similar target at Flixecourt. This was to be the last operation needed to complete the tour of Adje Bevelander and his crew, the recent increase in tempo of operations having been only too welcome to them as a spell of leave would be granted at the tour's end. It was this leave which was so important to the young pilot, as his wife had just presented him with a baby and he was looking forward to having the opportunity to spend some time with his new family. Over the target however, Bevelander's Mitchell, FR141, was suddenly seen to rear up above the formation after a flak shell burst close alongside it. The aircraft stalled and plunged earthwards. So close and yet so far from the end of their tour, there were no survivors.

Yet another close encounter with the Channel was only just avoided a few days later by Flying Officer Pitchforth, a navigator with 180 Squadron. Returning from a sortie in all too infrequent sunshine, Pitchforth began to feel uncomfortably hot as the sun's rays combined with the Mitchell's heating system.

Rising from his seat, he moved to turn off the heating system's stopcock, only to suddenly find himself hanging over the Channel at 8,000 feet as a hatch gave way beneath him. By great good fortune, the effect of the aircraft's slipstream was to keep pressure against the hatch door and the severely shaken Pitchforth was able to drag himself back in. A faulty catch was later diagnosed as being the cause of his near-ducking.

The early hours of 25th March brought to an end the temporary stay of a straggler at Dunsfold. This was an aircraft exotically named 'The Passionate Witch', a B-17G Flying Fortress of the USAAF which had dropped in badly damaged after a daylight raid over Germany a couple of days earlier. On landing, the bomber had run off the edge of the runway causing an undercarriage oleo leg to collapse and thus adding to the battle damage. While this damage was serious enough to ground the aircraft, it was nevertheless assessed as repairable and consequently an American repair crew was sent to Dunsfold to make the bomber airworthy. After much hard labour, the task was completed and as night fell on the 24th the American bomber, resplendent in the lurid nose-art which illustrated her name, awaited the arrival of a crew to ferry her home.

Enter one Lancaster. The night of 24th March also saw the launch of the sixteenth and final major raid in the Battle of Berlin, RAF Bomber Command having sent out a strong force which ran into heavy opposition from the German capital's formidable defences. Among the aircraft which suffered was Lancaster III ND572 PM-M of 103 Squadron. Prolonged attacks by a Focke Wulf FW 190 fighter had knocked out all turrets and killed the rear gunner. Flak then found the wounded bomber. In short time, the flaps and rudders were shot away, tanks holed and most of the cockpit instruments and intercom shattered. By supreme skill, Flight Sergeant Fred Brownings had coaxed his aircraft back to southern England but realised there was no hope of reaching home base at Elsham Wolds in Lincolnshire. With relief, the wireless operator managed a fix on Dunsfold, but with no radio, red Very flares had to be fired off by the bomber to attract the attention of the darkened aerodrome. Eventually the runway lights came on and the exhausted pilot turned on to final approach. At the last moment, Brownings realised he was

Lancaster ND572 meets B-17 'Passionate Witch' at Dunsfold on March 24th, 1944. (Mrs F. Brownings.)

too high and with a roar of straining engines the Lancaster went round again. At the second attempt Brownings crowned a tremendous effort by bringing his Lancaster safely down onto Dunsfold's welcoming runway. Without brakes, the aircraft's trauma was not yet finished and she swung violently. Hurtling across the grass, a sudden halt was brought to the Lancaster's progress when in the darkness it met the solid mass of another aircraft - 'The Passionate Witch'. Fearing the outbreak of fire, those of Brownings' crew who could vacated the wreckage as swiftly as possible. This resulted in back injuries for the Lancaster's navigator who jumped from the aircraft without realising that there was a long drop to the ground below. Other than this mishap, and the loss of the rear gunner, the rest of the crew escaped injury.

After a sleepless night due to shock, Brownings' surviving crew sadly surveyed the machine which had managed to bring them home. The navigator's long fall was due to the Lancaster having come to rest half mounted over the American Fortress, the British bomber was covered in hundreds of flak holes and pronounced a write-off.* With one wing shattered, the Fortress too was now beyond hope and the dismay of its repair crew was

*Contrary to what the crew believed to have been the fate of their aircraft, surviving official records maintain that Lancaster ND572 was repaired and went on to serve with 57 Squadron until it was destroyed in a mid-air collision in March

only heightened by the cat-calls of 139 Airfield's 'erks'. Observing the positions of the two aircaft, the wags suggested that somehow, in the night, the Lancaster had 'taken advantage of' the Fortress. The response of the Americans is not recorded.

A better example of RAF/USAAF liaison was demonstrated on 26th March when Wing Commander Lynn led a major effort by all three of Dunsfold's squadrons and two Boston squadrons. The formation joined no fewer than 378 B-26 Marauders of the U.S. 9th Air Force in attacking E-boat pens under construction at Ijmuiden. The raid had special significance for the Dutchmen of 320 Squadron as the attack was the first they had launched against a target in Holland. Extra care in aiming was stressed and, perhaps because of this, the Dutchmen were the only ones to claim hits.

A couple of days later, Squadron Leader Williams had some success in his continual struggle to persuade aircrews to wear all their protective clothing, including the standard issue flak helmet made of leather and containing strips of steel. There were many aircrew who could not be bothered to wear this protection but the Medical Officer's case was proven when during a raid on Bonnières on the 28th, accurate flak had ripped into the Dunsfold Mitchells. While 180 Squadron lost FL685 shot down over the target, several aircraft in 98 Squadron were also hit less severely, including that of Australian pilot Nevin Filby, on his sixth operation. Filby recalls that his first impressions of flak had been somewhat detached, noting, "funny stuff flak, red if close, black if not too close" while tracers were, "quite pretty and seemed innocuous." On his third operation, opinion hardened when his Mitchell took hits over Flottmanville-Hague. Rudder controls were severed and the main spar fractured, resulting in a fraught but successful landing back at Dunsfold where seven holes were counted. By the time of the Bonnières raid therefore, Filby was more inclined to pay heed for the first time to the advice of his navigator, Keith Herman, to wear the American-designed helmet. His decision to try the protection came not a moment too soon. Heavy and accurate flak from the Hesdin area again severed the main spar of Filby's Mitchell as well as severing an elevator cable. More crucially, shrapnel also ripped into the cockpit area, creasing Filby's helmet and leaving a small indentation in his left temple to permanently remind him of the incident. Dazed but still conscious, Filby was able to recover and, seeking landing priority, again made it home safely.

While such close shaves as these were usually played down with studied nonchalence, as crews tired it became harder to conceal normally hidden tensions. One pilot at Dunsfold watched with concern as his top gunner clearly struggled with his nerves. When, after an operation, the crew repaired to a pub, it became necessary to hold the gunner's first pint for him, such was the shaking of his hands. Despite being asked by his pilot to request a medical discharge from operations, (termed 'screening'), the gunner gamely struggled to continue and the rest of his crew resolved to put up with his "hose-pipe" style of gunnery which arose from his condition. Came the day however when the gunner could hide no longer. Returning from one operation, his pilot found the Mitchell difficult to trim and struggled to maintain level flight. On landing the reason was found to lie with the gunner who was discovered wrapped in eight heavy flak jackets.

By now the medical authorities were recognizing that battle fatigue was an illness rather than a sign of cowardice and thus release could be found for those unable to continue longer under the strain of operations. On another occasion, a New Zealand pilot returned from a raid with one of his crew terribly injured in the head. After helping in the struggle to extricate the wounded man from the aircraft back at Dunsfold the deeply shocked pilot simply announced "that's enough for me, I'm for screening" and his colleagues on the squadron both understood and accepted his attitude.

The end of March also brought two logistical movements which eased the problems of accommodation. Firstly, on the 26th, 98 Squadron was 139 Airfield's first unit to leave for Practice Battle Camp at Swanton Morley, in Norfolk. This commenced a series of rotational detachments which were to take each squadron in turn to Swanton Morley prior to the invasion. Included in the camp's training was practice of night flying in formation and 180 and 320 Squadrons were pleased that 98 would be the first to attempt this dificult technique.

Already, the Dunsfold squadrons had undertaken *Exercise Nightlight* in March which was designed to find the best means of night attacks on convoys. This rôle was one of the tasks now designated for the Mitchells in the invasion to come, the idea being for them to either undertake the bombing in their own right, or to illuminate targets for attacks by Mosquitos. 98 Squadron's temporary move to Norfolk was therefore also to involve practice in the dropping of 4.5 inch flares.

Secondly, on the last day of the month, one of the most unpopular orders ever to reach Dunsfold came when, with the exception of the station headquarters' staff, all personnel were directed to henceforth live under canvas. The aim of this move was to prepare the squadrons for the supposed rigors of life on the continent, post-invasion. All permanent buildings and accommodation were padlocked shut and field rations became the order of the day. If these conditions were not bad enough, the regime of living in tents was deemed too harsh for women and Dunsfold thus lost its popular complement of WAAFs. There were numerous other consequences. In response to the more basic field rations, trade at the 'Gibbs Hatch Family Restaurant' and the 'Sundial Café' increased dramatically, although restrictions were placed on usage when one crew member was heard discussing details of a forthcoming operation. Despite the unlikelihood of hostile ears having overheard, the operation was cancelled.

All units were also required to be 100% mobile and this led to an urgent need for more personnel to be trained as drivers. With no means to adequately cover this training within the service, the British School of Motoring was called upon and the aerodrome and locality soon became busy with airmen grappling with their new skills in driving school cars before progressing to 15 cwts lorries.

The HQ Signals section also had cause to rue the move. Instead of their permanent buildings, the section now found itself operating from four receiver vehicles and a three ton code and cypher truck. Attached to the latter was a lean-to tent which served as the Signals Traffic Office, everything being covered by camouflage netting. It was the obsession of the Signals Sergeant for drinking tea which nearly led to disaster, constant brew-ups being required on a primus stove in the Office tent. On the day in question a hapless erk had been sharply ordered to put the kettle on and make sure a brew was ready by the time the Sergeant returned from an errand. In his haste, the nervous airman filled the kettle from the jerrycan holding paraffin for the stove. The kettle was just boiling when the Sergeant returned, only to trip over a chair which in turn knocked the stove and kettle over. In the panic to rescue the code and cypher books, the Sergeant bent down and succeeded in setting his trousers alight, therupon bursting out of the tent yelling, "I'm on fire!" By this time, the tent and three tonner were well alight and it was a question of who or what should be dealt with first. Since the Sergeant appeared intent on lapping the airfield and therefore would be difficult to catch, the truck was dealt with first. Consequently the Sergeant required a two week sojourn in the General Military Hospital in Horsham before being able to return to duty.

One practice which also disappeared with the move under canvas was the amusing 'metal polish trick.' Over the cold winter months, the stove located in each Nissen hut became an increasingly favoured spot to place one's chair by. In such poorly insulated temporary accommodation, a seat a few feet from the stove was as good as sitting outside, and the air gunners in particular felt they were getting a raw deal. Thanks to their longer inspections, the gunners were often the last to return to the crew huts, and thus usually found the pilots and navigators already warmly ensconced in the best stove-side seats. But one cold day, enough was enough for one suffering gunner, and a small tin of metal polish provided the solution. Dropped down the outside chimney, the tin would eventually explode inside the stove, filling the hut with hot cinders, smoke and, more importantly, empty chairs as pilots and navigators scrambled for the door.

When 98 Squadron returned from Swanton Morley, the question arose of how to maintain the newly acquired skills of night flying. All crews were still committed to extensive and exhausting daylight operations but, nevertheless, limited night intruder sorties were operated. 98 Squadron therefore commenced such operations in April, their first night attack being on a

Noball target. In a rôle reversal of what had been practiced so far, the target was marked by flares dropped by Mosquitos and two of 98's Mitchells then attacked with bombs, the cover of darkness helping to limit the effectiveness of the flak defences. The move to night operations did not, however, preclude the continuation of daylight attacks. 98 Squadron lost Flight Lieutenant Cullen's FL181, shot down in flames on the 13th of the month, during a raid on enemy naval gun positions east of Dieppe and on the 20th, FL700 piloted by Sergeant Davis inexplicably crashed just after take-off for a *Noball* raid. The last aircraft off in a squadron formation of twelve, the Mitchell plunged into the ground four miles south of the aerodrome with no survivors.

In turn, 180 Squadron was detached to Swanton Morley, only to suffer a disasterous spate of accidents during night flying. No less than three aircraft, FV915, FV975 and FW110, were lost before the unit returned to Dunsfold on 27th April and, although 320 Squadron then followed, it was recognised that tight formations could not be maintained at night to the same degree as in daylight.

Another task which Dunsfold's Mitchells had to master at this time involved what were known as *Batseye* exercises. These were dawn reconnaissance flights which were practice for the job of flying over enemy-held harbours and spotting any shipping present. One such flight came in the early hours of 26th April when 320 Squadron was called upon to provide one aircraft for a *Batseye* exercise around the Thames estuary and Kent coastline.

The early morning call did little to increase the enthusiasm of Lieutenant Commander Johnny Mulder and his crew. Briefed for take-off at 05.45 hours, Mulder gained some comfort from the fact that the Mitchell he was flying was FR142 *Margriet*. This aircraft, named after the Dutch Princess, was something of a prized possession in the squadron since its recent transatlantic delivery flight had been in the hands of HRH Prince Bernhard of the Netherlands. The exercise itself involved little more than navigating from point to point over south-east England and consequently Mulder was not over concerned on boarding *Margriet* that one of his gunners, Sergeant de Vos, had not yet appeared and looked likely to miss the flight. As the Mitchell's

Mitchell FV914 of 98 Squadron over northern France on April 19th, 1944. (IWM-CH12842.)

engines roared into life, shattering the calm of the early half light, de Vos belatedly arrived at the dispersal and was just in time to clamber aboard before Mulder taxied out. *Margriet* thundered down the runway and took off into a sky which was already lightening to the east. As he passed to the south of London, heading towards the Thames estuary, Mulder noticed a number of flashes away to the north and, as a precaution, he therefore called to his crew to keep a good look out for other aircraft.

This order proved none too soon for, a few minutes later, as the Mitchell droned on across Kent, a Typhoon was spotted approaching. The British fighter swung towards *Margriet*, but then pulled away on identifying the bomber. Almost immediately afterwards, Corporal Trieling again called out and reported the approach of a Mosquito.

Flight Lieutenant McLurg had taken off from RAF Lasham at the same time that Mulder lifted off from Dunsfold. Having only recently arrived from instructor's duties in Canada, McLurg was taking part in the same *Batseye* exercise in Mosquito NS903 of

107 Squadron. Before take off, McLurg had been warned that enemy aircraft were operating over the south-east and this seemed to be confirmed when, like Mulder, he saw what he took to be the enemy's target indicator flares in the distance over London. As McLurg then turned on to the Canterbury to Faversham leg of his route, *Margriet* emerged from cloud to the north-west.

The Mosquito pilot immediately swung into a wide circle around the bomber, suspicious that it had appeared from the direction of London where he had already seen what he took to be signs of an enemy raid. By one of those fateful combinations of circumstances, identification of the 'bandit' was proving difficult for McLurg as his gunsight illumination was jammed on full intensity but as he completed his wary circuit he noted twin engines and twin rudders - the characteristics of a Dornier Do 217 of the Luftwaffe.

Aboard *Margriet*, McLurg's intentions became chillingly clear as the Mosquito closed to four hundred yards on the port quarter. Mulder just had time to hear de Vos's shouted warning before the intercom died under the hammering strikes of the Mosquito's guns. Mulder desperately wrenched *Margriet* into evasive action while his navigator, Sub-Lieutenant Wytman, fired off the colours of the day. For the cherished *Margriet*, the crew's efforts came too late. McLurg again curved into the attack and, with impressive accuracy, hit both of the Mitchell's engines. As he broke off his second attack at one hundred yards, McLurg felt his stomach sink. He could now at last see that the 'bandit' was without doubt an RAF Mitchell and he could only watch in despair as the bomber slowed and began to lose height. Aboard *Margriet*, Mulder saw both oil pressure gauges flicker to zero as the engines stopped. With the Mitchell sinking lower and lower, Mulder ordered his crew to bale out and struggled to put on his own parachute while still trying to keep the powerless aircraft under control.

Back in the fuselage, Wytman successfully baled out from his navigator's compartment, but Sergeant de Vos was left with a frightening discovery. Having assumed that a parachute had been put aboard for him by his fellow crew members, he now discovered that his late arrival on dispersal had led to only three

FR142 'Margriet' with Henk Voorspuy in the cockpit. (Royal Dutch Navy 4743.)

parachutes having been put aboard. Fortunately, as he prepared to make his own exit, Mulder heard de Vos call out, and the pilot therefore returned to the controls determined to put the aircraft down safely. This was good news too for Corporal Trieling, who had not heard the 'bale out' order until it was too low to jump. Luckily, the countryside below was relatively open and Mulder pulled off an immaculate landing in fields three miles north of Headcorn, in Kent. Ironically, the only injury suffered was that of Wytman, who broke his ankle on landing by parachute. He also had difficulty in persuading locals that he was not German, his story of having been shot down by a RAF Mosquito did little to help!

Poor *Margriet* was a sorry sight and beyond recovery. Nevertheless, a technical team was flown the next day from Dunsfold to nearby RAF Detling. The attention of the RAF guards was diverted, and *Margriet's* clock, compass and altimeter were removed as souvenirs.

While at Swanton Morley, 180 Squadron missed out on one of Dunsfold's most famous visitors. On 18th April, a Dakota had landed with Supreme Commander General Dwight Eisenhower aboard, accompanied by Air Chief Marshal Sir Trafford Leigh-Mallory, Air Marshal Sir Arthur Coningham, Air Vice-Marshal Embry and Group Captain Atcherley. The USAAF and US Army were represented by Major General Hoyt Vandenberg and Major

General L. Brereton respectively. The Supreme Commander had come from RAF Hartford Bridge while on a tour of inspections across south-east England, and from Hartford Bridge he was followed by a Boston of 88 Squadron. The Boston roared low over Dunsfold, laying smoke and thus demonstrating 88's designated rôle in the forthcoming invasion. Following an inspection of the aircraft and crews of 98 and 320 Squadrons, General Eisenhower addressed all personnel in one of the T2 hangars, stessing the urgent need to train and be prepared for the challenges ahead.

On 4th May Group Captain Dunlap and Wing Commander Lynn were ordered to RAF Northolt for a top secret briefing on the cross-Channel invasion, code-named *Operation Overlord*. A requirement of this indoctrination was that henceforth neither Dunlap nor Lynn would be permitted to fly on operations until such time as Overlord materialised, this being a security measure to protect against capture and possible torture which might reveal the operation's secret details. Up until this restriction Lynn had participated in operations regularly, sometimes as often as twice a day. Both he and his navigator, Waardenburg, had become so skillful in handling the lead positions (i.e. lead pilot and lead navigator), that they were constantly in demand for these duties. Lynn had established a reputation for being able to get the formation to and from the target with a minimum of trouble from flak batteries, while Waardenburg always seemed to bomb accurately in the face of any amount of enemy opposition, thus avoiding the necessity of a return engagement.

Lynn's 'press-on' character was not to everyone's liking however, particularly with some of the senior officers of the squadrons. As Wing Commander (Flying), Lynn had the authority to lead any formation and he frequently used this authority in electing to lead attacks on important targets. Unavoidably, this caused some resentment amongst the squadron commanders who considered Lynn's presence as weakening their own authority. Lynn's eagerness to participate in most operations is illustrated by the story of Keith Cudlipp, who joined Lynn's crew in May. Previously belonging to the crew of one of 98 Squadron's flight commanders, Cudlipp found himself

The April 18th visit. Front row; Leigh-Mallory, Eisenhower and Dunlap. (IWM-CH12784.)

a spare part when his pilot was posted away. Cudlipp wanted to stay on the squadron and was looking to join another crew when he was approached by Lynn, coincidentally looking for a replacement for one of his gunners who had recently been injured. Bearing in mind that Lynn was Wing Commander (Flying), Cudlipp imagined that his duties would not be over onerous, as he thought Lynn would only undertake the odd trip here and there. Therefore, when Lynn suggested "Come along to see how things go, and see how you like my efforts", Cudlipp accepted. Contrary to his expectations, the young gunner noted that ten days after joining Lynn, he had flown no less than fifteen operations.

The new gunner in Lynn's crew soon noticed an idiosyncrasy of his pilot which involved chewing gum. While refuting any suggestion of superstition, the South African nevertheless developed the habit of always chewing gum before an operation. On arrival at the dispersal point, he would then always stick the chewed gum on the underneath of his Mitchell's tail unit.

Then came the day when, just before climbing up into his aircraft, Lynn suddenly stopped in his tracks. Clearly agitated, he turned to his crew members: "I haven't got any gum, quickly, who's got some?" None of the crew were able to oblige their skipper and Lynn's frown deepened. "For Christ's sake, find me some gum!" he ordered. The three men scattered, chasing around the ground crews on the dispersals until Cudlipp struck lucky. One of the fitters, digging deep in his pockets with a greasy begrimed hand, proffered a fistful of nuts and bolts and other odds and ends. In the middle was what might be a very grubby piece of Wrigleys. Quickly, Cudlipp took the stick, spat into his handkerchief and rubbed it clean. It was chewing gum. A relieved Lynn took the wad and, ignorant of its history, happily gave it a rapid chew before sticking it on his aircraft.*

An attack by all squadrons on the marshalling yards at Cambrai led to drama both before and during the attack. It was the habit of Lieutenant Commander Spangenburg, 320 Squadron's Technical Officer, to stand at the end of the runway to see the aircraft off, rather than at the beginning of the runway, which was more the usual practice of well-wishers. He therefore became a familiar figure, with his little Austin saloon which he used to reach the far end of the airfield, assuring the aircrews that this position enabled him to be at hand to give technical advice until the last possible moment!

On this occasion, Spangenburg had safely seen off all the Dutch Mitchells and was turning to leave when FW100 of 180 Squadron came down the runway, obviously unable to gain altitude. The Mitchell flashed past the alarmed officer and crashed off the end of the runway. As the aircraft burst into flames, the Dutchman raced to the scene and managed to free one of the gunners trapped in the wreckage. Together they raced to the nearest slit trench where they joined the other members of Flying Officer Kennard's crew just in time before the bombs exploded. Himself shaken by the blast, Spangenburg offered a lift to the dazed airmen in his Austin which was parked only a short distance away. On reaching it however, they discovered it

---

*Keith Cudlipp had joined 98 Squadron at West Raynham on 20.9.42 and remained with the squadron until the end of the war. In that time he flew 83 Mitchell operations, with eighteen different pilots and crews. Almost seventy were completed with Alan Lynn from Dunsfold and Cudlipp received a well deserved DFC for his efforts.

Alan Lynn, Wing Commander (Flying) and the chewing gum. (Keith Cudlipp.)

riddled with shrapnel from the explosion and, like the Mitchell, a total write-off. Of those 320 Squadron Mitchells which Spangenburg had waved off, FR184 was hit by flak near Abbeville and did not return, having ditched in the Channel.

On 6th May 1944, a change of squadron command occurred when Wing Commander John Castle DFC handed over 180 Squadron to Wing Commander Ray Goodwin, newly arrived from Canada.

Only two days later, Goodwin's fellow Canadian and opposite number on 98 Squadron, Wing Commander Bell-Irving, led 139 and 137 Airfields in a strong attack against a *Noball* target at Bois Coquerel. For this operation, Leading Aircraftsman Reg Day was on his best behaviour since the young mechanic had been temporarily assigned to his commanding officer's aircraft FW109. Bell-Irving was in cheerful mood as he climbed into his machine and, noticing the somewhat overawed newcomer amongst his ground crew, he joked at Day's small size compared to his own bulk. Laughing, the Canadian dropped his own hat on Day's head, covering the mechanic's eyes and ears and he told him to take good care of the hat until he returned.

Less than an hour later, Bell-Irving led the two wing formations over the French coast at 13,000 feet in cloudless skies. As the target was approached, heavy and accurate flak bracketed the formations and, shortly after releasing his bombs, Bell-Irving's machine suffered a direct hit in the nose. Canadian pilot Max Harris was flying number two in the formation and stared across in shocked horror at the scene in his leader's cockpit. The remains of the aircraft slowly spiralled down out of control and despite scores of willing eyes which watched, no parachutes emerged.

When the squadrons touched down back at Dunsfold, Reg Day was still proudly guarding his commanding officer's cap. As the aircrews climbed out however, there was still no sign of FW109 and the grim news then quickly spread amongst the ground personnel. Day felt a lump come to his throat as he stared at the hat in his hands.*

Squadron Leader Ken Eager took over temporary command of 98 Squadron pending the arrival of another commanding officer. This replacement took place with the arrival on the 19th of Wing Commander Christopher Paul, a regular officer with a wealth of experience in both the pre-war RAF and Fleet Air Arm.

Within the new Wing Commander's crew were three very different characters, yet they lacked nothing in cohesion as an efficient team. Navigator Bill Williams was a dependable and calm officer, even in the face of the heaviest flak. Sergeant Harris, a former barrow boy from the East End of London, was tough and chirpy with the small and wiry athletic build of a boxer. His opposite was Zdenek Kokes, the Czech mid-upper gunner. Kokes, or 'Cokey Joe' as he quickly became known, had already served a tour with a Czech Wellington squadron and held his country's Military Cross. At the outbreak of war he had been an undergraduate at Cambridge University and had been separated from his parents and two sisters. The family continued to live in Amsterdam, where Kokes' father had been Czech Commercial Attaché to Holland, their house only a few doors away from local Gestapo headquarters. In England

---

*By a strange quirk of fate, one of Bell-Irving's crew escaped this disaster. Navigator John Bateman had only been with the crew for five operations and on the fateful day had been called to the Air Ministry in London. When he returned to Dunsfold that evening he learned of the deaths of his colleagues and the man who had taken his place for just one operation.

Wing Commander Bell-Irving (right) with navigator Flying Officer Vic Phipps. (K. Cudlipp.)

LAC Reg Day. The crest on the B-25 is that of the City of Derby. (Reg Day.)

Zdenek, with his continental charm and youthful good looks, was very popular with the ladies.

On arrival, Wing Commander Paul was delighted with his flight offices in picturesque Rose Cottage (formerly Broadmeads Cottage) and, like many before him, soon came to appreciate that Group Captain Dunlap and his staff spared no effort to support the operational crews. On returning from raids, there would always be two eggs, bacon and a hot bath and, despite shortages countrywide, a priority was to ensure that beer never ran out.

Organisationally, the aerodrome had now been transferred to 11 Group of Air Defence Great Britain (formerly Fighter Command). As a Second TAF unit, 139 Airfield was therefore now deemed only a lodger unit, pending its planned move to the continent after the invasion. From 15th May the Airfield had been formally renamed 139 Wing, still under the command of Group Captain Dunlap who, for the time being, retained responsibility for the station's discipline. On the airfield itself, even station headquarters had now moved under canvass, but worries continued that some of the tented areas were close to the operational areas of the aerodrome and might therefore be in danger from any mishaps in flying duties. This had already been demonstrated in early May when a 180 Squadron Mitchell crashed during take-off and blew up at the end of runway 26. Fortunately, the crew were able to jump out in time, but several ground crew tents in the proximity had been riddled with shrapnel.

The lesson had not been heeded however when, on 22nd May, Lancaster JB217 of 156 Squadron from RAF Upwood limped in for a crash-landing just after midnight. Badly shot up by a German nightfighter and unable to brake, the crippled machine overshot the runway and careered into the tented quarters of 2847 Squadron of the RAF Regiment. In the ensuing carnage, many men were injured and one decapitated by the Lancaster's propellers. This ended a disastrous spate of incidents which had befallen 2847 Squadron's gunners. One of their officers, Pilot Officer Monk, had recently died of his injuries following a motorcycle accident in nearby Loxwood and earlier in the month a crew member of one of the Bofors guns had attempted suicide. A one day pass had involved some sort of girlfriend trouble and the dejected man had returned to Dunsfold only to shoot himself through the chest with his rifle.

Unlike the RAF Regiment's tented site, that of 98 Squadron was well protected, its lines being sited in a pair of drives through dense woods just behind the western end of the technical site. Wing Commander Paul had arranged that each four man crew, regardless of rank, shared one tent. As squadron commanding officer, only Paul had a tent to himself. As is often the case in unusual circumstances, unusual talents were discovered by the bohemian lifestyle and no skills were more sought after than those of Leading Aircraftsman 'Paddy' Pooley. Pooley had joined the RAF in 1941 and had been with 139 Wing since its inception. He had previously spent seventeen years in the Army, including First World War service in the trenches where he had won the Military Medal in 1917. It was this latter experience which now made him a leading authority on life under canvas and his skills soon earned him the title of 'King of the Lazy Boiler.'

*Wing Commander Paul's crew. (L to R) Zdenek Kokes, 'Colonel'
Booth, Bill Williams, Paul, Fred Halsey, Mich Jansen. (Air Cdr.
G. J. C. Paul.)*

The woods themselves were filled with nightingales, who could
be guaranteed to break into glorious song whenever a Mitchell's
engines started up. On occasions their chorus was drowned by
the raucous competition of the airmen in party mood. In
particular, the Canadian aircrews of 98 Squadron needed little
excuse to build a campfire and hold a feast with the contents of
their food parcels from home. If no operations were pending this
could last well into the night, encouraged by beer.

There were attractions too to 180 Squadron's tented site. After
the accident involving the RAF Regiment's lines, the squadron's
tents were moved from an area close to the main runway.
Instead, they were re-sited beneath the beech trees in the
grounds of Sachel Court - home of the Land Army girls. In this
classic example of putting the cat among the pigeons, grumbles
against the outdoor life dramatically decreased!

Clearly, 139 Wing's operations were working to a crescendo by
the beginning of June. May had seen a switch to attacks on
marshalling yards and other railway targets, followed by three

days of raids on enemy airfields. All personnel realised that the invasion was only a matter of days away. Many aircrew were determined to be in on the occasion, typical of such types being Olaf Gronmark, formerly of 180 Squadron.

Gronmark had been one of the irrepressible characters on the squadron, 6' 4" tall and with the colourful life history of a Norwegian who had spent much of his life as a miner in Canada. Despite this background, Gronmark was normally a quiet and unassuming man who nevertheless inspired confidence and respect in anyone. While leading formations he had achieved the enviable record of never loosing an aircraft or crew member in his formation, to flak or fighters. 'Think like a German' was the advice he always gave to other pilots, and it certainly seemed to work.

On only one occasion did Gronmark lose his temper. Leading a 180 Squadron formation, the Norwegian was on his final bombing run when crew member Frank Morgan shouted a warning of aircraft above. Only a few feet up a box of 320 Squadron Mitchells already had their bomb doors open and the airwaves exploded as Gronmark let fly with language learned from the mining camps of northern Ontario. Almost immediately, the bomb doors closed as the Dutch aircraft went round again. By the time the formations landed back at Dunsfold, the big Norwegian was back to his unperturbable self.

After a demanding and eventful tour at Foulsham and Dunsfold, Gronmark and his crew had been posted 'on rest' as instructors with 13 O.T.U. (Operational Training Unit) based at Bicester. Boredom had soon set in and so one week-end had seen them flying down to Dunsfold where Wing Commander Castle confirmed he would be glad to see Gronmark back, if this could be arranged. Returning to Bicester, Gronmark blithely told the Chief Instructor that he and his crew were posted back to 180 Squadron and it took several days before the ruse came to light. 2 Group Headquarters demanded that Gronmark report immediately back to 13 O.T.U. but a crew conference of war nominated the burly Norwegian to ask to see the Group commander, Air Vice-Marshal Embry, in person. Embry promised to find a way around the red tape and he did. After a

On May 26th, Flight Lieutenant Knowlton took CBC reporter Don Fairburn on an op. in 'Sneezy'. (L to R) Eppstadt, Purvis, Hastings, Knowlton. (Dr L. Hastings.)

training course in GEE-H, Gronmark and his crew returned to Dunsfold for their second tour, just in time for the invasion.

On 3rd June, 1944 the arrival of Operations Order Number 3 outlined the 2nd Tactical Air Force's plans for Dunsfold's Mitchells:

INTENTION : To cause maximum delay to the movement by road and rail, by enemy forces at night, in the area prescribed.

GENERAL PLAN : All Mitchell and Mosquito squadrons in the Group will be used, throughout the hours of darkness, to delay enemy road movements in the following inclusive areas:

Lessay - Caen - Lisieux - Argentan - Domfont - Fougeres -Avranches.

Any movement is to be attacked whenever seen in the area, but particular attention is to be concentrated on the following roads :

Avranches - Coutances - Lessay; Fougeres - Vire - St Lo; Domfont - Flers - Caen; Argentan - Falaise - Caen; Evreux - Lisieux - Caen.

Mitchells will be employed to attack static targets, decided upon as a result of tactical information received from various sources. Attacks will be carried out by one of the following methods :

i) aircraft fitted with GEE-H to bomb, or act as pathfinders to illuminate the target by means of flares or T.I.s for attack by non GEE-H fitted aircraft.

ii) aircraft not fitted with GEE-H to make individual, but closely co-ordinated attacks on static targets visually by the light of flares or T.I.s dropped by pathfinders.

iii) in suitable weather, and moon conditions, flying independently to attack selected targets by visual means.

Upon receipt of this order, only one question regarding D-Day remained for Dunsfold's squadrons - when? On 5th June a further priority order led to the RAF Regiment suddenly sealing off the camp, much to the frustration of those men who had grown accustomed to the proximity of the Land Army girls, still only yards away but now screened behind hastily erected barbed-wire fences. All non-service letters, telephone calls and telegrams were halted while ground crews worked feverishly to apply broad black and white invasion stripes to the wings and fuselage of each Mitchell. Clearly, the moment was at hand. As dusk fell heavy activity was noted in the skies and Dunsfold's crews impatiently awaited their own call to arms.

Chapter Seven

D - DAY

As the evening of 5th June wore on, all three squadrons were placed on readiness for operations and, as midnight approached, crews were briefed on their respective targets. At twenty-three minutes past midnight, twelve aircraft of 320 Squadron were first into the air, with orders to attack a bridge over the River Dives. At 01.13 hours, twelve aircraft of 180 Squadron took off to attack a road and rail crossing north of Argentan, followed at 02.16 hours by a final formation of eleven aircraft from 98 Squadron, heading for a defile south of Thury Harcourt. While most crews were convinced that the operations were in preparation for the invasion, no official information was forthcoming. The only unusual order was not to fly below 3,000 feet over the Channel.

By the time they crossed the French coast, 320 Squadron were down to eleven aircraft, due to FR167 having turned back over Beachy Head with a malfunctioning GEE box. Led by Commander Burgerhout, those who reached the target area were then frustrated to find 10/10 cloud at 5,000 feet and 9/10 at 2,500 feet. Burgerhout was left with no option but to abandon the mission and return to Dunsfold.

180 Squadron fared little better, again due to the poor weather conditions. Led by Wing Commander Lynn, only eight aircraft identified the target and bombed by the light of target indicator flares without being able to see any results. Of the other four aircraft, two returned to Dunsfold with their bomb loads intact while another found and bombed the airfield at Argentan. The final aircraft of the eight jettisoned its load in the Channel.

Of 98 Squadron's eleven Mitchells, led by Wing Commander Paul, five located and bombed the primary target at Thury Harcourt with the aid of target indicators dropped by Lasham's Mosquitos. The remaining six aircraft attempted to attack the secondary target of the aerodrome at Condé-sur-Vire but only aircraft 'P' managed to bomb, encountering light and inaccurate flak from the defences. Two other aircraft of this group returned before reaching the target due to equipment failures while the final two could not locate the enemy aerodrome and brought their bomb loads back.

On the return journey, evidence was seen that the invasion was indeed on. As dawn broke, crews of 98 Squadron reported the sea to the north full of ships and the skies black with aircraft. 180 Squadron likewise gained some evidence when, as they crossed the coast near Le Havre, a gap in the cloud cover revealed the wakes of many ships. Chaplain Tom Warner was flying in the aircraft of Flight Lieutenant Gareth Lyden and, contrary to orders, the crew pursuaded their pilot to drop lower for a better look. As the Mitchell emerged beneath the cloud the dark form of a destroyer was spotted below and the warship instantly opened fire with all guns. Lyden quickly climbed the Mitchell back up into the safety of the cloud, but not before they had time to see the largest armada of warships ever assembled. Landing back at Dunsfold, Warner excitedly rushed back to the intelligence tent, arms full of flying gear. In the darkness, he neglected the guy ropes with disastrous consequences.

All aircraft returned safely without encountering flak and, at 07.30 hours on the 6th, Group Captain Dunlap announced in the Airmens' Mess Hall that the invasion had indeed commenced. At 14.00 hours all security restrictions were lifted from the aerodrome and before the forthcoming night's operations, the crews took the opportunity to relax and read the first press reports of the invasion. The steady build up at Dunsfold towards the invasion had led to a number of war correspondents visiting the squadrons in order to participate in, and report upon, the operations. While a BBC radio news team recorded from one of Dunsfold's Mitchells over the invasion beaches (one such BBC man to visit Dunsfold having been the well-known Richard Dimbleby), several other aircraft carried newspapermen, with varying results.

Perhaps the most factual account came from Ronald Walker of the London daily 'News Chronicle'. Walker had arrived at Dunsfold on Monday the 5th and his account written up on the morning of the 6th appeared in the press the following day.

FW172 of 180 Squadron takes off for Normandy. (National Archives of Canada PL-31251.)

Wednesday, June 7, 1944

NEWS CHRONICLE

In the clouds at H-Hour on D-Day

By RONALD WALKER News Chronicle Air Correspondent who flew to Normandy with advance bombing crews

BOMBER CREWS DIDN'T KNOW THIS WAS 'IT'
I COULD NOT EVEN SEE THE CHANNEL BELOW

RAF TACTICAL BOMBER BASE Tuesday morning

The crews of the three Mitchell bomber squadrons of this station who were sent on bombing missions to France in the early hours of this morning did not know that they were taking part in the invasion of Europe. They had been carefully briefed about the nature of the targets they were to attack and how they should be bombed, but the Group Captain commanding the Wing was more than careful not to give them that information. When I left them later this morning, when they had eaten their bacon and egg breakfast, and were making for their tents in the first sunlight, they still did not know.

NOW GOING BACK

I had flown with one of these squadrons to bomb a road and rail junction in Normandy, as part of the campaign to destroy the German means of military movement. Almost four years previous I had flown out of France in the brilliant sunshine of another June day. Now we were going back. We were going back, not only with great and well equipped armies, but with an air strength bigger than Germany had thought possible, which had already hounded and beaten the German, not only in his own country, but throughout Europe. Knowing something of the real significance of this night's operations, it was easy for me to listen in to the rythmic rumble of the engines 'Going back, going back, going back.' On previous occasions I had been over France and around its coast, but this was the real thing. For weeks off and on I had been camping on this station with the officers and men, all under canvas. Crews moaned about having to do two operations each day and sometimes three, but the moan is a reverse measure of the real spirit of the RAF. One of these three squadrons belongs to the Dutch Air Force. The enthusiasm and skill of these exiled Dutchmen has to be seen to be fully appreciated.

CAMP WAS SEALED

It was only yesterday morning that the pulse began to quicken. Suddenly and without previous warning - even by the usual 'bush telegraph' of the RAF Station - the camp was sealed. No-one could leave without a very special pass. People could come in, but once in they had to stay. All except official communications were severed. This announcement caused great excitement and much speculation. Endless discussions went on in the tents fed by the news that the Group Captain had called for this or that Officer. Then came the announcment of 'ops' that night. The pilots and crews sat and waited. At the dispersal points the ground crews worked on the Mitchells, readying them for the night, while painters hurriedly decorated them with the wide black and white stripes, which are now the identifying marks of aircraft of the Allied Expeditionary Air Force.

HUMOROUS SIDE

The suspense was not without its humour. A road bends around one end of the camp. Here it is the custom for quite a number of young women to wait for their Air Force friends in the evening. Last evening they waited in vain. As anxious young women peered through the bushes into the camp, young men on the other side of the barbed wire waved their arms in the tic tac signal, which means that an Operation or order is cancelled. One desperate young man was heard to shout, 'I shan't be able to come tonight.' Laughter followed the puzzled young ladies as they drifted away. There was a very big muster in the big mess tent. Dinner was quickly eaten and the crews went off to wait for further news. Finally came the news that the briefing would be fairly late. The sun was setting when the pilots and crews of the Dutch squadron, the first to be called, gathered in the big tent used as the briefing room. Electric lights blazed on the big maps showing the targets for the night and the routes to be flown. The babble of conversation in the strange mixture of English and Dutch died as the Group Captain began to speak. What he said he told in turn to each of the squadrons. He told them that the preparatory phase of the invasion was finished, and that the air forces had more than fulfilled the task of smoothing the way for the surface forces. The Germans knew that we were about to strike; but when and where?

GROUP CAPTAIN EXPLAINS

The Group Captain explained that Allied night fighters would be flying over the area in great numbers, and big forces of RAF heavy night bombers would be pounding enemy communications and troop concentrations in a given area to the north of our several targets. Our task was to smash a road and rail junction, one of many communication targets in Normandy. When I reported in the crew room, just before take-off, a young Australian Air Gunner looked at me very hard and then forcefully expressed the opinion that anyone who went flying on night operations when they did not have to must be mad.

FROM DOMINIONS

Many of these crews are made up of men from the Dominions, particularly Canada and Australia. I happened to fly with a crew three quarters British. The pilot was Flt.-Lt. A. C. Maclaren, of Glasgow, the navigator, Flying Officer R. Stigant, of Gosport, and the two gunners, Flying Officer M. C. Demers, of Saskatchewan, Canada, and Flt.-Sgt. J. D. Davies, of Shropshire. It was dark when we finally climbed aboard. The aerodrome was speckled with lights, outlining the runways and the taxi-ing tracks. From all directions came the roaring of engines running up and the flames spouting from the exhausts flickered wherever one looked. The all but full moon did not appear until we had climbed for several thousand feet to emerge above the first cloud layer. We set course for a point on the French coast west of Dieppe. I had hoped to be flying by day so that I could bring back a picture of the Channel crammed with ships making for the beachhead, plus something of the happenings on land. This was not to be. The Squadron was detailed for night operations. I did not even see the Channel. It lay concealed beneath a cloud layer several thousand feet in depth. Above was a scene of rare beauty composed of the moon, shining on the endless expanse of cloud, shining cold and very remote from the world of war beneath. It was 2.15a.m. when we approached the target area. Vainly we searched for a gap in the clouds. There was none. The pilot pushed the stick forward and held it there. The needle on the rate of climb indicator dropped below the level and the Mitchell pushed its nose into the woolly cloud base and we were engulfed in a ghostly world where nothing could be seen except the exhaust flames turned to a vivid colour. At less than 4,000ft we finally emerged into some open air. Up to this moment there had been no sign of an enemy in the apparently dead and dark land beneath us. Now we could see fields, cut through with roads. We ran up to bomb and then tracers from light flak came sailing up towards us, drawing curves of coloured lights against the dark land. It lasted but a minute or two, and then was gone as we began to climb again through the cloud. We flew home in the upper world of moonlight and finally, the Mitchell touched down again on the runway.

TARGETS INVISIBLE

In the interrogation room, we found that many of the Mitchells had brought their bombs back because the thick clouds had completely hidden their targets from them. It was one of this Wing's most disappointing night's operations. There was the consoling knowledge that not only D-Day had arrived, but H-Hour - the actual moment for invasion.

For Squadron Leader Fisher's crew of 180 Squadron, surprise came with the discovery that they were billed as heroes of the night. Having taken off at 01.15 hours their aircraft, S-Sugar, had carried a passenger in the form of Colin Bednall, a correspondent with the London Daily Mail. Bednall had already flown twice with the crew on operations against V-1 sites, the first such mission had proved to be the proverbial 'piece of cake,' but the second had met heavy flak opposition. Two Mitchells were shot down and this had clearly made a lasting impression on Bednall, who had subsequently written, 'Today I saw and experienced flak so thick you could have lowered the undercarriage and taxied on it!' In the early hours of 6th June, Bednall had again joined S-Sugar for their attack on the road and rail crossing near Argentan. The target was to be illuminated by a Mosquito dropping flares but, from leaving the coast, thick cloud had been encountered. Despite confirmation from the GEE-H box that they were in position no flares were seen and, after a few circuits, S-Sugar's allotted time over target ran out and Squadron Leader Fisher turned for home with discomforting thoughts of a night landing back at Dunsfold with eight 500lb bombs still aboard. Nothing unusual was seen and a strong feeling of frustration and anti-climax pervaded the return flight. A safe landing back at Dunsfold was followed by bacon and eggs and then sleep. Later in the day the morning papers arrived in the flight crew room and featured on the front page of the London Daily News was a stirring article by Colin Bednall entitled 'I was over the D-Day beaches.' The dramatic account which followed borrowed heavily on the imagination of the writer and Squadron Leader Fisher's crew could scarcely believe it referred to their operation of the previous night.

Despite the flowery language used, the journalists at Dunsfold were nevertheless volunteers when joining crews to share the dangers of operations. In some cases this led to firm friendships being made, one such being between the Australians of Pilot Officer Nevin Filby's 98 Squadron crew and Australian war correspondent Peter Gladwin, later to become an editor of the Daily Telegraph. Filby was now regularly flying 'W' -William, and an American friend had dubbed this colourful crew the 'Wallaroo Warriors' in recognition of their aggressive spirit. Gladwin also wrote admiringly of his fellow contrymen, describing their jaunty singing on the way home from operations despite, on one occasion having only 'one rudder, one elevator and half a wing flapping.'

On the night of 6th/7th June, all squadrons were again busy over the invasion area, this time with more success in bombing targets. An observer who joined Commander Burgerhout's seventeen aircraft from 320 Squadron proved to be General Down of the British Army. Burgerhout and his crew were startled to learn that only 24 hours previously, the General had gone ashore with the land forces. He had subsequently been flown out by Auster and was now viewing the situation from the air. Once again, no losses were suffered by the three squadrons, despite at least one crew going in to bomb, unofficially, at only 3,000 feet, determined to achieve the best possible results for the crucial battle going on below.

On a similar night operation, several aircraft of 98 Squadron were sent to knock out a bridge being used by the enemy. Nevin Filby took his Mitchell in at only 500 feet until his navigator Keith Herman pinpointed the target using the GEE-H box. Filby pulled up to 1,000 feet and deliberated the tactics for his four 1,000lb bombs. Even at 1,000 feet, the bombs' instantaneous fuses threatened damage to the releasing aircraft but Filby elected to take the risk and made a diagonal run up to the target, clearly illuminated in the moonlight. Two good near misses were seen either side of the bridge, but no hits and Filby returned to Dunsfold to be told that his was the only aircraft to have identified the target at all. He never did find out whether the bridge was subsequently downed but a sobering discovery was the number of gaping holes in the wing undersurfaces and belly of his Mitchell, caused by fragments from the aircraft's own bombs. The Australians had again enjoyed good fortune.

On the night of 7th/8th June, the honeymoon ended when shortly after take off a large flash illuminated the sky around a formation of 320 Squadron's Mitchells climbing over Horsham. This came from the collision of aircraft FR150 and FR182, one blowing up immediately and the other five minutes after crashing in flames. Due to the explosion of the bomb loads, the task of locating the bodies of the crews proved a grim task the next day. 320 Squadron also lost aircraft FL179 'T' over the target that same night, possibly due to night fighters since a 98 Squadron crew reported having to dodge the attentions of a Junkers Ju 88.

A new tactic was revealed in the enemy nightfighter's arsenal on the night of 8th June when Lieutenant Gronmark's Mitchell of 180 Squadron enjoyed good fortune. Detailed to attack a railway junction from 12,000 feet, Gronmark had just crossed the French coast south east of Cherbourg when a single searchlight came on ahead of his aircraft. Unusually, rather than sweeping the sky to pick up the Mitchell, the light instead kept ahead of the aircraft, moving along the same track and waving up and down. After a short while, Gronmark's puzzled crew saw the light go out and the mystery was then promptly solved when a burst of tracer came at them from below on the port side.

As the gunfire sped past his starboard wing, Gronmark wrenched the Mitchell into violent evasive action and dived to 9,000 feet. By so doing, Gronmark's mid-upper gunner was presented with a dream target. Perfectly silhouetted against the moon was a single engined fighter turning into the attack from the five o'clock high position and smack in the sights of Jack Smith. As his first burst snaked from the Browning machine guns, Smith was blinded from the dazzle of the tracer ammunition. No-one had thought to change the day tracer rounds to the night-time variety and consequently Smith lost his target. Quickly, Frank Morgan, the wireless operator/air gunner, picked up the fighter again from the vantage point of the cockpit, sitting alongside Gronmark. As the German curved in once more, Morgan gave a running commentary so that Smith was ready again when Gronmark dived to starboard beneath the fighter. At Morgan's call, Smith opened fire as the enemy aircraft streaked over the Mitchell, the German receiving a long burst before it disappeared into cloud. As it did so, a red blinding flash was seen, turning to a glow through the cloud cover. The anxious watching eyes aboard the Mitchell were convinced that the fighter had been badly hit, it did not reappear and Smith claimed probable damage to the enemy machine. Thankful of their own skilled teamwork, Gronmark's crew later learned that they had survived an enemy technique known as 'Wild Boar' where a night fighter would combine with searchlights to locate its prey. Several other aircraft were not so lucky. Four nights later, FR205 of 320 Squadron disappeared while undertaking a similar lone night intruder sortie over Lisieux and the next night 98 Squadron lost FW129 and FW184 in like circumstances.

Another 180 Squadron crew to meet a German nightfighter was that of Flight Lieutenant Lorne MacFarlane, RCAF. While on a night operation and flying over the Bay of Biscay MacFarlane recalls:

"My mid-upper gunner came running down from his turret and said 'Did you see that?!' We never saw anything. 'We nearly had it that time', he went on. 'We just met a 'plane head on and he cleaned our top off, I thought he had me too!'

"A German night fighter, flying in the opposite direction, had cleaned the aerial off the top of our Mitchell. That was the closest call we ever had. Just a few more inches and we would have all been gonners. The German probably went home and changed his pants too, I bet."

Meanwhile, the Mitchell formations continued their daylight raids against the enemy and the operation mounted on 10th June, 1944, must go down in Dunsfold's history as the aerodrome's most spectacular war-time success. For more than 24 hours all three squadrons had been held in readiness for an attack on an important German headquarters and tank concentration, identified by intelligence sources. At last, word arrived that the time was right despite poor cloud conditions and that evening 53 aircraft were mustered for an attack using GEE-H in order to bomb blind.

This planning seemed to be vindicated when the formation found itself in clear air at 12,000 feet but with solid cloud below. Joining 226 Squadron from Hartford Bridge, the Mitchell force was now 71 aircraft strong but, if this was not enough, four squadrons of Typhoons provided a further 40 aircraft carrying rocket projectiles. The Typhoons were to attack the armoured vehicles while the Mitchells' target was the headquarters itself, a château in the village of La Caine. As the final bombing run commenced, all aircraft awaited the order to bomb from the leading Mitchell using GEE-H, flown by Wing Commander Lynn.

By a great stroke of good luck, a gap appeared in the cloud cover just as bombing commenced and the resultant camera evidence showed that the squadrons had been directly over the château. The German headquarters appeared to have been severely damaged and this was confirmed by the intelligence source who had watched the procedings from nearby. In addition it was reported that a senior German General and his staff had driven up to the chateau at the precise moment that bombing commenced. Information received later confirmed that the château had served as the headquarters for the Germans' Panzer Group West, and as such its destruction had dealt a severe blow to the enemy. The senior officer present had been Major-General Ritter von Elder von Dawans, who had perished along with two Majors, two Captains and 13 others of his personal staff. When Canadian troops subsequently captured the ruins, they discovered a large wooden cross over a common grave holding those killed in the raid. A couple of months later, Group Captain Dunlap and Wing Commander Lynn flew to the continent and visited the site of the château, photographing the cross which still stood.

The spirits of the Dutchmen were raised when, on 12th June, an afternoon visit was paid by their Queen Wilhemina, accompanied by Prince Bernhard and Air Vice-Marshal Embry. Once described by Winston Churchill as, 'the only man in the Dutch Government,' Queen Wilhemina encouraged the crews with a morale boosting speech and the presentation of several decorations, including one to the squadron's popular command-ing officer, Commander Burgerhout. There was a great depth of respect and enthusiasm for the Dutch royal family within the squadron, encouraged by the tradition of granting twenty cigarettes and two shillings to all ranks on every Dutch royal birthday!

While the Queen was at Dunsfold, 320 Squadron mounted an operation against enemy tank concentrations spotted in the Forêt de Grimbecq. A full strength of 18 aircraft was sent, thundering down Dunsfold's runways to the wave of Queen Wilhelmina herself. For the Dutchmen it was one of their proudest moments, but practicalities soon returned when the formation ran into stiff defences over the target area. Two aircraft were lost. FR191 of Lieutenant Commander van der Wolf ditched safely in the Channel and a speedy rescue of the crew was effected within 20 minutes by a British destroyer. Likewise badly hit, Daan Brand's Mitchell, FR149, was in no shape to even reach the French coastline and he therefore ordered his crew to bale out in no-man's land near Caen. While hope was initially held that the crew might manage to gain the allied lines, this was not to be. Brand himself was soon caught by a German Sergeant. The latter, with strict military formality, consulted a small reference booklet in order to identify the Dutchman's unusual badges of rank. Eventually, the German snapped to attention having identified Brand as the equivalent of a Captain and then led him off into captivity where he joined the rest of his crew for the remainder of the war.

Two days later, on the night of 14th/15th June, 320 Squadron were able to continue their revived good fortune during a raid by twelve aircraft against an ammunition dump at Condé-sur-Vire. Aircraft 'P', piloted by Lieutenant Manchot, was attacked by two German night fighters over France, one a twin engined Messerschmitt Me 210 and the other a single engined Mes-serschmitt Me 109. By the flying skill of the pilot and effective shooting by the Mitchell's gunners, the Germans were eventually driven off and the only damage suffered was due to the violent evasive manoeuvres carried out.

The same night had also brought reports of increased enemy aerial activity over south-eastern England. Rumours spread of mysterious sightings and an official communiqué was issued on 15th June, confirming that the Germans were using pilotless aircraft, the V-1. This brought Dunsfold into a new front line with immediate effect and on the afternoon of the 15th itself, a V-1 passed close to the aerodrome, resulting in a remarkable telephone conversation. At the time, a call was received at 98 Squadron's flight offices from a member of the squadron ringing from nearby Cranleigh, the man querying the possibility of transport back to the aerodrome. As the raucous note of the flying bomb passed the aerodrome, it was then heard over the line from Cranleigh. The caller, enthralled, gave a running commentary from his call-box as he watched the V-1's approach. This was followed by sudden silence as both the bomb's motor, and the commentary, ceased. Then came the shouted words, 'Its stopped and its diving!' An explosive crash cut off any further words. As crash teams and ambulances sped from the airfield the worst was feared, but word was soon returned that the individual had survived relatively unscathed. The telephone box was a complete write-off!

Also quickly on the site of the explosion were Dunsfold's intrepid newshounds, conspicuous amongst them being one Ernest Hemingway, famous American writer and then a war correspondent for the U.S. magazine 'Colliers'. Hemingway had recently arrived at Dunsfold to cover the operations of 98 Squadron and had already shown a preference for holding court in the Officers' Mess with tall stories of his own hell-raising life and escapades. It was from the Mess that Hemingway heard the V-1 go by and, on learning of its crash in Cranleigh, he sped out of the aerodrome with the other correspondents.

At the site of impact, several pieces of still smouldering wreckage were obtained by Hemingway and his cronies and quickly spirited away before the arrival of the local police. This was strictly forbidden and a number of witnesses came forward having recognized Hemingway amongst the scavengers. Consequently, policemen arrived at the aerodrome and soon ran the American to ground at the bar of the Officers' Mess. The big man had no option but to contritely own up and, along with the other newsmen, he was escorted to his quarters in order to hand over his 'souvenirs'.

Ironically, the next day saw the arrival of temporary visitors anxious to avoid the onslaught of the V-1s!

140 Wing consisted of 21, 464 RAAF, and 487 RNZAF Squadrons, currently based at RAF Gravesend and operating the potent Mosquito FB VI aircraft. As the V-1s headed for London, the Mosquitos had quickly found themselves at risk from their own airfield and local anti-aircraft defences, particularly at night when the nervy gunners fired on anything airborne. Although all three squadrons were already under notice to move to RAF Thorney Island on 20th June, the threat was considered severe enough to find a temporary alternative base for operations. As a result, 12 Mosquitos of 21 Squadron operated from Dunsfold on the night of 16th June, undertaking a patrol over Normandy. The following night, 16 aircraft from the Australian 464 Squadron attacked road and rail facilities around Cherbourg while two more Mosquitos of 21 Squadron and three of the New Zealanders of 487 Squadron also used Dunsfold rather than Gravesend.

Meanwhile, the RAF Regiment gunners had not been idle against the new threat. On 14th June, 2879 Squadron had arrived on the aerodrome in order to take over from 2847 Squadron who had now been on the airfield since May 1943. From 3rd June the latter squadron had come under 11 Group and this headquarters had arranged for a small overlap when 2879 Squadron moved in from RAF Swanton Morley. Consequently 2847 Squadron had the perfect opportunity to show off their skills to the newcomers when, on 17th June, a second V-1 rattled low over the aerodrome.

Quickly off the mark was Bofors gun L.1, and its crew successfully engaged the flying bomb as it sped by. 40mm gunfire raked the stubby winged intruder and a great cheer went up when it faltered and plummeted to earth in the distance. If the gunners thought they would be lauded from on high, they were mistaken. Great concern was expressed that considerable damage could have been caused by either wreckage or spent ammunition falling on the aerodrome and its aircraft and a couple of days later 11 Group decreed that aerodrome anti-aircraft guns were *not* to open fire on flying bombs. In the interim even a Mitchell crew had managed to join the fray

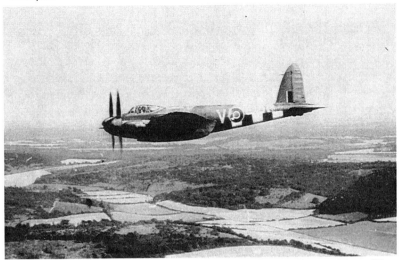

Mosquito FBVI MM403 of 464 Squadron. (Australian War Memorial.)

against the new menace. On the night of the 17th, Dunsfold's aircraft had already tangled with incoming V-1s on take-off for attacks on enemy troop movements near Thury-Harcourt, having to dodge the aerodrome's own anti-aircraft fire in the process. When therefore, on the return journey a V-1 came up astern of Nevin Filby's Mitchell, the Australian pilot manoeuvred to allow air gunner Joe Carey a chance to engage the speeding target. Unfortunately, the V-1 rapidly outpaced the Mitchell before Carey's fire was able to take effect.

The middle of June not only brought Mosquitos and V-1s, but also the tragic start of a run of bad-luck for Colin MacLaren's crew in 180 Squadron. Their 'star' rôle on D-Day had been followed by good news which arrived on the 17th, notifying Flight Sergeant Johnny Davies of his commission and promotion to Pilot Officer. Maclaren had immediately requested that his crew be granted a stand-down from operations that night in order that they might go up to London, both to celebrate and arrange for Johnny's new uniform. The request was, however, turned down when it became apparent that a 'maximum effort' operation was pending and it was the turn of MacLaren and his crew to lead 180 Squadron. As such, MacLaren's Mitchell was also detailed to carry an extra crew member for the operation in the form of the squadron's Gunnery Leader.

This officer, Flight Lieutenant W. S. Fielding-Johnson, was one of Dunsfold's most respected and experienced personnel, possessing the distinction of having served as aircrew in both World War 1 and World War 2. Being well over forty at the outbreak of World War 2, he had to move heaven and earth to be accepted for flying duties. Too old to qualify as a pilot or navigator, and being well beyond the normal age limit of air gunners, he nevertheless pulled every conceivable string in high places. By dint of great pursuasiveness, 'F-J', as he was known, finally managed to be accepted as an air gunner. He arrived at Dunsfold in February 1944 from 107 Squadron and his contageous enthusiasm immediately proved a great encouragement to his younger associates who noted that 'F-J' already held the DFC in addition to a Military Cross and Bar from the First World War.

On the 17th he joined Colin Maclaren's crew in Mitchell FW249 for what was obviously a top priority daylight target. At the briefing the crews were told that their aiming point was to be a German Headquarters where it was suspected Field Marshal Rommel might be found. 139 Wing's entire strength of 54 aircraft was to attack in close formation and bomb on the orders of their lead aircraft. As Flight Lieutenant Maclaren's aircraft was to lead 180 Squadron, the onus of bombing accuracy therefore lay with its navigator/bomb aimer, Flying Officer Ronald Stigant, who recalls the operation as follows:

"After assembling over Dunsfold we headed for the south coast, reached our operational height of 7,000 feet and rendezvoused with our fighter escort over the Channel. The blue of the sea was streaked with the white of the wakes of the large numbers of supply ships making their way to and from the invasion beaches. Most of the trip was in bright evening sunshine and, from the co-pilot's seat, I map read to the target.

"After identifying the target, which was a château located deep amongst trees, I went to the nose compartment and prepared to bomb. I opened the bomb doors and asked Colin for one or two final minor corrections to our course as we now came to the most anxious moments of the flight. Flying as we were over an area known to be heavily defended by the enemy's flak guns, it was nevertheless necessary to fly straight and level until I could release our bombs. For the rest of the crew this stage could seem to last an eternity, but for me there was always a last minute check to make sure this was indeed the right place. Then I would watch as the target slowly came along the guide-lines of the bomb sight until, at last, I pressed the bomb button and let go our load.

"Closing the bomb doors, and with our Mitchell already turning away onto the first leg of the homeward journey, I had no chance of watching where the bombs fell. It seemed to me that eighteen aircraft, flying in close formation was hazardous enough, but for three times that number to be over a target and dropping bombs all at the same time, seemed to border on the suicidal and yet there were no collisions and no bombs hit our own planes, not this time anyway!

"With all this to think about we hardly needed any enemy opposition but, as we were about half way along the first leg home, Johnny Davies, in the mid-upper turret, began reporting that he could see a motorised convoy moving along a road below. Before he could finish, however, he gave a piercing cry and fell silent. An anti-aircraft shell had burst beneath us and several pieces of shrapnel had hit the aircraft.

"Our other gunner, French-Canadian Marcel Demers, came on the intercom and reported that Johnny had been severely injured and that he was unable to remove him from the turret. Marcel also reported that F-J had been hit but, typically, F-J quickly broke in to say that he was alright and that Johnny must be cared for first.

"We immediately left the formation and I gave Colin a course to the nearest emergency landing strip, the Royal Naval Air Station at Ford, near to Chichester. Colin took the Mitchell down to pick up speed and we raced low over the Channel while calling the control tower at Ford. We were given immediate clearance and, as we came in, landed and taxied to a halt,an ambulance was at our wing tip.

"Johnny was rushed in the ambulance to the airfield's hospital but F-J insisted on walking there. As he left with Marcel, blood was oozing from a gaping hole in the heel of one of his flying boots. Colin and I went to Flying Control where we were later joined by Marcel. He told us that Johnny was dead.

"Darkness was just falling when the three of us went out to our 'plane and flew back to Dunsfold."

Due to the importance of the target, Johnny Davies died without experiencing the proud moment of trying on his first officer's uniform.

Intelligence reports later revealed that Rommel had not been in the château attacked.

On 20th June, Dunsfold again had the dubious pleasure of playing host to the talents of Ernest Hemingway. Following his V-1 encounter earlier in the month, Hemingway had become fascinated in this new form of warfare and particularly in the measures the RAF were adopting to combat it. Already, Hemingway had visited a Typhoon squadron based in the New Forest, but he was unable to see the end results of their strikes against the V-1 launch sites as the Typhoons could not carry a passenger. Hemingway quickly appreciated that this was not so in the case of the Mitchell. He therefore applied for, and obtained, permission to again visit Dunsfold and join 139 Wing on a raid against a *Noball* target. By the time Hemingway arrived for his trip in the afternoon, dramatic events in the morning had set the scene.

The day had dawned clear with excellent visibility and a strong early raid of 60 Mitchells and 24 Bostons had been mounted against a V-1 site near Mozenville in northern France, south-west of Abbeville. As the bombers swung into their final approach to the target, deadly and accurate flak rose to meet them.

In 180 Squadron, Squadron Leader Ford was leading 'B' flight's box with the Norwegian Gronmark maintaining position at his wing tip. As the flak erupted one of Gronmark's gunners, Frank Morgan, watched a shell burst directly in front of Ford's aircraft, FV988. While the Mitchell did not itself seem unduly damaged, Morgan clearly saw both Ford and his navigator, George Lister, slump forward in the cockpit. The Mitchell's nose dropped and it fell away below the formation while Gronmark quickly manoeuvred to take over the box's lead position. Only much later did Morgan and his fellow crew members learn that Ford's doomed aircraft took a direct hit on its way down. No parachutes were seen before the crippled bomber blew up in mid-air. From the same squadron, Flight Lieutenant Shapton was also soon in trouble. Badly hit, and with one gunner wounded, Shapton nevertheless managed to nurse his aircraft back over the Channel for a crash-landing at Friston.

Despite these sacrifices, bombing results were inconclusive and, on return to Dunsfold, a repeat attack was ordered for the afternoon. While the surviving aircraft were quickly bombed up again, Hemingway joined Alan Lynn's crew who were now only too aware of the dangers that lay ahead. Nevertheless, Hemingway still showed no signs of apprehension as he first posed with Lynn for photographs, the writer presenting an imposing yet

War Correspondent Ernest Hemingway joins Wing Commander Lynn for the op. on June 20th. (IWM-CL198.)

incongruous sight with his large frame squeezed into RAF battle dress, flying gear and helmet. His steel-rimmed spectacles and shaggy beard did not detract from the overall impression of something a little out of the ordinary.

Lynn this time led two formations and, as expected, murderous flak opened up as soon as the French coast was crossed. This time, it was the turn of 320 Squadron in the second formation to suffer losses.

The Dutchmen's problems had begun over the Channel when Commander Burgerhout had discovered that his radio was malfunctioning. A few minutes later it stopped working altogether. As leader of the second formation, it should have been the responsibility of Burgerhout's navigator to radio the bombing order to the other aircraft of the group. Now that this was not possible, Burgerhout reluctantly made the decision to turn back. Helped by his navigator, Van der Kop, Burgerhout gesticulated to his wingman, Den Tex Bondt, in the formation's number two position and managed to convey the nature of their problem. Den Tex Bondt nodded his understanding and gave the thumbs up signal before calling up the formation to announce that he was now in command. Burgerhout eased out of the lead position and Den Tex Bondt carefully moved into place. Burgerhout then banked steeply to take his aircraft back to the coast and his crew watched as their formation continued on its way. Suddenly eight puffs of flak were seen to explode immediately in front of the formation. Then they were followed by others and the fourth one hit the leading Mitchell, FR151 of Den Tex Bondt. Within seconds the aircraft was ablaze and dropped from the formation in a fiery dive. Horrified, Burgerhout and his crew realised that, but for a faulty radio, the doomed aircraft would have been theirs.

The same incident produced a remarkable reaction aboard another of 320's aircraft, that of Sergeant Van Berkum. Coincidentally, he too had experienced radio problems during the flight, the intercom in particular being badly affected. Van Berkum had found he was hardly able to understand his air gunners and navigator and for that reason, he had requested Corporal Aartsen, his wireless operator/air gunner, to come forward and take up position beside him in the cockpit. Upon crossing the enemy coast, Van Berkum noticed that his parachute was not in its usual place and he therefore asked Aartsen to place his parachute beside him. At the same moment, a hail of flak burst around them, claiming Den Tex Bondt's aircraft as already described and scattering the formation in sudden confusion. Five more bursts of flak churned the sky between Van Berkum's and the next aircraft and, caught in the air pressure, the Mitchell lost height steeply in a turn to port before Van Berkum managed to regain control. While struggling to right the aircraft, the pilot called up his turret gunner, Corporal Theunissen, to report visually on the engines, but despite repeating the message several times, Van Berkum received no reply. Navigator Bloemgarten reported that the turret appeared empty and when Aartsen left the cockpit to check, no sign was found of Theunissen.

Back at Dunsfold, an investigation into the incident noted that there had been a request from the pilot for Corporal Aartsen to pass his parachute. At the same time, Van Berkum's Mitchell was blown out of the formation by a near-miss and was momentarily out of control. By a cruel quirk of fate, also at the same moment, the turret gunner of another aircraft in the formation had called 'Bale out,' over the VHF radio, directed at the crew of Den Tex Bondt's aircraft, which he had just seen hit by flak. This call was certainly heard in Van Berkum's aircraft by Corporal Aartsen, also, it would seem, by Corporal Theunissen. Putting two and two together in the confusion, the unfortunate turret gunner had decided his own aircraft had been hit and he therefore baled out over the target area.

At the head of the two formations, Alan Lynn had listened to the drama unfolding behind him and heard the reports of Den Tex Bondt's aircraft going down in flames. As soon as Waardenburg had released his bombs therefore, Lynn swung the Mitchell hard away from the target. For Hemingway, this was too soon and he rashly asked if Lynn would go around again so that he might observe the results of the bombing. Unimpressed by the American's show of bravado, Lynn curtly refused the request. Back at Dunsfold, there were few sorry to see the writer leave as his often-voiced opinions on danger, bravery, stress and the like were considered somewhat 'over the top' by these calm veterans of constant operations.

Noball targets such as the one Hemingway had seen attacked were clearly of great importance to the Germans, illustrated by the formidable flak defences which were positioned around them. One method used to try to nullify such defences was the practice of sending in fighters to shoot up the flak batteries at low level. This task was often performed by fighters of the USAAF, normally Thunderbolts, and on one such occasion led to a puzzling incident. After the Mitchells had bombed and turned back for Dunsfold a Thunderbolt, in American markings, climbed up to the bomber formation and appeared to start a mock attack through the close cover of Spitfires. As the British fighters turned into the American's approach, the Thunderbolt broke away and the Spitfires resumed station. A minute later, the Thunderbolt returned, again attempting to break through the close escort and again being shooed away by the Spitfires. When, inexplicably, the Thunderbolt curved in for a third attempt, the matter became serious. At this time, aircrews were constantly being warned about captured allied aircraft infiltrating their operations. In view of the Thunderbolt's strange persistence, doubt now crept in as to the intentions of the mystery aircraft and the escort commander decided to take no chances. Once more the British fighters turned into the approaching Thunderbolt, but this time they opened fire. Out of control and in flames, the American aircraft dived away and the watching bomber crews were left to wonder, 'was it, or wasn't it?'

An urgent plea from the British Army on 22nd June led to a successful operation by the Wing, ranking in importance alongside the attack earlier in the month against the Château de La Caine.

Progress from the invasion beach-head was slowing down by the latter half of the month and, in particular, the Germans had succeeded in rallying strong forces around Caen. Just to the north of Caen itself, on the eastern side of the Orne river and the Orne canal, stood the Colombelles Steel Works and here the German army had dug in, keeping the opposing 51st Highland Division pinned down on the western side of the river. The target presented was therefore an extremely difficult one. Only 1,000 yards separated the Scottish troops from the Germans, while some 40 batteries of enemy 88mm flak made aiming difficult. Nevertheless, a remarkable effort was provided by Dunsfold's 98 and 320 Squadrons, joined by other Mitchells and Bostons from Hartford Bridge. The works were obliterated without any 'bomb creep' into the Highlanders' lines and the Scottish troops seized their opportunity to storm across the waterway and dislodge the Germans. No aircraft were lost and a personal letter of thanks from the 51st Division's commanding General underlined the importance of the attack.

Dunsfold's squadrons next attempted a strategic, rather than tactical, attack against the V-1 menace. Intelligence sources had discovered that much of the V-1 campaign's success depended on the officer with overall responsibility - a Colonel Wachtel who commanded Flakregiment 155 (W). It was decided to try to nullify the Colonel's technical knowledge and expertise when investigations revealed that he and his staff were housed in a château near Beauvais. The Colonel was expected to be at home between the hours of 4 p.m. and 6 p.m. for tea and consequently, Dunsfold's Mitchells attacked in the late afternoon of 25th June.

Above NO-K of 320 Sqn. over the Cean steelworks, target for June 22nd. (IWM-CL217)

Three days later this man was the target for Dunsfold's Mitchells, Colonel Max Wachtel.

The château was accurately plastered with bombs, but it was later learned that, although the Colonel had indeed been at tea, this was in a summer house some way from the aiming point. The German officer thus observed the bombing in safety and with a great deal of interest and admiration. 320 Squadron lost FR204 shot down by accurate flak on this operation.

For Colin Maclaren's crew of 180 Squadron, 27th June started out as any other day, marked out only by being the birthday of navigator Ron Stigant. After the excitement of D-Day, the crew's morale had plummetted following the death of Johnny Davies, but on the plus side news was received that F-J was recovering well in hospital from his wounds. A fresh gunner had been found to replace Johnny, but the team spirit had been hard-hit. It was therefore hoped that the 27th might bring a lull in operations and with it the opportunity to celebrate Stigant's birthday in style.

Although Maclaren's crew were on the battle order to fly a night operation, filthy weather seemed almost certain to preclude the mission going ahead. As the day wore on the weather worsened, but there was still no word of cancellation and eventually the crew reported for briefing at the appointed time. The operation was to consist of a GEE-H bombing raid on a number of French villages, undertaken by three aircraft of 180 Squadron and one from 320. The crews were briefed that the aim of the raid would be to harrass and disturb the enemy ahead of 2nd Army's front and prior to a break-out by the Allied armies.

The flight to the target area was uneventful. Take-off was fifteen minutes past midnight and immediately afterwards Ron Stigant went back to the navigator's compartment and remained there for most of the trip. The GEE-H box was much like a very small television set. The screen was darkened and had two bright green lines running across it, one below the other. Stigant fed into it the two co-ordinates that constituted the bombing point. These co-ordinates then took the form of a blip, one on each line, and these would move towards the centre of the line as the aircraft drew closer to them. Taking the top line first, a course was steered until the blip was in the correct position and then the course was altered to keep that blip dead centre. It was then a matter of tracking along that course until the other blip reached the centre of its line. When both were lined up, one immmediately below the other, Stigant released the bombs, using the bomb door lever and the bombing button which were in the navigator's compartment. By bombing on instruments, Stigant was not even aware of the results, nor indeed noticed the flak which other aircraft reported in the Coutances region. Nevertheless, a portion of this flak hit and damaged the Mitchell's fuel lines and, even as the Mitchell followed the GEE-H co-ordinates for Dunsfold, the aircraft was already losing fuel. All the way back, this continued and pilot Maclaren worriedly watched as the needles on his fuel gauges dropped lower and lower. Maclaren, sizing up the situation, concluded that there was still a chance to make it back to Dunsfold and his guess seemed vindicated when, in due course, the aerodrome lights appeared ahead and Mitchell FW101 settled into its circuit for final approach. As MacLaren gingerly throttled back the engines, they both stopped. Derek Porter, resident of Cranleigh, now takes up the story :-

"1944 was a year of great expectations for us all. Squadron activity had clearly increased at Dunsfold, more and more military convoys sped through Cranleigh. The build up to the great day was obvious -invasion of Europe. The exact date had been a popular topic of conversation, with many a pint of beer plied upon those thought to be in the know.

"Living as I did in such close proximity to the aerodrome, I naturally shared some of its life. Moreover, as I was employed by the Southern Railway at Cranleigh Station, it was all too obvious to me that the air war was not being fought without its casualties. A common and sad task was the sending home by rail of deceased aircrew to their next of kin.

"June arrived and of course, on the 6th, D-Day. Black and white invasion stripes could be seen on Dunsfold's Mitchell bombers and scattered leaflets left upon the station platform at Cranleigh bore messages from Eisenhower and Montgomery. We gathered around radios to listen to the latest BBC report and, on occasions, I would stand with other local people on the aerodrome's perimeter and wave to the returning crews, to us, heroes all.

"On the night of the 27th June, I lay awake in bed, listening to the distant noise of doodlebugs in procession to the east of us. Eventually drifting off to sleep, I was woken up by a muffled thumping and final crash that can perhaps best be described as 'that expensive noise' made when a vehicle crashes. This was not an uncommon occurrence, for on the other side of the road was a very steep sided, six foot deep ditch, complete with stream which bordered a duck pen. More than one Canadian soldier had made the acquaintance of this ditch in the blackout conditions, usually influenced by a certain amount of drink. I was not therefore altogether surprised when a loud North American accented voice could be heard shouting, 'Help!, help! Can't anybody wake up in this God-damned burgh?'

"Leaping up and pulling back the blackout curtains, I could just make out in the darkness three vertical white stripes in the duck run on the opposite side of the road. The only possible explanation for these stripes was that they were the invasion stripes around the fuselage of an aircraft and it dawned on me that the commotion represented something more than the ravings of a drunk.

"Dragging on my clothes, I ran out of the house and across the road, with our local chimney sweep close behind me. I tried to open the gate to the duck run, (which, I might add, was an extremely muddy and smelly plot), but could not do so. The impatient chimney sweep, with laudable athletic prowess, vaulted the gate but, in so doing, caught his trailing leg in the wire netting, somersaulted and landed face down in the evil smelling ooze. The saying that chimney sweeps bring luck seemed somewhat amiss on this occasion. Guided by his tirade of profanity, I wisely decided to kick down the gate and walked through. This did little to appease the muddy sweep, but did serve to allow entrance for the rapidly approaching posse of rescuers and the St John's Ambulance men, who had left their vehicle by a small wooden bridge leading to the now vandalised gate. The latter helpers had been summoned by the duty lady Fire Watcher, who had observed the crash and logically concluded that first aid and an ambulance would be sorely needed.

"Taking a few steps forward through a flock of bewildered Khaki Campbell fowl, I was confronted by the mangled nose of a B-25 Mitchell. Shining my torch through the shattered perspex, I could see the pilot to be fully conscious, still strapped in his seat and badly shocked. His only physical injury was a thin trickle of blood running down his face from a small head wound and, in response to my question as to his general condition, he replied 'OK, but my legs are trapped. Have I hurt anybody?'

"By now quite a number of people had arrived and two crew members were safely aboard the ambulance, leaving just the pilot and the missing navigator who could not be located. A strong smell of petrol dictated that the rescue should take place rapidly and the sight of an elderly person about to light his pipe drew yells of alarm and candid observations as to the level of his IQ.

"An RAF doctor arrived, but still no crash tender. A morphine injection deadened the pilot's pain while we tried to release his legs, but to no effect. It was clear that the nose of the aircraft would have to be lifted back to its proper position to release him and this we achieved by rigging up a tripod winch over the nose and applying plenty of muscle from willing helpers.

"Meanwhile, the search continued for the missing man. He was eventually found within the wreckage, the searchers having walked over him several times. Badly injured, this officer was rushed off for medical attention. We helpers drifted back to the road for a well earned cup of tea which, despite severe rationing, was being liberally dispensed by local ladies.

"Daylight revealed a remarkable scene. The Mitchell was mainly complete, the fuselage being fractured midway between the trailing edge of its wings and the tail unit, the whole being bent roughly ten degrees out of true. The nose was crumpled, with all perspex glazing shattered and fractured just forward of the cockpit. Tracing its path, I was struck by the extremely short length of its slide, which had obviously been broadside on. It could be seen where the aircraft had first struck a twenty foot long hedgerow, then continued, still airborne over a ten yard wide garden, before striking the corner of a long, low, wooden building with its right wing tip. This must have turned the aircraft, still perhaps some four feet above the ground, roughly ninety degrees to its flight path. It then hit the ground, decelerating rapidly as it demolished a large shed, housing a number of ducks, and it came to a halt in an area of open ground, just wide enough to accommodate its bulk. Its nose was only twenty feet from a bungalow and its tail fifteen feet from a house on the opposite side of the plot.

"Who says there isn't a thing called luck? It needed no imagination to contemplate the results of even a three degree variation, left or right, from its final track."*

This aspect of luck was also to sorely tax 180 Squadron during this period, as illustrated by two dramatic incidents.

Firstly, a new arrival in June had been Squadron Leader Bob Wood, posted in to take over as flight commander of 'A' flight. An accomplished pilot, Wood was nevertheless relatively new to operational flying and expressed concern that the current length of bombing run as practised by his flight was too short to achieve good accuracy. Despite the flak defences, Wood was convinced that it was necessary to fly a straight and level bombing run in excess of ten seconds. While the existing crews were not convinced, Wood was determined to try his theory. After only three or four operations, his aircraft was bracketed by

---

*Author's note: In 1988 I received a letter from former Flt. Lt. Ron Stigant of Ontario, Canada. Ron had seen my request for information on Dunsfold in the magazine of the RCAF and wrote of his service with 180 Squadron at Dunsfold in 1944. This service was abruptly ended on the night of 27th/28th June 1944 when returning from the above night raid over France. Maclaren's superb crash landing at 0300 hrs. on the outskirts of Cranleigh saved his crew although Ron Stigant was seriously enough injured to require three years of treatment in an RAF hospital before being released in 1947. This was the officer that Derek Porter found so difficult to locate. The crew member whom Derek initially assumed to be a drunk was French-Canadian gunner Marcel Demers. Soon after his release from hospital, Ron Stigant emigrated to Canada where he lives today. He writes that his wife was most indignant to learn that his would-be rescuers had walked over him several times!

flak during a long bombing run. Fortunately, the crew had enough time to bale out but, when Wood gave the order to do so, it was discovered that the parachute of one crew member had been damaged. Wood did not hesitate to hand over his own parachute and elect to stay with the plane. The Mitchell plunged down out of control and its pilot stood no chance. The theory of a brave man had been disproved, but the cost of the lesson was great.

Secondly, fate's fickle finger beckoned to a young American on the squadron, Pilot Officer Rex Haddock, a 23 year old from New York City who had volunteered to serve in the RAF. Previously with 98 Squadron, Haddock had moved across to 180 Squadron and quickly proved to be a great personality as well as a reliable mid-upper gunner, fitting in to his new squadron as though he had belonged there from the beginning. Flying Officer Ken Wright RCAF was a 180 Squadron pilot who had previously flown with Haddock. As he recalls, the circumstances under which Haddock had become spare and had subsequently transferred from 98 had been somewhat traumatic, to say the least:

"He had lost his crew on 98 Squadron in a crash just off the end of Dunsfold's main runway. Rex had had a premonition that, if he were going to 'go for a burton', it would be shortly after take-off with a full bomb load, when an engine failure could have disastrous results. So how could he avoid this eventuality? He would sit right on the forward escape hatch prior to take-off, remove his oxygen and intercom, no safety belt on and his parachute chest pack all ready and secured to his harness. Only when safely over 1,000 feet or so would he then take his position in the mid-upper turret.

"So it happened that one day, when just over 500 feet, he heard and felt the loss of one engine. Without hesitation he went out of the hatch, pulled the ripcord and felt the jerk of the canopy just before hitting the ground. He heard the roar as the Mitchell crashed and blew up a mile or so beyond and realised that the only thing he could do was to pack up his parachute and walk back to the aerodrome - no one would be searching for a survivor.

"Although this action had worked well for him, the squadron was not going to recognise this take-off position and print it in the training manuals! When he joined 180 Squadron, however, he insisted that he would not continue to take up this position. Radio checks prior to take-off confirmed that he was either in the turret or seated with his lap belt on, even though he had been told to feel free and assume the crash position if he so wished. He said he was in a lucky crew now."

So Haddock had continued thus until the last day of June 1944. Night operations called for three aircraft to be dispatched singly to bomb tank concentrations at Thury Harcourt and last off at 01.45 hours was FW169 EV-Y carrying Haddock and flown by Flying Officer Struthers. The latter had also previously enjoyed his fair share of luck, Struthers having survived a crash landing at Friston in badly damaged FL689 back in February. It had been on this earlier operation that Struthers' original gunner, Warran Officer Hammond, had been killed, ultimately leading to Haddock's transfer as a replacement.

For this night operation, a fifth member also joined the crew for the first time, Flight Sergeant Rook being a new spare air gunner and no doubt impressed by the good fortune so far enjoyed by Struthers' crew. Immediately after take off fortune deserted. Inexplicably, the Mitchell turned sharply at low altitude and clipped the tall trees of Butchers Copse near the village of Chiddingfold, cart-wheeling into the ground and erupting into a mass of flames.

When the ambulance reached the inferno, only Flight Sergeant Exon, another survivor of the Friston crash, was found alive but terribly injured. Rex Haddock, from his earlier almost identical experience on 98 Squadron, had managed to bale out, but the Mitchell had been too low and the American had hit the ground before his parachute opened. All five men were buried in Brookwood Military Cemetery, Exon having not survived the journey to hospital.

Chapter Eight
'Things That Go Bang in the Night!'

July 1944 brought several changes of command. On the 1st, the aerodrome itself passed from the hands of Group Captain Dunlap, who henceforth was to maintain operational command of 139 Wing, while station responsibility passed to Squadron Leader J. Secter, RAF. The same day, Commander Burgerhout left 320 Squadron for a temporary spell as a Staff Officer with Air Vice-Marshal Embry, his place being taken by Lieutenant Commander Mulder. On 4th July, 1944, Wing Commander Ray Goodwin was posted away from 180 Squadron, to be replaced by Wing Commander N. de Warren Boult.

Behind these command moves lay a number of tensions. Both Goodwin and Burgerhout had held deep reservations over the frequency of operations which were now very much the norm. On one occasion, two daylight and one night raid had been called for within 24 hours and the squadrons' commanding officers had expressed concern over the fatigue now becoming obvious among the crews. 180 Squadron in particular suffered a spate of minor accidents exacerbated by the strain of night operations following day. In the final week of June, three of the squadron's Mitchells had been damaged in two incidents on consecutive nights. In both instances, pilots had mis-judged taxiing at night and, while there were no injuries, the accidents were proof of the heavy demands then being made on crews. The Canadian Goodwin was known to have voiced his criticism of higher authority on the situation and this may have had something to do with his abrupt departure from the squadron. After expressing his own concerns, Burgerhout also seemed to be heading for trouble. When his permanent posting was announced however, outraged protests from his crews led to Group headquarters reconsidering the situation and promising that Burgerhout could return in September after a rest.

The aircrews themselves were not slow to invent their own means of relieving the tensions of operational flying. The normally quiet country lanes around the aerodrome witnessed some remarkable scenes when a number of Australian aircrew adopted a new practice of driving 'under the hood.' This usually took place when returning from pub crawls by car and involved the driver putting his head between his knees so that he could not see where he was going. A colleague would then stand up and act as navigator, calling out directions such as 'left four degrees, steady, steady, prepare for ninety degree starboard turn' etc. At least one car, the possession of an Australian air gunner known as 'Mullet Head,' was completely written off after collision with a telegraph pole, but no-one is recorded as being seriously injured.

Such escapades on public roads may have influenced the consession to civilised living which came when the aerodrome's permanent mess facilities were re-opened in the evenings, despite all personnel still being required to live under canvas. Closing time at the Sergeants' Mess usually saw a conglomeration of aircrew N.C.O.s board their bicycles in various states of sobriety and, subject to there being no night flying, a race would be organised down the runway. Added to the hazards of the darkness, alcohol and bicycles, were the loaded revolvers which all air crew had been ordered to carry since D-Day. One night the massed start came to grief when two Australian members of Jack Curtis' 180 Squadron crew crashed and brought down a heap of bodies and machines. One of the Australians claimed a foul had been committed, 'elbowing while under way', which required satisfaction there and then. Drawing his revolver, he commenced firing at his fellow countrymen, who promptly replied in kind. The rest of the mob desperately tried to dig foxholes in the runway with their fingernails, but the shooting stopped when the two Australians ran out of ammunition. The ride home resumed, thankfully with no-one the worse for wear. The same Australian pair also started the questionable habit of shooting out the candle in their tent after they had got into bed. This soon came to a halt when 180's commanding officer received reports of bullets whizzing around the campsite and through other tents. Likewise, in 98 Squadron's tent lines one evening, the usual commotion of songs around the campfire was drowned by the sound of pistol shots as Flight Lieutenant Joe Knowlton and his crew set up beer cans for candlelit target practice. The next morning, penitent and hungover, they were carpeted by Wing Commander Paul who could not find it in his heart to more than admonish the contrite Canadians. Later in the day, Group Captain Dunlap queried the unusual night noises, but was happy to leave the fate of his countrymen to the discretion of their commanding officer.

The aerodrome's RAF Regiment squadron received its share of excitement on the 4th when a USAAF Liberator bomber, abandoned by its crew, crashed in near-by Shalford. Dunsfold provided the guard of one Corporal and three men to watch over the wreckage, a task made no easier by the knowledge that only 44 of the 52 bombs aboard the aircraft had been recovered from the scene.

The beginning of the month also saw an end to the overlap between RAF Regiment units. The successful but ill-fated 2847 Squadron was moved out to the gun belt set up in Kent to counter the V-1, leaving 2879 Suadron alone with their two flights of 20mm Hispano guns. Frustratingly, orders were soon received to first restrict, and then to withdraw altogether, permission to fire at any flying bombs.

In the middle of the month, Dunsfold once again played host to Mosquitos, this time from 137 Wing at Lasham. On the nights of both the 13th and 14th, squadron strength formations used Dunsfold instead of Lasham, where weather seems to have been a temporary problem. It was by now not infrequently that Dunsfold acted as diversion aerodrome for the intensive intruder operations being mounted from Lasham. A typical occasion involved a Mosquito of 613 Squadron which, returning from a night intruder sortie, had reported losing fuel on the way home, presumably from flak damage. The crew had told the Flying Controller at Lasham that it was probable they would not make the base before fuel ran out and shortly afterwards they reported sighting an airfield with a lighted runway. Announcing his intention to join the circuit and land, the pilot then suddenly radioed "Damn, the lights have gone out!".

Lasham's Flying Controller was Flight Lieutenant Lawrence, a hat salesman by trade. Calculating the time which had elapsed since the Mosquito had reported crossing the coast at Deal, Lawrence quickly worked out that the aircraft in distress was over Dunsfold. When he heard the crew report that the airfield lights had gone out, Lawrence put through an emergency telephone call to Dunsfold and asked the Controller there if they had just extinguished their lights. "Yes, we've just closed down for the night," came the reply. "Well put them on again," said Lawrence, explaining that he had one of his Mosquitos in the Dunsfold circuit and short of fuel. The Dunsfold Controller responded immediately and quickly read off Dunsfold's runway and landing information to Lawrence, who then repeated it to the Mosquito. This method was adopted as each airfield had its own individual local airfield control frequency, so the Mosquito from Lasham would not have the Dunsfold local frequency. Neither was there sufficient time to allow the international distress frequency to be opened, which would have been the normal option in less critical circumstances. The Mosquito touched down safely at Dunsfold with its crew thankful for Lawrence's quick thinking.

It has to be acknowledged that at this time, 2 Group's Mosquitos were receiving the lion's share of glamour and publicity while their hard-working Mitchell colleagues soldiered on much less in the public eye. What the readers of the popular press sometimes overlooked was that, particularly on night operations, it was sometimes only with the help of Mitchells that the Mosquitos gained any success. Operating as a team, one to one, the Mosquito would fly as low as possible to spot enemy ground targets. When he thought he had something, the Mosquito called in the Mitchell, flying at a higher altitude on the same track. The latter would then accurately illuminate the area with flares for the Mosquito to attack. On other occasions, such as the D-Day operations, rôles would be reversed and the Mitchells would bomb by the flares dropped by Mosquitos. Despite this lack of public recognition, the Mitchell crews pressed on uncomplaining.

Group Captain Dunlap found himself back in the action when a late request arrived for 98 Squadron to provide an aircraft for a night sortie on 20th July. Having not expected any such call, Dunlap had stood down 98 Squadron after operations earlier in the day and by the time the order arrived he was fully aware that Wing Commander Paul and his crews were well ensconced in 'The Three Pigeons' in Guildford. Nevertheless, determined to fulfill the request from Group, Dunlap quickly assembled a scratch crew from his headquarters staff and, using a 98 Squadron Mitchell, flew the sortie on behalf of the unit.

Since the end of June the Wing had enjoyed an unusual spell of successful operations without losses, the only casualty having been FW253 of 98 Squadron which overshot the runway on take off on 12th July. The law of averages meant, however, that losses were soon bound to mount again and a raid on Glos-Montfort on the 23rd of the month illustrated this inevitability with a vengeance. Over the target, Squadron Leader Paynter's FV985 of 98 Squadron was about to release its bombs when they exploded, ripping the Mitchell apart with such force that there was no hope for the crew. Due to the practice of close formation bombing, three other aircraft of 98 suffered grievously. FW122 dived away to crash in flames while veteran FL186 crash-landed in Normandy when Flying Officer Berry realised he could not reach the Channel. Flying Officer Harris had more success in nursing badly damaged FV931 back for a safe belly landing at Tangmere. The day's losses increased to five aircraft when FW118 of 180 Squadron did not return from a night intruder operation.

The very next day again saw a crippled Mitchell drop in to Tangmere when Wing Commander de Warren Boult's short career with 180 Squadron came to a rapid end during an attack on a wood at La Hogue. The target was known to conceal some eighteen hundred German troops who had brought the Allied advance to an abrupt halt. As such, the attack was designated top priority and Alan Lynn therefore chose to lead the operation.

Despite the fact that little opposition was expected, many of the crews involved remember this operation as one of their worst. The formation first flew along the battle line of the armies below, but as a sharp turn onto the target was made, all hell broke loose. The sky erupted as heavy flak, seemingly from nowhere, reached for the Mitchells. Aboard Lynn's aircraft, Cees Waardenburg was trying to operate the GEE box, but either through jamming or simple malfunctioning, he was unable to obtain results. Also in the aircraft that day was Squadron Leader 'Buddy' Rees, the Wing's Navigating Officer, who therefore instead went forward into the nose to use the bomb sight. By now, Rees had no time to identify the target through the flak bursts so Alan Lynn called up the formation, "Round again, I say round again."

This order was none too well-received in the face of the determined flak, but all seemed to be going well as the second run-in commenced and Rees reported that he could see the target despite the ground haze. Suddenly, however, Rees shouted "Oh Christ, I've missed it!" Another box of Mitchells, out of position due to the second run-in, had passed underneath Lynn's aircraft at the critical moment, blotting out the target at the very moment Rees was ready to release the bomb load. As the flak gunners were now beginning to get the range it seemed the only course was to give the attack up as a bad job and the Mitchell crews waited for the order to turn for home. Typically, Lynn had other ideas.

After confirming that Rees knew exactly where the target was, Lynn paused for only a couple of seconds thought before he again called up the formation. "This is Red Leader calling, Red Leader calling, round again, I say round again." A stunned silence initially greeted the order, but then, crisp and clear over the ether, came a single four letter anatomical expletive. Despite the tenseness of the situation, many of those listening could not help bursting into laughter. Lynn himself was furious. "Who the Hell was that?" he demanded, "I'll have him court martialed." Not surprisingly, there was no confession forthcoming.

Turning again to the task in hand, Lynn led a third run over the target. By now, flak was not the only hazard as there were Mitchells all over the sky, bringing a real danger of collision. By some miracle, no aircraft were shot down although many were damaged. One of the worst hit was the Mitchell of Boult, leading 180 Squadron. Boult had taken with him, as co-pilot and fifth crew member, Squadron Leader Griffiths who was new to the squadron. Over the target, heavy flak scored a hit in Boult's cockpit, killing Griffiths immediately and severely wounding Boult and his navigator, Flight Lieutenant Burgess. Despite their wounds, Boult and Burgess together managed to guide their crippled bomber back for a belly landing at Tangmere. Both officers were subsequently awarded the DFC for this tremendous effort, but Boult was unable to fly operationally again due to his eye injuries.

Although Lynn's leading box had managed to bomb the target, many aircraft were out of position and had been unable to do so. Back at Dunsfold, results were assessed as being poor, and there were even crews who reported not being able to find the target in the general confusion. As one member of Lynn's crew put it, "Couldn't find the target? They only had to look where the flak was and they ruddy well would have found it!"

After the customary bacon and eggs and a good stiff drink, the crews were sent to bed with the depressing information that a return visit would be required the following morning. Taking off at 0630 hours, this time the Germans were caught unawares and a good job was done. Intelligence reports later revealed that the Germans had concealed up to eighteen of their deadly 88mm flak guns in the woods in order to cover their troop concentrations.

The final week of July saw the Wing attack petrol dumps and gun emplacements, 320 Squadron bearing the losses of FR185 over Fontainebleu on the 26th and FR158 on the 29th. Amongst the operational pressures, 139 Wing also concentrated in July on improving their take-off and forming up practices. These were still taking too much time and using up a lot of fuel as the existing method was to line up on the perimeter track with only one aircraft being allowed on the runway at a time. Instead, the Wing now practiced a take-off technique originally used by General Dolittle for his raid on Tokyo, flying Mitchells from the aircraft carrier USS Wasp. Olaf Gronmark was one of those who enthusiastically extolled this method, whereby two lines of three planes each formed up on the runway staggered in their box order. In this way, a whole box would run down the runway and become airborne more or less as one unit, with the added improvement that visual contact could usually be maintained even when climbing through cloud. When 180 Squadron received their replacement commanding officer on 1st August, Wing Commander R. Edwards DFC, AFC therefore took over an efficient and tested unit, playing a full part in the operations of 139 Wing. Edwards' contemporary on 98 Squadron, Wing Commander (now Air Commodore retired) Christopher Paul recalls with professional pride the skills involved in mounting an operation:

"As soon as an operation order was received from Group, the pilots and navigators would be called to the Wing briefing room. Here Squadron leader John Pawson, who filled the combined posts of Operations and Intelligence, would have large scale maps marked up. Having given the target, route and bomb load he would then add any Intelligence information. Incidentally, Pawson was noted for his habit of keeping pet white mice in his uniform pockets. At intervals he would drop morsels of food into his pockets to keep the mice occupied!

"Next the Flak Officer briefed us. To him we attached considerable importance. Then would come the Armaments Officer, with details of the bomb load and any special features such as delay fuses. Five inch lens cameras in two aircraft in each box recorded bomb bursts and would, of course, record only those bombs with no delay. Finally came the Signals Officer with details of call signs, emergency calls and target co-ordinates which would indicate the release point for bombing. My own call sign was FOUNTAIN TWO ZERO, the box of Mitchells which I led was always IVORY BOX and the other two boxes of 98 were BLUE and RED respectively. When in formation I used the call sign FOUNTAIN LEADER.

"While this briefing was going on, the gunners were over on the squadron dispersals, drawing their ammunition and checking turrets. The armourers, having collected bombs from the distant dump, would be fitting fuses and loading the bombs into the aircraft.

"Then, from the Wing briefing, we would hasten round the perimeter track to our own squadron briefing rooms. There we would give a quick general briefing to the whole squadron and thence, in flying clothing, we went out to our aircraft. Here I would be met by our fitter, 'Colonel' Booth, and rigger Fred Halsey, who helped us in. 'The Colonel' always made it his special task to see that I was properly installed and fastened in. With everybody aboard, and the hatches closed, the armourer would remove the bomb safety pins and display these to the navigator/bomb aimer. Then we were free to start up. Start up time was always specified at the main briefing. Under normal circumstances it would be 55-60 minutes from the commencement of that briefing. When necessary, we could reduce this time to 35 minutes.

"Next, the aircraft would taxi out, line up in pre-arranged order on the runway and take off in succession. As the leader of each box made a wide sweep round the aerodrome his formation, taking short cuts, would rapidly join up. In turn, the boxes then came together to complete the squadron formation. We reckoned to be able to set course in squadron formation at 2,000 feet, in an hour and a half from the start of the first briefing and, when necessary, in only a minute or two over one hour."

The first week of August brought tragedy to Wing Commander Paul's crew. Doctor Fox of nearby Hascombe had generously made available a lake in the grounds of his house, used for both swimming parties and dinghy drill by the Dunsfold aircrews. It was an exercise in the latter on 3rd August that led to Flight Sergeant Harris, Paul's belly gunner, breaking his neck. Diving some thirty feet into the lake, Harris hit a submerged wooden board head first and, although still conscious and able to speak, the gunner seemed to be paralysed from the neck down. Rushed back to Dunsfold, it was obvious that Harris would need immediate surgery and he was therefore gently lifted into the squadron's Airspeed Oxford communications aircraft and flown to the RAF hospital at Wroughton in Wiltshire by Wing Commander Paul and his fellow crew members. Harris was operated on almost immediately and the operation was initially thought to have been successful. Wing Commander Paul and the others stayed overnight, but the next day were informed that their ebullient gunner had died.

Harris' replacement only lasted three days until it was found that he reacted badly to flak. It would therefore have been understandable for Wing Commander Paul's crew to have suffered some drop in morale as a result of these incidents, but the next replacement proved to be a formidable character in his own right, and a worthy successor to Harris.

Mich Jansen, a Belgian, had been a reserve pilot flying Fairey Battles in the Belgian Air Force. When Belgium fell to the Germans, Jansen fought to the last with his squadron. He then fled to France, but made his way back to Brussels and joined the Resistance. Twice he was captured and sentenced to death, but both times he was sprung from prison by the Resistance and eventually had to leave Belgium by way of France, Spain and Gibraltar. Upon reporting to Belgian headquarters in London, Jansen was offered a desk job, but instead the enthusiastic pilot replied that he still wanted to fly. As he was already in his forties, Jansen was refused by the Belgians, so instead he joined the RAF as an air gunner and had reached the rank of Flight Lieutenant when he joined Wing Commander Paul at Dunsfold. It was clear to all in Paul's crew that Jansen would have little chance if forced down and captured in enemy territory, so together they evolved a plan that, in the event of being shot down, they would stay together and, due to language ability, Jansen would be in charge. Happily, there was never an occasion for the plan to be put into operation.

A humorous interlude was provided on 4th August when Dunsfold's control tower was notified that radar had picked up airborne intruders approaching the aerodrome. Fortunately, flying was interrupted only briefly while those on the ground enjoyed the spectacle of a Spitfire called up to shoot the intruders down. Under the gunfire of the sleek fighter several barrage balloons, which had broken away from London's defences, slowly subsided to the ground!

The Germans' flak defences claimed more successes on the 9th when again, Dunsfold's ground crews were dismayed to count the number of gaps in the formations returning from attacks on munitions dumps. Three of 320 Squadron's aircraft did not return, FR160 and FR186 only just managing cliff-top Friston on the return journey while FR143 ditched in the Channel. The latter had been badly hit by flak on the approach to the target, but the pilot had struggled on to bomb successfully. As he turned for home, however, the very same flak battery again blasted the aircraft, badly injuring two of the crew. Fortunately, two Air Sea Rescue aircraft were quickly on the scene when the Mitchell ditched and the crew were rescued. Similarly, accurate flak shot down FW113 and FW175, both of 180 Squadron, in the vicinity of the target.

The night of 12th August saw the commencement of operations by the Wing in the Falaise area of France, where the Germans were now in full retreat. Like angry bees, the Allied air forces swarmed in the air above the enemy, exacting terrible retribution. By the light of flares, the Mitchell crews could see the enemy falling back as quickly as they could, and their bombs could not miss. But as the night sky filled with aircraft, 98 Squadron almost suffered a repeat of the incident in May when Lieutenant Commander Mulder of 320 Squadron had been shot down by a Lasham Mosquito.

On this occasion, one of 98 Squadron's aircraft was likewise attacked by a Mosquito, but with no compunction, the Mitchell's air gunners drove the Mosquito off with six well-aimed bursts of fire which came close to evening up the score. On another night, Major Gronmark of 180 Squadron (now promoted and on his third tour) was attacked by night fighters when flare dropping for the rest of the squadron from 12,000 feet. From the brief

glimpses which his crew had of their attackers, Gronmark*
suspected over-eager Mosquitos again, especially when the
Wing's Intelligence Officer later reported that Mosquitos had
claimed attacks on 'Dorniers' over the battle area. The Norwegian's suspicions were eventually confirmed when one returning
Mitchell crew reported persistent night fighter attacks all the
way back over the Channel. The same night a Mosquito reported
chasing a 'Dornier' from France to the English coast. On landing,
machine gun fire damage to the Mosquito was found to have
been caused by Allied guns, of the calibre carried on Mitchells.

On 13th August, a possible change of use seemed to be in the
air for Dunsfold, with the visit of Group Captain Alvey and
other officers of 38 Group, keen to assess Dunsfold for its
suitability for units operating Stirling bombers towing gliders. A
full survey was carried out on the 15th and satisfactory trials
were later undertaken by Wing Commander Bertram and
Squadron Leader Taplin from 38 Group, using an Albemarle
aircraft to tow a Horsa glider. Despite the satisfaction expressed,
nothing ever came of these plans for Dunsfold.

The same day as the 38 Group assessment, Dunsfold saw the
departure of one of the most popular crews in 98 Squadron, that
of Flight Lieutenant Joe Knowlton. Already renowned for their
antics at pistol practice in Dunsfold's woods, the enthusiastic
all-Canadian crew had recently received further noteriety. On
the raid against the Colombelles steel works, the crew had been
accompanied by Stanley Nash, correspondent with the Daily
Sketch. Nash had obviously been impressed with the Canadians'
cool professionalism when he subsequently wrote, "I sat with F/L
J. L. Knowlton, who wore on this assault a pair of ordinary
sunglasses and patent leather shoes." Knowlton and his crew
had only arrived at Dunsfold on May 11th, but by August they
had finished their tour.

*Post-V.E. Day, Gronmark and his crew even volunteered for operations against
the Japanese in the Far East. Perhaps fortunately, this move did not materialise,
but led to the crew at long last having to go their separate ways. Gronmark was
subsequently awarded one of Norway's highest decorations and post-war went to
Norway to rebuild the Royal Norwegian Air Force. He later served as Air Attaché
in London.

Knowlton was justifiably recommended for a DFC, but he promptly refused the award since the same recognition was not extended to the rest of his crew.

While crews quickly came and went, the Mitchells themselves had to soldier on through scores of operations, metal often patched time and again after flak damage. Nevertheless, crews maintained confidence in this rugged and stable aircraft. On 17th August, a daylight attack by 139 Wing on an enemy munitions dump gave rise to solid evidence of the the Mitchell's inherent strength. As 320 Squadron bombed, they passed beneath a formation of 266 Squadron from Hartford Bridge who released their bombloads at the same time. One 500 lb. bomb destroyed the starboard rudder fin of 320 Squadron's FR186 - B, the aircraft of Lieutenant the Baron Steengracht van Moyland. Despite also suffering heavy flak on the return journey, the aircraft made Dunsfold and landed safely.

Sporadic losses still, however, ate into the Mitchells. In addition to the operational dangers which claimed FW258 of 320 and HD329 of 98 Squadron over Falaise on the 19th, 180's FW124 at Elboeuf on the 21st and HD316 of 180 which ditched twelve miles short of Beachy Head on the 25th, a spate of accidents also now claimed three aircraft. On the 18th, 98 Squadron lost FW173 when its undercarriage collapsed while visiting RAF Finmere and FR190 of 320 Squadron was written off when it overshot on landing at RAF Long Newnton in Gloucestershire while on a cross-country exercise on the 31st. While no injuries were sustained in either incident, the tragic accident closer to home on 30th August had a very different ending.

On 29th August Wing Commander Paul and his crew had finished their tour with 98 Squadron. This coincided with Wing Commander Lynn completing his second tour of operations at which time the South African was obliged to relinquish his post as Wing Commander (Flying) for the Wing. Therefore, Wing Commander Paul temporarily took over from Lynn, while his own position on 98 Squadron was filled by Wing Commander George Hamer.

Lynn's Dutch navigator, Lieutenant Cees Waardenburg, DFC, had just completed his 100 operations as navigator to Lynn and therefore, at long last, was allowed to claim his own aircraft in order to continue operations as a pilot. Keith Cudlipp, one of Lynn's gunners, takes up the story of the events of 30th August.

"Cees, Johnny Pritchard and I were in our tent between the control tower and the Ops. room. With us was Flying Officer Harry Payne who had just been posted to the Wing as an air gunner, and didn't yet have a crew. In the meantime, Alan Lynn had told him to come along with us until he was sorted out.

"That day, Cees and Harry had bowled into the tent to find Johnny and I listening to the radio, a short play called, I think, 'Beetle Doctor', which was quite interesting. Alan Lynn walked in and asked Cees if he would take our aircraft up for an air test and Cees jumped up, looked at us and said "O.K., any of you coming?" Harry Payne, who hadn't yet flown much on Mitchells, showed his willingness to go, but Johnny and I decided to stay, in order to listen to the end of the play. They were only going around the houses, so off they went.

"I think it was about twenty minutes later when someone ran out of the control tower and shouted that an aircraft had gone down near Godalming. There were only two aircraft up that afternoon and a few minutes later the other one landed, so we realised then that it was Cees who had come to grief. I think that finished us for quite a while, as we were a very close crew. Even Alan Lynn said he wasn't interested in doing any more operations."

Details received later showed that the exhuberant Dutchman had been low flying over the grounds of Peper Harow House, a stately home where Land Army girls were at work. An eye witness watching from the road had first seen the aircraft when it roared up from behind a line of trees but on a second pass the Mitchell had dropped too low and its tail clipped a tree. The aircraft, FW268 EV-O, flicked over onto its back and spun into the ground by a Canadian Army vehicle park on Shackleford Heath. The wreck immediately caught fire and burned out, both men were killed instantly. On 2nd September the two airmen were interred in the village graveyard of Rudgwick, some five miles from the aerodrome. This was a break from tradition as normally, fatalities were either sent home to their families or buried at Brookwood Military Cemetery. In the case of Waardenburg and Payne, Lynn wanted them buried close to where he lived in Rudgwick with his wife. The Dutchman's remains were later moved in 1964 to the Dutch section of Mill Hill Cemetery in London, but the grave of Harry Payne remains there today as a testament to the tragic and accidental loss of two young lives.

Chapter Nine

Arnhem

Once again, the beginning of the month saw a flurry of activity amongst commanding officers and units.

On 1st September, Commander Burgerhout made a welcome return to take up the reins of 320 Squadron again and the following day Squadron Leader A.G. Sudworth took over command of the station from the departing Squadron Leader Secter. At the same time, 2826 Squadron of the RAF Regiment arrived for aerodrome defence duties, replacing 2879 Squadron which had left for Middle Wallop at the end of August. Unfortunately, the gunners found themselves bottom of the list of priorities for accommodation with the result that they temporarily moved into 'The Kennels' in Dunsfold village. A dog's life indeed!

The pressure of operations at Dunsfold showed little sign of relenting as support was constantly needed for the ground forces fighting their way into occupied Europe. A further result of the bitter land battles was that more and more casualties needed the urgent attention of doctors back in England and the Canadians were not slow to realize that their former airfield was still sited conveniently close to the Canadian casualty station in Cranleigh, and hospital in Horsham. Consequently, Canadian Army officers visited Dunsfold on 3rd September in order to confirm the final arrangements for the aerodrome to become an air evacuation centre. Henceforth, Dunsfold was used by Dakota air ambulance aircraft carrying wounded Canadian troops from the battles on the Continent.

September 8th, 1944, brought two dramatic incidents which are still clearly recalled today by many witnesses.

Late that day, 139 Wing were briefed for attacks on a number of gun positions in the Boulogne area. As the squadrons took off in the early evening sunshine, the Mitchells of 226 Squadron arrived overhead to join in with the operations but those on the ground at Dunsfold detected a strange note amongst the Hartford Bridge formations. Necks craned upwards as Mitchell FV936 was seen diving down from its box, heading for Dunsfold's circuit. Clearly, the aircraft was in considerable difficulties as one engine could be seen to have stopped while the other screamed at full power. Below, Dunsfold's personnel stood transfixed as the stricken aircraft's pilot struggled to control his machine. With only partial command of his speed, he overshot Dunsfold's runways and just succeeded in clearing the roof of 'The Sundial Café' before miraculously pancaking safely into a small field alongside the Horsham Road. An investigation into the accident later revealed that the Mitchell's port engine reduction gear had failed. This had caused it to run at maximum revolutions but, in his haste to feather it, the young and inexperienced pilot had shut down the starboard engine by mistake. In view of the eventual safe outcome, no action was recommended against the pilot and the incident's record even notes that he did well to bring the aircraft down safely in the circumstances!

Meanwhile, 98 Squadron had been detailed to provide twelve aircraft for the Wing's attacks against the Boulogne guns, two boxes of six aircraft each attacking separate targets. Take off for both formations was at 18.50 hours, Squadron Leader Spong leading the A Flight box, and Squadron Leader Brown that of B Flight.

Within the 'A' Flight formation, a Canadian crew found themselves without their usual machine. Flying Officer Denis Loveridge and his crew had begun operations on 12th July, using FL176 'B', one of 98 Squadron's veteran aircraft and one of the original seven named after Snow White's dwarves, 'B' being 'Grumpy'. From then on, as a new crew, the Canadians were obliged to use any spare aircraft until late in the month when Loveridge began to regularly claim FV976, suitably coded 'L'. Squadron records indicate that after 22 operations, Loveridge and his crew had a break commencing 8th August before returning to the fray on the 19th. As an experienced captain, Loveridge again claimed priority use of 'L' which then saw the Canadians through a further nine sorties (including no less than three on one memorable day, 26th August) until the Boulogne guns attack of 8th September. For some unrecorded reason, 'L' was unavailable and consequently Loveridge found himself assigned to aircraft FW188.

FW188, VO-B, was a relative newcomer to Dunsfold. It had arrived in Britain on 8th January 1944, passing to 12 MU at Kirkbride on 10th February before delivery to Dunsfold on 24th August. On 98 Squadron it replaced FL176 'B' -'Grumpy' which had flown its final sortie on 8th August and retired as the Mitchell with the highest total of operations to its credit - 125 bombing and 3 air-sea rescue sorties. As the regular aircraft of Warrant Officer Dodd, the replacement FW188 was christened 'B-Beer' and had then seen off five operations in safety. The superstitions that aircrew attached to particular aircraft are well documented and one can only guess at whether any of the young Canadians of Loveridge's crew expressed unease when their usual trusted mount was switched. If there were any fears, they were to prove fatally justified.

Over the target, given as map reference 709499, Squadron Leader Spong's six Mitchells made a good run up despite intense flak. As bombs were released, no results could be seen due to the cloud cover and the 98 Squadron formation suffered no damage as it turned for the return trip to Dunsfold. Aboard two aircraft, however, problems were reported.

Aircraft 'J', FW262, had a complete hang-up of all eight bombs while Loveridge in 'B-Beer' discovered that just one bomb had failed to drop. Over the Channel, Loveridge's crew were heard struggling to free the bomb, even to the extent of lowering a man down into the open bomb bay to hack at the release mechanism. Despite all efforts, neither Mitchell succeeded in jettisoning their unwanted cargo into the sea and for both pilots, the prospect of a landing with bombs still aboard held little appeal.

Back in the circuit, Spong was the first of 98 Squadron to touch down at 20.20 hours, turning off the runway to follow the aircraft of 180 Squadron who had returned shortly before and were now threading their way along the perimeter track to squadron dispersals. Third aircraft back from 98, two minutes behind their flight commander, was 'B-Beer' with Loveridge attempting as soft a landing as possible.

As the Mitchell's wheels touched, the bomb jolted free and exploded. A blinding flash split the sky as, with a screech of tortured metal, the blazing bomber careered along the runway. Sergeant Ted Burn, a pilot of 180 Squadron, watched aghast from his aircraft on the perimeter track as B-Beer's entire tail unit was hurled through the air while other debris scythed across the airfield.*

For the crew there was clearly little chance of survival and although Flight Segeant Churchard was found alive, he died at midnight from terrible blast and burn injuries. Vicious metal shards also cut into a number of ground personnel who had been counting the bombers in as they landed. Among these onlookers was Flight Sergeant Joe Palmer, who had arrived a day or so earlier to join the staff of station sick quarters. Palmer had accompanied Squadron Leader Williams, the Senior Medical Officer, to watch the aircraft return and was horrified at the sudden explosion as the aircraft slid along the runway in a mass of sparks and flames. Palmer was quickly on hand to treat the ground personnel injured but, tragically, a piece of shrapnel from the explosion also reached out way across the airfield to where Sergeant Albert 'Tubby' Jones, a Fitter IIE from station workshops, was watching in front of the hangars. Gravely injured in the chest by the flying metal, Jones was rushed to the crash tent, but little could be done and he died soon afterwards.

Overhead, the circling crews grimly watched the scene as they awaited their own turn to land. The runway in use was quickly changed and the final three aircraft of A Flight slipped safely in, including Currell, the relieved pilot of 'J', still with a full bomb load. Just minutes later, Squadron Leader Brown brought 'B' Flight safely back with reports of excellent bombing results on their own target.

The Canadian crew of 'B-Beer' (Flying Officer Denis L. Loveridge, pilot; Flight Lieutenant Robert F. Logie, navigator; Flight Sergeant George Churchard, wireless operator/air gunner; and Pilot Officer Russell D. Durling, air gunner) were buried at Brookwood Military Cemetery, as was Sergeant A.C. Jones. In another sad irony, by the time of the burials word was received of the promotions of Churchard and Durling, to Pilot Officer and Flying Officer respectively.

---

*Ted Burn had an amazing escape from death after the Wing moved to Belgium. Burn was lying on his bunk in his billet when someone in the next room decided to hammer a nail into the wall in order to hang a picture. Instead of a hammer, the individual used the butt of his loaded Smith and Wesson .38 revolver. The gun went off and the bullet went through the wall and into Burn's head. Miraculously he survived, though he was affected by the injury until he died in 1991.

Ivor Ward with 'B-Beer's' remains in 1988.

Right, one of the models made from the wreckage.

The tragic remains of 'B-Beer' were unceremoniously bulldozed off the damaged runway and into the trees lining the Wey and Arun Junction Canal on the aerodrome's eastern boundary. Throughout the post-war years, souvenir hunters removed shell clips, fuel tanks, an armoured seat backing and at least one of the propellers. Thanks to the cover of the trees, however, much of the remaining debris survived in fair condition, preserved paintwork including half of both letter 'B's, located either side of the nose. In 1987, an enthusiastic employee of British Aerospace began to pull the remains out from their hiding place of over forty years. Ivor Ward spent painstaking and laborious hours sifting and moving the tangled pile of wreckage to a new site, appropriately enough to the place where 98 Squadron's dispersals had once been. In late 1988, British Aerospace regretfully announced that the wreckage would have to be found a new home. Ivor put out an S.O.S. to the author and a local Councillor, John Neale, offered the wreckage a new home. A small team was quickly assembled to salvage the major pieces and, fittingly, one of the volunteers was former 98 Squadron fitter Reg Day who had served at Dunsfold from August 1943 until October 1944. In conjunction with the author, craftsman David Carter subsequently melted down some of the wreckage and turned it into miniature replicas of 'B-Beer'. These now serve as fitting memorials to the sacrifice of Pilot Officer Loveridge and his crew.

The following day saw repeated attacks against the Boulogne guns and FW125 of 180 Squadron was lost to the accurate flak defences. It was to be for a different type of tragedy, however, that the day is remembered by so many who served on the aerodrome at the time.

Two fitters of the station workshops had just left the station for an evening out when they were passed by a black Canadian soldier, pedalling furiously on a bicycle in the direction of Hascombe and Godalming. Besides the relative rarity of seeing a black soldier in Canadian Army service, the Dunsfold men also remarked upon the fact that the cyclist was risking a charge by not wearing his uniform cap.

A few hundred yards further along the road to Guildford, close to 'The Leathern Bottle' public house, the two airmen came across an awful scene. Led by her small dog and crawling in great pain along the grass verge was eighteen year old Dorothy Hillman, a young pregnant housewife, of nearby Palmers Cross Cottages.

Horrified, the men saw that she was covered in blood coming from no less than eleven stab wounds. Instantly guessing that there had been some link with the soldier they had just passed, one of the two flagged down a motorist to set off in pursuit, while the other stayed to comfort the girl. The motorist, who chanced to be a local Justice of the Peace, willingly agreed to take the Hascombe Road to see if the Canadian could be caught. As they dropped down into the village of Hascombe, they spied ahead of them the still furiously pedalling soldier. As they hung back and debated on how best to tackle the situation, good fortune took a hand. From the opposite direction appeared a police car, which was quickly enlisted in the chase. Detective Sergeant Storr and P.C. Gunning, of the Godalming Police, quickly apprehended the soldier who was identified as Private Horace Beresford Gordon. Damning evidence was found on the man, including an open knife and blood stains on his uniform and handkerchief. Back at the scene of the crime, a field service cap belonging to Gordon was found.

At his trial, Gordon was found guilty of the attack, his swift arrest being due in no small part to the quick thinking of the two airmen. In hospital, despite losing her baby, Dorothy

Hillman had seemed well on the way to recovery. Almost two weeks after the attack, however, the stab wounds in her chest and abdomen turned septic and she died. Before her death, she recovered sufficiently to both positively identify Private Gordon and make a statement. Apparently the Canadian, despite the girl's state of eight month's pregnancy, had stopped her and asked for sexual favours. On her refusal, he had drawn a knife and pushed her into the hedgerow, before stabbing her repeatedly. Despite an appeal, Gordon's guilt and sentence were confirmed by the Lord Chief Justice in December 1944. On 9th January 1945, Gordon was hanged at Wandsworth Prison in London.

On 12th September, FW167 of 98 Squadron failed to return from attacks on Breskens when it fell to the flak at Vlissingen on the Dutch coast, and on two successive days, 13th and 14th September, 180 Squadron lost two more aircraft, FW232 and FW207, both on take-off for operations.

The latter accident meant short-lived good news for one of the crew of Warrant Officer Seymour. A welcome order on 12th September gave instructions for at least the aircrews to return from under canvas to their previous accommodation. For 180 Squadron, the good news was somewhat tainted due to the fact that their tented area had been within the grounds of Sachel Court, home of the Land Army girls. Their more established accommodation in Hall Place and number 5 site was on the opposite side of the airfield and distance could not always be relied upon to make the heart grow fonder! For Seymour's navigator, the return of creature comforts came too late. When FW207 lost power on take-off, the ensuing crash-landing near Dunsfold village injured all four crew and navigator Flight Sergeant Styles later died in hospital.

In mid-September, 139 Wing were involved with dropping flares and bombs on the enemy's positions on the Brabant-Beveland Causeway and the Walcheren-South Beveland Bridge, where the German Army was still preventing access to the Port of Antwerp, liberated at the beginning of September. During this period, a briefing for a daylight raid brought some intriguing information. Crews were warned to look out for a new type of Allied aircraft in addition to the usual escort of Spitfires. Sure enough, these mystery aircraft were spotted and identified as the new Meteor jets, the first such jet aircraft seen by the Mitchell crews. Because of the jets' greater speed, the Meteors had too much difficulty staying with the bombers and it was decided to instead use the new aircraft against the V-1 threat.

15th September saw an intriguing incident in the history of the aerodrome which has yet to be entirely explained. On this day, a young RAF fitter, attached to the 9th USAAF Troop Carrier Command headquarters at Eastcote, Middlesex, was detailed to drive two men to RAF Dunsfold. Leading Aircraftsman A. Calvert understood the two to be Dutch saboteurs, returning to the continent, but he had no idea as to their mission or why they were to fly from Dunsfold. All he knew was that after a foggy journey down from Eastcote, he was directed to one of Dunsfold's more distant dispersals where it had been arranged for a transport aircraft to fly in to collect the two men. Calvert believes this to have been a Dakota and, on leaving the airfield, he thought no more of the incident until the end of the war. Then, he read reports of an infamous Dutch double agent nicknamed 'King Kong', whom the Dutch government had sentenced to death. This man was one of the two that Calvert had delivered to Dunsfold.

Despite the purely co-incidental Dutch connection of 320 Squadron, the weather perhaps gives one clue to the reason that Calvert was ordered to Dunsfold. Many airfields in Great Britain were fogbound that day, yet Dunsfold was clearly open for flying. It is known that the Dutchmen were flown to Brussels and, at this time, Canadian Dakotas were starting to shuttle casualties into the aerodrome, often from Brussels. No doubt there would have been spare passenger space on the return trips. There is also evidence that 'King Kong' had been de-briefed by Canadian Intelligence officers. It is still a mystery as to why the USAAF 9th Troop Carrier Command became involved, although it is possible that the unidentified partner of 'King Kong' was an American-run agent. Certainly, no member of 320 Squadron was aware of fellow countrymen visitors on the aerodrome and station headquarters did not log the movement.

'King Kong' was in fact a 6' 3" Dutchman with the real name of Christiaan Antonius Lindemans. Lindemans had made contact with intelligence officers as the advancing Anglo-Canadian 21st Army Group moved through Belgium towards Holland. Lindemans presented himself as a long serving member of the Dutch underground, and offered his services to the Allies. Despite his success in meeting with some members of the staff of Prince Bernhard (then commanding the Free Dutch Forces), Lindemans could not win the trust of the Prince himself, who formed an immediate dislike of the man. When Allied intelligence officers returned Lindemans to Holland, his mission was to warn Dutch underground resistence leaders not to continue sending Allied pilots along an escape line which had been penetrated by the Germans. Lindemans had, however, in his brief time with the Allies, somehow learned the secret that the German 'Enigma' code had been broken. This fact Lindemans was able to pass on to his German masters, with the result that the Ardennes offence of January 1945 was prepared using a different code and the Allies suffered badly. At the end of the war, Lindemans came under suspicion and was arrested by the Dutch authorities, ironically not for the 'Enigma' coup, but instead, because he was erroneously suspected of having given away plans for the Arnhem operation. Before his trial could take place, Lindemans committed suicide in hospital.

Wing Commander George Hamer assumed command of 98 Squadron on 16th September, 1944 and was just in time to lead some of the unit's most harrowing sorties.

On 17th September, 139 Wing began maximum effort operations supporting *Operation Market Garden*, the allied airborne forces' drop on bridges at Arnhem and Nijmegen in Holland. All three squadrons were detailed to bomb the military barracks at Ede and, at the pre-raid briefing, one crew member of 320 Squadron expressed great satisfaction at the target. Several years previously the barracks had been the place where he joined the Dutch Army as a conscript! The Mitchell crews were witness to a remarkable sight as they swept in behind the transport aircaft and gliders, stretching in a seemingly endless column to the landing zones. At nearby Ede, however, eight tenths cloud obscured the target, and many aircraft therefore returned with their bomb loads intact as they were under orders to bomb only if the target was definitely identified. Of those that did bomb, several reported bombs falling wide but at least some aircraft of 180 Squadron managed to attack in good visibility through cloud gaps. As bombs were released, German troops could be seen boarding their lorries to go to the landing areas.

For the next three days, bad weather curtailed operations and it was not until the 22nd and 23rd that operations were again attempted against Arnhem. Due, however, to a combination of poor weather and the uncertain situation on the ground in the target area, these strikes were recalled and it was then 25th September when Arnhem support operations were finally resumed. Watched by Princess Juliana of the Netherlands on a visit to the aerodrome, each of Dunsfold's squadrons took off to attack a separate enemy strongpoint in the battle area. On this occasion not only heavy flak but also considerable enemy fighter opposition was encountered, including sightings of the Luftwaffe's new Messerschmitt Me 262 jet fighters. Wing Commander Hamer had safely lead eleven aircraft of 98 Squadron through intense and accurate flak only to meet Focke Wulf FW 190s which had broken through the bombers' fighter cover. In quick succession, Mitchells FW194 and FW211 were shot down. All members of the crews of Flight Sergeant Williams and Pilot Officer Harrison were reported missing.

On 26th September, the Wing again operated against enemy strongpoints in the Arnhem area and also against a road junction at Cleve, just over the border in Germany itself. This latter operation represented the first attack on the Reich homeland by Dunsfold's Mitchells while the day also saw the withdrawal of airborne forces from Arnhem. The bold gamble had failed and it would be some time yet before 320 Squadron could return to their homeland.

Chapter Ten

'The Charmer'

The close of September and the first days of October saw the Wing continuing daylight raids on enemy targets along the German/Dutch border and against the enemy troop concentrations still in the Arnhem area.

On 6th October, Curly Motheral of 180 Squadron once again survived a close call, but in tragic circumstances. Flying Mitchell FW221, Motheral collided with FW244 when climbing through cloud in formation. Motheral's aircraft only suffered slight damage but FW244, flown by Flying Officer Crank, also of 180 Squadron, crashed at Blacknest Farm, Dunsfold, killing all on board. The investigation found no-one to blame, the accident being termed a sad outcome of operational necessity.

Operations then ceased as rumours strengthened that the Wing was to move to the Continent. These rumours proved true as 139 Wing had received orders to move to Melsbroek (now Brussels International Airport) in Belgium. In true RAF style, the airmen were among the last to know of their destination. One 'erk' recalls being told of his destination by a civilian at a bus stop in Cranleigh, while an air gunner first heard the news from Mrs Evans in 'The Three Compasses'!

As packing up began, a new crew joined 180 Squadron, led by a strange character, Lieutenant James Armstrong, of the South African Air Force. By his brash behaviour, excessive drinking and loudly professed interest in women, Armstrong instantly built a poor reputation for himself. It was rumoured that already he was disliked and mistrusted by his own crew. Nor could anyone understand where the money came from to enable Armstrong to spend every spare moment of his time up in London. Other crews resented the new pilot's arrogant manner, which seemed to lead him to ignore anyone under the rank of Flying Officer. Luckily, Dunsfold did not have to suffer the presence of Armstrong for too long due to the Wing's move to Belgium, the new pilot not having progressed onto operational flying by the time of his departure. It is interesting, however, to follow the career of this officer a little further.

Murderer Neville Heath at the time of his arrest in 1946. (Photo J. C. Standing.)

After only a couple of operations with the Wing on the Continent, Armstrong was flying Mitchell FV967 from Melsbroek against the bridges at Venlo, in Holland. The operation had started controversially when, during the briefing, Armstrong had openly argued with one of his gunners, who complained of feeling unwell. Armstrong had publicly accused the man of cowardice and the confrontation was only calmed by the intervention of the indomitable Fielding-Johnson. Recovered from his wounds of June, and promoted to Squadron Leader, F-J had just returned to the Wing as Gunnery Leader. Sizing up the situation and knowing of Armstrong's reputation, F-J volunteered to fly the operation instead of the sick gunner. Over the target, heavy flak was encountered and other crews noted Armstrong's clear lack of experience as he failed to take any form of evasive action. For too long he flew straight and level and flak inevitably found the Mitchell. An engine burst into flames and aboard the aircraft pandemonium broke out. Instead of taking action to put the fire out, Armstrong panicked and immediately ordered his crew to bale out. F-J, as unpurturbed as if he were a passenger in a family car, removed his flak helmet and then his flying helmet, carefully coiling up his intercom cord. He then placed the flying helmet in the flak helmet, did up the snap fasteners and slid the helmet onto his arm. Throughout

171

this cool performance Armstrong was jumping up and down in his seat, screaming at F-J to 'Get out!' Eventually the crew were all clear and landed safely within liberated territory before returning to Melsbroek where Armstrong's first priority was to ask for leave following his 'stressful' experience. From F-J's comments on the new pilot's performance there was no delay in posting the odious character back to England and he was not seen on the squadron again. This was not, however, the last that was heard of Armstrong. Post war, his features adorned the front page of every newspaper in the country under his true name of Neville Heath, arrested for the brutal and sadistic murders of several women. 'Armstrong' had been dismissed the Service in December 1945 for conduct prejudicial to good order and for wearing military decorations unlawfully. He had then, masquerading as either Colonel Heath or Group Captain Rupert Brooke, preyed on young women. At his trial in 1946, he was found guilty of the murders and hanged at Pentonville Prison on the 16th October.*

Commencing on 9th October, the move from Dunsfold to Belgium began, and followed 414 Air Stores Park who had left Hascombe two days previously. In recent days it had never seemed to stop raining and much equipment had to be packed away wet. The RAF provided the services of 314 Supply and Transport Column to manage the move,one section being detailed to lead the ground parties to Tilbury Docks (via, strangely, Salisbury Plain), while the other section would remain on the aerodrome to help with clearing up. With their cavernous Dodge trucks and despatch riders, 314 STC swarmed about the airfield, making speedy work of what seemed a logistical nightmare. Many airmen broke into the airfield's locked permanent quarters to 'borrow' equipment and soon after arriving on the Continent, it was heard that 139 Wing had received a 'rocket' from higher authority, complaining about the state of the airfield. Aerial photographs had even been taken as evidence of the mess that had been left behind and Squadron Leader Sudworth, the station commanding officer back at Dunsfold, sourly noted that "this unnecessary wastage of valuable equipment and labour is deplorable". Barrack damage alone amounted

---

*In recent years a television series, 'The Charmer', starring Nigel Havers, was basedlooselyonArmstrong'slife.

to the then princely sum of £175 and many weeks were spent cleaning up, clearing and overhauling the aerodrome's facilities.

One of the last items to be surreptitiously spirited away to Belgium was the local policeman's bicycle. When the air parties of the Wing left for Belgium on 18th October, Curly Motheral had been given the job of checking 180's offices, crew and locker rooms for anything left behind. As he did so, the local village police constable pedalled up to the flight office and approached Curly. The Canadian recognised the constable as the same law officer who had the irritating habit of waiting outside 'The Three Compasses' at night. Many an airman was caught for such trivial offences as riding two on a bike, or riding without lights. The constable would then appear at the Wing Commander's office the next day to report these 'criminal' acts, making the C.O. more than a little testy with his crews, since he had many more serious things to think about. Therefore, when the constable approached Curly Motheral, the pilot saw his opportunity for retribution. The policeman was seeking a particular airman for punishment. In his most official manner, Curly assured him that the wanted individual could be found on 320 Squadron's dispersals in the distance. The quickest way, the constable was advised, was through a patch of scrub and trees which would conveniently obscure his view of 180's dispersals. The policeman marched off and, as soon as he was out of sight, his bicycle was hung up inside the bomb bay of Curly's Mitchell, the engines started, and the Canadian* disappeared into the blue towards Brussels! Perhaps even today that bicycle is bumping its way around the cobbled streets of the Belgian capital. It is also rumoured that for many months a signpost stood on Melsbroek airfield, its finger signs pointing to Hascombe, Godalming, Cranleigh and Guildford. Another souvenir!

Following the departure of the Wing, relative peace descended on the aerodrome. The Dakotas landing Canadian wounded had

---

*By now, Motheral was considered one of the 'old men' of the Squadron since, at thirty one years old, he was some ten years older than the majority of aircrew. Because of this seniority and supposed maturity, Curly was often called upon to be in charge of burial parties of Canadian airmen at Brookwood Military Cemetery. He soon acquired a trademark with his habit of appearing in the crew room and calling for 'six volunteers for a plantin' party.'

used Dunsfold until 26th September when the Air Evacuation Unit left and many other aircraft, flying to and from the continent, used the aerodrome during bad weather conditions. Some were not so fortunate. The aerodrome's air traffic control staff were called upon to erect anti-collision lights on nearby Leith Hill after a tragic incident on 26th November 1944. In poor weather, no less than three USAAF Dakotas, ironically from a Pathfinder squadron, smashed into the hill in succession while returning from operations. In the crashes, two aircraft burnt out completely and the third partially. While thirteen bodies were pulled from the wreckage, somehow two men survived with only minor injuries.

As the aerodrome's temporary wind-down continued, 2862 Squadron RAF Regiment had moved to number 2 site on 11th October for its winter quarters while on the 19th, 2791 Squadron were able to move in to the aerodrome from their quarters in Dunsfold village. Together, the two squadrons began to help with clearing up the aerodrome after 139 Wing's departure, assisting the rear detachment of 314 Supply and Transport Column* who took over Broadmeads Cottage while their forward element remained on the continent. The job also called for 28 armourers who arrived on the 27th of the month to assist with the disposal of the bombs left behind. This latter work was perhaps not performed as thoroughly as it should have been. More than two years later, in December 1946, a left-behind RAF bomb was discovered in a copse bordering the airfield and necessitated the attentions of a bomb disposal team from Biggin Hill.

The opportunity was also taken to start work on minor runway repairs and on taking up the Canadians' experimental bituminous fabric runway which was removed and the grass re-sown by the end of October. This latter work at least prevented a repetition of one of the aerodrome's most spectacular crash-landings. After heavy rain, the experimental runway had

---

*Jock Adams and Donald Maughan were fellow despatch riders and best friends in 314 STC. Post-war they lost touch as Jock settled in Reading while Donald married a Belgian girl and took up residence in Ghent. Despite numerous efforts to trace each other it was not to be until 1989 that they met again. Both had made contact with the author, the only former 314 STC personnel to do so and had thus been put in touch again.

retained far too much surface water and from the air it took on the appearance of a canal or river. Inevitably, one day a swan was observed 'on finals', only to discover to its painful cost that the 'waterway' was somewhat unrelenting!

An indication as to future plans for the aerodrome had come on 11th October when two officers of 84 Group Support Unit visited Dunsfold with a view to moving in. Instead, however, an officer of 83 Group Support Unit was then attached to Dunsfold pending the future move of that unit to the aerodrome but in the interim, the aerodrome enjoyed a quiet spell for the remaining two months of the year. In December a contract was let for a new drainage system which was installed on the aerodrome while the two RAF Regiment squadrons converted from Bofors guns to become rifle squadrons since it was felt there was now little need to protect against possible air attack. The lull in activities was also welcome in that those remaining on the aerodrome were able to enjoy an active social life over the festive season. One participant in the Christmas spirit proved to be 139 Wing, now on the continent. Not to be defeated by shortages in war-torn Belgium, a Mitchell was dispatched back to Dunsfold. There it was loaded with beer from 'The Three Compasses' while cakes and mince pies were brought from the 'Gibbs Hatch Family Restaurant'. By way of thanks, the Mitchell's pilot waggled his wings on departure to the 'Gibbs Hatch' staff, all while slanting the bomber between two large trees in the restaurant's grounds!

In spite of the welcome respite, it was nevertheless appreciated that 83 Group Support Unit would be arriving in the New Year and the tempo of flying could therefore soon be expected to increase again. Meanwhile, the aerodrome's attentions were devoted towards preparations for the station concert party revue, 'Elizabeth Didn't Approve', in Hascombe Village Hall.

The following verse, penned at Dunsfold in 1944, gives an idea of the spirits of the Mitchell crews while on operations. Though no great poet, G. H. Olson, a Canadian air gunner with an otherwise Australian crew of 98 Squadron, plainly projects the optimism and pride which was typical of so many young men at Dunsfold, despite the dangers faced.

AN 'OP' ON DOODLE BUG LAIR

We were down at the Crew Room
One bright summer's day
When we all got the word
We'd soon be on our way.

We climbed into the planes
All ready to go
And warmed up the engines
And taxied out slow.

We raced down the runway
And took to the air,
We were off on a mission
To the Doodle Bug Lair.

Past the White Cliffs of Dover
And out over the sea,
We flew tight formation
It was lovely to see.

In the distance lay France,
Almost hidden with haze,
When the pilot calls up
And to the crew says.

Put on your flak helmets
There may be some flak
So we put on our helmets
And answered him back.

Those Jerries are clueless,
We've been here before.
And at that moment
We passed the French shore.

We made a sharp turn
And started our run
When the flak started bursting
This was not to be fun.

The bomb doors were open,
Our target in sight.
So we flew through the heavens
Like eagles in flight.

At last came the words
We were all waiting for,
Bombing - Go! so we dropped them
And closed the bomb door.

The bombs fell in a cluster
I'll bet they made a bang.
And the Observer shouted
Oh Boy, what a Prang!

We weathered the flak
And were over the sea
And no-one was missing
We were thankful to see.

Back over the Channel
In formation we flew
There was Red Box leading
Then Ivory and Blue.

We made a nice landing
Back at our base
And climbed out relieved
With smiles on our face.

One more mission completed
One last 'Op' to go.
We felt quite contented
It had been a good show.

Just keep up the good work
Our C.O. tells us,
He's not a bad fellow,
A nice pleasant cuss.

On bacon and eggs
We had a good feed,
And now a good sleep
Is all that we need.

98 SQUADRON

We're the Airmen of the nation
We're the soldiers of the skies,
With the miles of space around us
As we fly up there on high.

As we fly high in the heavens,
That's where we gain our fame,
And that's where we add more glory
To old 98's great name.

Some are Pilots, Observers, Gunners,
Others fix the planes below,
But in this we're all united
In this greatest fight we know.

We're not heroes, we're just airmen,
We're the masters of the blue,
And we know that hearts are beating strong
In every Mitchell crew.

As we look into the sunset
As the sun sinks in the West,
We are proud to be the members
Of the Squadron that's the best.

And when this struggle's over
And we go home once more
We can say we flew with 98
In the Second Great World War.

We are proud of 98 Squadron
And will keep its records high
And we're proud of all its members
Who are masters of the sky.

No other ones can beat us
We're the finest in the land,
And with old 98 Squadron,
We'll always make our stand.

G. H. OLSON

Chapter Eleven
The Approach of Peace

The advent of 1945 saw the end in sight for the Axis powers. In the Far East, Allied advances in Burma and the Phillippines continued to push the Japanese Army back, while in Japan itself Tokyo and other major cities were bombed in daylight by USAAF B-29 Superfortress long range aircraft. The German Army's winter offensive had been halted in the Ardennes on Christmas Day and the Allied armies in the west were now poised to strike into the Reich from France, Luxembourg, Belgium and Holland. The Russians were fighting their way through Czechoslovakia and Hungary on the eastern front, with their sights also firmly fixed on the borders of the Fatherland.

At Dunsfold, as expected, 7th January, 1945 saw the arrival of the headquarters staff and Flying Training Wing of 83 Group Support Unit from RAF Westhampnett, led by Wing Commander C. W. Passy DFC and quickly visited the next day by the Group's renowned AOC, Air Vice-Marshal Harry Broadhurst. While the unit remained, Dunsfold was to see much of this famous officer on his frequent visits to the aerodrome. Broadhurst (later Air Chief Marshal Sir Harry Broadhurst) had a distinguished record as a senior commander with a great deal of personal operational experience from earlier in the war. Known as 'Monty's favourite airman', Broadhurst had forged a strong working relationship with Montgomery's forces when in command of the Desert Air Force supporting the 8th Army in North Africa. It was also Broadhurst who had perfected the 'cab-rank' system of fighter bomber support for advancing troops. Montgomery had therefore made sure he was able to call on Broadhurst's services again when the latter was rapidly promoted to command 83 Group in Europe.

83 Group Support Unit was exactly as titled, a support facility for 83 Group then based on the continent and operating in close conjunction with the advancing Allied armies. 83 GSU's task was to train and ferry new pilots and repaired, modified or replacement aircraft across to the Group's operational squadrons. As such, it was a unit where neither men nor machines stayed for very long, albeit large stocks of aircraft, numbering up

Back at Dunsfold, Spitfire PV202 prepares for its first post restoration flight on February 23rd, 1990. (Peter Arnold.)

to 200, were normally maintained. The Flying Training Wing's duties included converting pilots onto the particular type of aircraft they would soon be flying in earnest, i.e. Spitfires,* Typhoons, Tempests and an occasional Auster for the artillery spotting squadrons. The aircraft themselves, either new or repaired examples, were usually ferried to 83 GSU by ATA pilots, frequently women. New aircraft then had radios, gunsights and guns fitted and tested by air firing.

*One 83 GSU aircraft was Spitfire XIV, RN689. Today, this aircraft is still maintained and flown by Rolls Royce as G-ALGT. RN689 was on the strength of 83 GSU for two periods: 24.2.45 to 1.3.45 and 17.5.45 to 12.7.45. Another of the unit's Spitfires was Mk. IX PV202 which was delivered to 412 RCAF Squadron from Dunsfold in January 1945 and returned to 83 GSU in May. During its operational career it destroyed two FW 190 and one Me 109 enemy fighters. Post-war it was converted to a two seat trainer and served with the Irish Air Corps until 1968 when it passed to the British civil register. An extensive rebuild programme, completed in December 1989, saw PV202 returned to her 1945 RAF colours. Fittingly, her first post-rebuild flight on 23.2.90 was back at Dunsfold, final assembly and flight testing facilities having been provided by the DH Group in the aerodrome's south-eastern corner.

On arrival at Dunsfold, the unit was in the midst of heavy demands upon its services. On New Year's Day the Luftwaffe had thrown one last major attack against the Allied air forces on the continent. Using the element of surprise to full advantage, the Germans had caught many squadrons unprepared on their airfields and 83 Group alone lost scores of aircraft. Back in England, 83 GSU therefore became a crucial element in restoring squadron strengths as swiftly as possible. The move to Dunsfold improved their facilities but atrocious weather and heavy snow falls hampered their operations. Both 2826 and 2791 Squadrons of the RAF Regiment were drafted onto snow clearing duties and soon Dunsfold's runways were clear enough for flying to re-commence. In addition to the activities of 83 GSU, other units also made use of Dunsfold for visits on training exercises. On 19th January, two Liberators performed circuits and bumps, while on 2nd February, no less that fourteen Dakotas practised likewise.

Despite the arrival of 83 GSU and the gradual build-up of flying again, Dunsfold lost its self accounting status when, on 15th January, 1945, it became a satellite of RAF Odiham. Notwithstanding this rôle relegation, 83 GSU continued its hectic flying programme. On 19th January the unit suffered its first accident at Dunsfold when a Spitfire Mk XIV of the Flying Training Wing crashed at Willards Farm, Dunsfold. Flying Officer Fisher just had time to bale out and was injured. Warrant Officer Cunningham too had a fortunate escape when he force landed Typhoon RB501 at Holdhurst Farm, Cranleigh on 4th February and emerged from the crash unscathed.

The remainder of 83 GSU, still based at Westhampnett on the south coast, also began to take the opportunity to become familiar with what was becoming their new home. Dunsfold thus began to receive numerous visits from the unit's aircraft and the first of several mishaps occurred on 9th February when Typhoon MN704, flown up from Westhampnett, crashed on the aerodrome's outskirts owing to shortage of fuel. Pilot Officer Beattie was killed instantly. The same day a pilot of an 83 GSU Tempest, on a similar visit, was lucky to escape unhurt when he had to make a wheels up landing on the aerodrome with engine trouble. In another early incident, a Typhoon's brakes locked on

Typhoon 1b 7S-X of 83 GSU at Dunsfold. (Air Commodore J. W. Frost via Chris Thomas.)

landing, causing it to cartwheel spectactularly down the runway. While the aircraft was a total wreck the pilot emerged suffering only from shock.

Another change of station commanding officer had occurred on 6th February, 1945 when Squadron Leader G. Hampson replaced Squadron Leader Sudworth and over the following two days further departures were seen as 2826 and 2791 Squadrons of the RAF Regiment left for the continent. This only provided brief respite on the pressure for space since on the 22nd, the remainder of 83 GSU moved up to Dunsfold, hastened by water logging at Westhampnett. In their new home, the GSU appreciated having a decent aerodrome to themselves with good runways, hangars and office accommodation. The only worries came from the staff of Flying Control, who viewed the surrounding hilly countryside with some apprehension.

The instructional flying staff of the unit were usually experienced 'tour expired' pilots on rest, but there were also many inexperienced pilots on the conversion courses yet to fly operationally. It was these latter types who, it was feared, might find the hilly terrain a problem in addition to familiarising themselves with new aircraft. On 3rd March, Warrant Officer Saunders' newly learned skills on Spitfires were put to the test when his engine cut immediately after take off. He managed to put the aircraft down at Blacknest Farm in Dunsfold village and escaped with only minor injuries before the machine burnt out.

The start of March also saw more postings arrive on the unit. On the 3rd, some of the personnel of 610 Squadron joined 83 GSU, their squadron having been suddenly disbanded while in the middle of an Armament Practice Camp at RAF Warmwell. Other new arrivals included a 25 strong group of Canadian armourers detailed to support the rocket firing Typhoons and Tempests. After only a few days, all 25 were on a charge for not conforming to routine mess times and procedures. George Cotterman, one of the offenders, recalls that the incident came about one morning. Arriving for breakfast at 07.45 instead of 08.00 hours, they were forbidden entry and told to wait. Undeterred by officialdom, all 25 marched across to 'The Three Compasses' where Mrs Evans obligingly served up egg and chips. Fortunately for the armourers, the officer detailed to hear the case was a fellow Canadian and the decision went their way!

Also with effect from the beginning of March, Group Captain A. R. F. de Salis OBE had taken over command of 83 GSU and with his arrival the unit formally created its own Ferry Flight, using twin engined Anson aircraft. The Ansons had already been carrying passengers and freight to the continent and to these cargoes were now added pilots, both on their way out to operational squadrons and on their way back from ferrying aircraft. Even these routine flights were not without possible drama, Flight Lieutenant Hamer crashing an Anson at Heesch on the continent on the 30th of the month, luckily without casualties.

The Flying Training Wing also continued with its share of mishaps. On 7th March, Spitfire TB624 burnt out when it force landed just half a mile from the aerodrome following engine failure shortly after take-off. Flying Officer Chittenden was then killed in another Spitfire when he crashed in bad weather near Shoreham on the 29th.

The following day an Australian instructor, Tom Hall, recalls that the continuing bad weather led to tense moments for several pilots. Hall had come to Dunsfold as a Flying Officer on rest on 14th March, 1945, having completed 122 operations on Hurricanes and Typhoons with 175 Squadron of 121 Wing. On 30th March, he was detailed to lead a formation of replacement aircraft and pilots and, while conditions were bad on take-off, improving weather was promised over the continent. Hall remembers:

> "We got out over the Channel OK, but had to go over the cloud, which was becoming too low as we approached the French coast. After flying for some time in loose formation, I called up and checked the weather at our destination (B100 Airfield at Goch, in Germany), where I learnt there was a cloud base of only about 800 ft. I didn't tell the replacement pilots flying with me, but I went over to another operational RT Channel and called for a course to Goch. It was duly given (my own reckoning had been out by about 5 degrees), as well as an ETA on current air speed, which meant that we should start descending in about eight minutes time. I went back to our communal channel and told the boys that we were on course and would soon go down through the overcast. At the appropriate time, I got them to spread out, warned them to stick to their set gyro compass reading and down we went at a steady speed. We broke cloud at about 900 ft. and straight ahead was Goch airfield. After landing, the boys congratulated me on my superb navigation. I just crossed my fingers and neglected to mention the help I'd been given."

The Flying Training Wing was well served by several experienced instructors, resting after operational tours. One, Squadron Leader Bob Spurdle, was a fearless New Zealand fighter leader, whose service career had already covered 564 operational sorties. His final tour had been in command of 80 Squadron in Germany, and his posting to Dunsfold as a Briefing Officer, on 15th January, quickly proved boring for this energetic officer. Along with Squadron Leader Vincent, Spurdle therefore volunteered to drop with the airborne forces crossing the Rhine. Their job, once on the ground, was to liaise with the RAF's fighters and fighter bombers which provided the troops with close ground support. Dropped on 24th March, Vincent returned to Dunsfold on 4th April, but Spurdle volunteered to stay on with the ground forces in search of more action in the final days of the war.*

*See 'The Blue Arena' by Squadron Leader Bob Spurdle DFC and Bar, William Kimber 1986.

Another experienced young New Zealander, B.J. Doyle, was more pleased than Spurdle at his posting to 83 GSU in April - for two reasons. Firstly, he had recently married a London girl, whom he would now have the opportunity to see more frequently. Secondly, after an operational tour on Spitfires, he was now under orders to convert to Tempests in order to join the New Zealand 486 Squadron in Germany. The prospect of coming to grips with the superb Tempest, as opposed to the Typhoon, was a particularly welcome one and Doyle therefore eagerly anticipated clocking up his six hours on the new machine. Although a posting to 486 meant another operational tour, he also appreciated that he would have the opportunity to see Germany and no doubt the war would soon end anyway. Forty four years later, Doyle clearly recalls that his first Tempest flight made him grateful for Dunsfold's long runways. He had been advised to make his landing approach at 120 mph, which he did. At about 500feet, he closed the throttle and moved the stick back to round out. To his consternation, the Tempest made no response but continued to descend at the same rate until it struck the runway and rebounded into the air. At this point, the young New Zealander opened the throttle and went round again, making his next approach at 140 mph and keeping power on until he rounded out. This time he made a good landing and his appreciation of the new type was firmly cemented.

Another of 83 GSU's antipodean types at this time was an Australian pilot awaiting allocation to an operational squadron. To get to this stage, he had to amass his six or seven training hours, but although he had been at Dunsfold for some months, he had still only managed to tot up four hours. As the normal stay at the GSU was about ten days, the Australian's instructor was beginning to lose patience. Every time he was allocated an operational training flight, the Australian would be missing for some reason, on sick parade, at an interview at Australia House, etc. etc.

Eventually, the instructor became determined to see that the 'reluctant pilot', as the Australian was dubbed, should serve his part as a replacement on an operational squadron. When the instructor presented his complaint to higher authority, however,

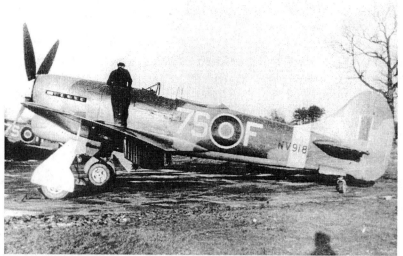

Tempest NV918 of 83 GSU. (Air Cdr. J W Frost via C Thomas.)

he was told a story which went some way to explaining the Australian's reluctance.

Back in 1943, the pilot had been allocated to an operational squadron in the south of England. The squadron's commanding officer was conducting formation flying practice low over the Channel when he ordered a turn to port, which forced the Australian newcomer down into the sea. The aircraft cartwheeled over before sliding under the waves the right way up and eventually settling on the sea bed. The pilot came to, still pushing the throttle and realised that the green haze was water. He released his straps, blew up his Mae West and shot to the surface. By a stroke of great good fortune, the aircraft had come to rest on a sand bank, with only about 30 feet of water over it. A boat from shore soon picked the Australian up and after recovering from shock, he was posted to another squadron in southern England.

On arrival, the commanding officer advised him to go up for a bit of local flying to familiarise himself with the area. The pilot had done this and had just re-entered the aerodrome's circuit when his engine cut out. He quickly calculated that he was in a good position to make it in over the fence of the aerodrome in a steep glide. His approach was good, just to the left of a hill and then over a road and railway line which ran parallel with the aerodrome's boundary. He was about to bring off a good landing when, at the last moment, a train emerged from a tunnel in the hill and the Australian seemed bound to collide with it. The pilot had no alternative but to try to pull the aircraft's nose up to clear the train. Without power, this action caused the aircraft to spin in just short of the railway line. When a rescue team reached the crash site, they found that the cockpit was nevertheless intact and the right way up. The shocked, but only slightly injured, Australian was still in his seat and after only a short spell of hospitalisation he had then been posted to Dunsfold for reallocation. After hearing this story, his instructor no longer pushed the reluctant pilot to complete his hours!

With the end of the European war now in sight, the pace of life at Dunsfold began to slacken. 314 STC left the aerodrome, and as the peak of 83 GSU's deliveries had now passed, it appeared that the aerodrome would start to wind down its activities. On 3rd April, however, the first news arrived that Dunsfold had been chosen to become an Air Arrival Centre for evacuated POWs from Europe. *Operation Exodus* designated Dunsfold and Ford as the arrival aerodromes for the Sussex Group of reception centres. Aerodrome personnel were instructed to immediately commence preparations according to the following requirements :-

1) POWs to be segregated from other personnel as far as possible;

2) Light refreshments and hot drinks to be provided;

3) Latrine facilities to be set up.

4) Medical facilities, including provision for delousing, to be provided.

5) A tented reception area to be set out, including waiting rooms for the POWs awaiting transportation.

Initial plans earmarked Dunsfold for British Army and South African Army (non European) POWs, and it was estimated that up to 3,750 men could be processed each day. Clearly, great demands would soon be made on the aerodrome's facilities and feverish activity commenced to draw up plans for receiving the large numbers of aircraft that would be involved.

Before the arrival of any POWs the aerodrome received another unusual visitor on 7th April, when a USAAF Waco troop-carrying glider was retrieved and brought to the aerodrome from nearby Ramster Park, Chiddingfold. The glider had made an emergency landing in a field there on the 4th when the tow rope had parted from its parent aircraft en route to the continent. No record remains of the glider leaving Dunsfold so it must be assumed it was subsequently scrapped on the airfield.

Another visiting aircraft, on 14th April, brought the return of a familiar face to Dunsfold when the control tower logged the arrival of an Auster aircraft, NJ808, from Rearsby, in Leicestershire.

From the small aeroplane stepped two Dutch pilots, one of whom was John Ot, returning to the aerodrome for the first time since he had left 320 Squadron in 1944. Since then, Ot had transferred to a newly formed Dutch Air Force squadron which was to operate Austers from the liberated part of Holland, flying food supplies into areas which were still German occupied and helping to evacuate sick people. The squadron's pilots had gone to the Auster parent factory at Rearsby to convert to their new aircraft, and it was from there that Ot and Sergeant Danne had taken time off to pop down to Dunsfold. The purpose of the trip was to pick up Ot's log book and flying boots which were with his wife, still living nearby. This return visit was to prove as traumatic to Ot as his last operational flight from the aerodrome.

The flight back to Rearsby was to be with Ot at the controls, his colleague having flown the first leg into Dunsfold. Take-off from Dunsfold's ample, long runway was a simple matter for the light aircraft. Ot then banked left as he passed over the Guildford to Horsham road and the aerodrome's northern boundary. Immediately ahead lay Elmbridge School, on the outskirts of Cranleigh, and the two Dutchmen noticed that the playing fields were being put to good use by the boys of the school.

At that moment, the Auster's engine stopped. With precious little altitude, Ot's brain worked rapidly as the frail machine glided earthwards. Dead ahead and below, the boys of Elmbridge stared upwards, alerted by the sudden cutting out of the

Auster's engine. Ot had no option but to struggle to keep the aircraft airborne over the packed playing fields, but beyond lay the school buildings and only a small field before the tree lined road leading into Cranleigh. With inches to spare, the Auster cleared the roof of the school's staff quarters before dropping heavily into the small grass field. As the aeroplane bounced from the impact, the field's length was quickly used up and the two Dutchmen could only watch and wait as their aircraft plummeted on towards the road ahead. Crashing through bushes, the Auster shot across the road, but came to grief at the far side where it hurtled between two holly trees, just far enough apart to accommodate the width of the fuselage. Both wings and tail planes were stripped off, as was all fabric from the fuselage frame and it was therefore a much "plucked" Auster that eventually slid to a halt upside down in the grounds of Rydinghurst House.

Help was quickly at hand as boys and masters from the school raced to help, soon joined by some of the inhabitants of Elmbridge Road. One of the first on the scene was again Derek Porter who had helped out at the Mitchell crash the previous June. When he reached the shattered aeroplane it was clear that Ot was in a bad way, with one eye jolted from its socket and a broken neck. Sergeant Danne had been thrown from the wreckage and was also seriously injured.

While the emergency services were called for, much discussion took place on the advisability of moving Ot from the wreckage and Derek Porter recalls that the matter was settled by one of his neighbours. This man was a Lancaster Flight Engineer home on leave, and he ordered that Ot be gently lifted from the cockpit. The RAF man then carefully eased the damaged eye back into its socket before any further damage could occur. This quick action probably helped Ot to eventually continue flying with the Dutch Air Force post war, although the eye gave problems over many years. Ot was taken for months of specialist treatment at the Canadian General Hospital in Bramshott while his fellow Dutchman was treated at the Canadian Hospital in Horsham.

The volume of flying undertaken by 83 GSU, albeit a non-operational unit, continued to produce numerous mishaps.

On 17th April, another accident illustrated that there could also be danger in the normally straightforward task of shepherding fresh pilots to the continent. Flying Typhoon SW400, Tom Hall was briefed to lead seven replacement pilots on a trip to Eindhoven, Holland and Rheine, Germany. On the take-off run, DN495, the aircraft of replacement pilot Flight Sergeant Wood, swung and caused mayhem as he nearly succeeded in bringing down several of his colleagues with him. The pilot escaped injuries, but the new machine broke in half and was a write off. Two days later, another machine was written off when Tempest EJ689 overran its landing and continued out of the aerodrome before coming to rest in Parsons Field, Lakers Green, Alfold. Luckily, Flight Lieutenant Latham emerged no worse than thoroughly shaken by the incident. On 20th April, Typhoon DN495 was written off on arrival at Wevelghem and on the 21st, Flight Lieutenant McCurdy crashed into the sea off Shoreham in a Spitfire. The following day it was the turn of an illustrious visitor to come close to grief. Wing Commander Michel Donnet, the celebrated Belgian fighter leader, was approaching the aerodrome in Mustang KM121 when engine trouble forced him down on the outskirts of Godalming. Fortunately for the future of Belgian military aviation, Donnet emerged unscathed.*

Neither were all accidents due to flying duties. One night a Canadian pilot, nicknamed Macca, invited some colleagues and a few WAAFs to a local dance. They went in the flight runabout truck which was not supposed to leave the station. On the way back, with Macca at the wheel and somewhat the worse for a few drinks, the vehicle slid off the road and tipped onto its side. Flying Officer Tom Hall, the experienced Australian pilot, suffered a flattened nose, while another Canadian pilot lost the top of a finger. Due to the numerous minor injuries, all the vehicle's occupants finished up in a Canadian Army hospital and the matter could not be hushed up. A great fuss ensued and an enquiry set up where it was clear that the Transport Officer would be aiming to have the book thrown at Macca. The

---

*Post-war, General le Baron Michel Donnet went on to command the Belgian Air Force. His courageous wartime leadership had only been possible after he had escaped from German-occupied Belgium in a stolen light aircraft. One of those who helped him to escape, and subsequently also made his way out of Belgium, was Mich Jansen who had served in Wing Commander Paul's crew on 98 Squadron at Dunsfold in 1944.

Canadian authorities could see the way things were going and suddenly Macca found himself posted back onto an operational Canadian Spitfire squadron. This effectively aborted the enquiry, but within a few days word was received that Macca had been killed on the first operation of his new tour.

By 18th April, preparations had been completed for the reception of the expected POWs. Number 2 hangar had been converted for use as the Air Arrival Centre and had been decked out with flowers and decorations. Outside, a medical inspection tent had been set up and all that was now awaited were the POWs themselves. After several false alarms and numerous delays, the first aircraft, a Stirling, arrived with 28 POWs at 21.50 hours on 21st April, followed shortly afterwards by a second Stirling with 42 more men. Thereafter, throughout May and June, aircraft poured into Dunsfold, sometimes seeming to fill the circuit from dawn to dusk.

Amongst the arrivals were a number of exotic sights, including many ex-Indian Army personnel who were later transported by rail from Cranleigh station. On one occasion, a returning flight was met by VIP transport and screened from onlookers, the 'buzz' being that one passenger was Odette Churchill, the courageous secret agent who had been captured and tortured by the Germans.*

As the POW trickle had increased to a flood, Dunsfold's flying control team had had to be augmented by more staff sent from Bomber Command. Likewise, many of 83 GSU's personnel were called upon to lend a helping hand. Frank Webb, a Canadian Typhoon pilot, recalls the emotional scenes as the liberated men stepped onto British soil once more, frequently falling to their knees in order to kiss the ground. Among them Webb personally greeted a former school friend from the same small Prairies town in Canada, and Webb was soon advised not to mention that he was a Typhoon pilot. Apparently, many of the former prisoners had suffered the experience of having to take cover from the ground attack 'Tiffies' going about their business in the skies above the battlefields of Europe.

Another returning soldier was John Biden of the Middlesex Yeomanry, a Territorial Army unit. In the summer of 1939, Biden had joined his fellow part-time soldiers for their seasonal

*It has not been possible to confirm this rumour.

camp, but he was not to see England again until he landed in Dunsfold in 1945. After service in France and the Middle East, the young signalman had been captured in Crete in 1941 while attached to Australian infantry. In 1945, as the Russians approached his PoW camp on the German/Polish border, Biden elected to walk westwards with two Scottish companions, Alec Reid and Kenny Knox. After many adventures, they reached Brussels where they managed to hitch a lift to Dunsfold aboard a Dakota of the RCAF. This was the first time that any of the three had flown and it was only the experience of later years that made them reflect that the Dakota had no glazing in its windows, and a gaping hole where the door should have been in the fuselage. The only advice given to the first-time fliers came from the pilot who instructed them to be sick in the oil drum provided for the purpose, rather than on the fuselage floor.

On landing at Dunsfold, Biden recalls the rousing welcome, especially from the Canadian groundcrews. An overnight stay at the aerodrome was necessary before the Red Cross then sent him on to Horsham for a new uniform and interview. Unable to control his impatience any longer, Biden skipped the procedures and took the first available London train to the girlfriend waiting to become his wife.

Less fortunate than the young signaller were other former POWs who managed a lift back to England in a Curtis Commando of the USAAF on 6th May. As the aircraft headed for the American airfield at Membury in Wiltshire, it collided with the aerial of an RAF radio station on Gibbet Hill, Hindhead. Although Dunsfold's medical services raced to the scene, all 31 men on board were found dead on impact, along with a Canadian officer from the radio station.

On 8th May 1945, the war in Europe ended with the German surrender and VE Day was celebrated in style. While London was supposedly out of bounds, at least 15 to 20 airmen hitched a lift there in a removal van, only to find it impossible to buy drinks as every establishment in the capital was crammed full to the doors with revellers. For those who remained at Dunsfold, a victory dance was held in the station cinema and Air Vice-Marshal Broadhurst arrived by air from the continent. His means of transport was a small Fieseler Storch which had been captured from the Germans in the Western Desert. Repainted in RAF markings, this versatile aeroplane had become Broadhurst's personal mount, along with a Spitfire marked with a sole letter B, and both these aircraft soon became his trademark and frequent visitors to Dunsfold. During the Normandy campaign, he had even taken Prime Minister Winston Churchill up in the Storch to survey the battle lines. On VE night at Dunsfold, however, the Storch came to a sad end. An exhuberant pilot fired a Verey flare into the frail aeroplane which caught fire and was totally destroyed. Fortunately, the AOC was able to pursuade the Germans to donate another Storch to him when he returned to Germany.* As VE Day drew to a close, free beer was made available to all ranks, leading one wag to note in 83 GSU's daily diary 'Never was so much drunk by so few in so short a time!' Other personnel elected to celebrate in a more sedate manner and several pilots, including Frank Webb, spent the evening in 'The Crown' at Chiddingfold, where a 'glow of respectable relief and good neighbourliness' pervaded the atmosphere.

After VE Day, life became relatively relaxed at Dunsfold. Bridge was popular, almost to the point of addiction, and a regime of flying and classroom exercises was brought in for half days only. Other diversions included a trip on a destroyer around the Isle of Wight. The end of hostilities did not, however, necessarily mean all danger was past.

The first reminder of this came on 9th May as a group of returning POWs had a harrowing experience when their Lancaster crashed on landing. Fortunately, none of those on board were hurt. Then, on 18th May 1945, Tom Hall was asked to test Typhoon JR531, which had been reported as having an intermittent engine problem. Hall recalls:

---

*Broadhurst's first Storch had a remarkable history. It had been captured from the Germans in the desert by the 8th Army, when it was discovered one night by British troops having just landed behind Allied lines for sabotage purposes. The engine had been kept ticking over for quick getaway purposes. It had served Broadhurst well as a communications aircraft through the African campaign, to Sicily and then to Italy before being brought back to England. After its destruction, a replacement example was flown back to Dunsfold, where it managed to survive the end of the war along with a number of other captured German aircraft including a Junkers Ju 52 and a Messerschmitt Me 108. On his eventual retirement from the RAF, Broadhurst joined the Hawker Siddeley's management and was thus again a frequent visitor to Dunsfold.

"I took off, got the wheels up, and held the aircraft down to build up speed. As I pulled up into a climbing turn to port, with plenty of speed, the engine cut out. The drill was always to go straight ahead, but as there was nothing but pine forest in front of me, and due to my initial early speed, I managed a fairly steep gliding turn back over the aerodrome boundary with wheels up. I had few worries, as the aircraft was so tough. I knew that it would hold together and, after the initial impact, it slithered along in a great cloud of dust. A check of the aircraft, after it had been lifted up, revealed that the carburretors were empty and the reason for the engine cut out was because the wing petrol tank valves had been put back in an upside down position. The purpose of these valves was to stop petrol flowing from one wing tank to the other when banking the aircraft. The effect of having them upside down was to cut off the petrol supply to the carburretors."

On 28th May, Squadron Leader Hampson stood down as station commanding officer when he left for Derby to seek election as the Conservative candidate for Belper in the forthcoming General Election. He was replaced on 7th June by Wing Commander Jim Hallowes DFC DFM, a former Battle of Britain ace and renowned fighter leader with over twenty German aircraft destroyed to his credit, including a share in a Heinkel He 111 which was the first enemy aircraft to be brought down on British soil. With his arrival from RAF North Weald, Dunsfold ceased to be a satellite of RAF Odiham and instead returned to a self-accounting basis. The following day, Dunsfold took over the parentage of RAF stations Friston, Lasham, Gatwick, Beachey Head and Wartling, the latter a G.C.I. radar station.

By June, 44,474 former POWs had passed through Dunsfold and the station's motor tranport had driven over 16,000 miles in just four weeks. After the first arrivals on 21st April, the station log had recorded the following movements throughout April and May:

Date	POWs	Transport	Date	POWs	Transport
22.4.45	346	16 Stirlings	13.5.45	2,895	36 a/c
23.4.45	777	29 Stirlings	14.5.45	3,113	124 a/c
24.4.45	1,069	38 Dakotas	15.5.45	3,117	96 a/c
26.4.45	53	2 Dakotas	16.5.45	1,417	50 a/c
27.4.45	214	9 Halifaxes	17.5.45	272	12 a/c
28.4.45	1,014	44 Lancasters	18.5.45	672	28 a/c
30.4.45	41	2 aircraft	19.5.45	896	31 a/c
03.5.45	385	15 a/c	23.5.45	1,406	60 a/c
04.5.45	1,564	66 a/c	24.5.45	1,196	51 a/c
06.5.45	1,021	43 a/c	25.5.45	750	30 a/c
07.5.45	212	8 a/c	26.5.45	2,499	60 a/c
08.5.45	1,667	72 a/c	27.5.45	532	21 a/c
09.5.45	3,953	160 a/c	28.5.45	936	33 a/c
10.5.45	1,662	71 a/c	29.5.45	503	20 a/c
11.5.45	2,090	97 a/c	30.5.45	1,631	68 a/c
12.5.45	1,752	69 a/c	31.5.45	96	6 a/c

With effect from 8th June, both Dunsfold and Ford received responsibility for accepting all ex-POWs from the Middle East theatre of operations and after 11th June, all repatriated POWs were supposed to be directed to either Dunsfold or Ford. This resulted in a further 300 POWs arriving from the continent on the 13th, followed over the next two days by 1,500 Canadian troops on the first leg of their repatriation from western Europe. Records show that 47,529 former POWs were welcomed before the aerodrome's role as an Air Arrival Centre formally ceased on 25th June 1945.

The ending of the POW flights did not bring tranquility to the aerodrome as 83 GSU maintained flying duties, still with the inevitable mishaps. On 25th May, Sergeant Pearson had overshot the runway at Lasham in Typhoon MN135 while Warrant Officer Lowrie crash landed Typhoon EJ907 near Petworth on the 29th. Both pilots were uninjured, bearing testimony to the ruggedness of the Typhoon in such situations. Flying Officer Eastman was not so lucky on 9th June when his Spitfire RM840 crashed near Lymington in Hampshire and Lieutenant Capstickdale SAAF was hospitalised when he crash-landed another Spitfire at Halton on the 13th. The next day, tragedy hit 83 GSU on their own doorstep at Dunsfold.

Flight Lieutenant Lewis RCAF, killed in the Typhoon accident on June 14th, 1945. (Photo Colin Brown.)

Leading Aircraftsman Jack Palmer and his 83 GSU colleagues were leaving the dispersals at midday for the cookhouse when they became aware of six Typhoons diving down towards the dispersals by 'The Compasses' gate, practicing rocket attacks. Suddenly, the note of one aircraft's engine made them look up and they were horrified to see a Typhoon at only some 400 feet in a vertical power dive. At seemingly the last moment, the Typhoon managed to turn slightly, missing the dispersals as it plunged behind the trees lining the bank of the Wey and Arun Junction Canal.

A muffled explosion was heard by the onlookers and one WAAF was physically sick on the spot as it was obvious the pilot would have stood no chance. From the end of one of the runways, Dave Howe, a Canadian pilot, was waiting to take off in a Spitfire Mk IX. He too watched the stricken Typhoon plummet earthwards and, as crash crews raced across the airfield towards the crash point, he also noticed a solitary object fluttering down from the sky and coming to earth a quarter of a mile away. When the crash crews reached the spot, a smoking crater showed where the aircraft, EK432, had buried itself into the soft earth of the canal bank. Several moorhens fluttered about on fire and shattered trees pointed to where the heavy fighter had smashed its path into the ground.

The pilot of the doomed Typhoon had been Flight Lieutenant Lewis, a fellow Canadian of Howe's. Lewis' body was found in the six foot deep crater and a subsequent Court of Enquiry heard that he was an experienced and steady pilot who had successfully completed a Spitfire tour in the Far East. He was familiar with the type and indeed had been the leader of the second section. His number two testified that Lewis had been unable to pull out of his dive at the prescribed 4,000 feet. His speed on impact would have been approaching 450 m.p.h. and Lewis had clearly been unable to control the Typhoon.*

The cause of this loss of control was attributed to an undercarriage door which had broken free, causing an unspecified aerodynamic attitude from which it was impossible to recover. At the Enquiry was another Canadian pilot, Frank Webb,† who had participated in the investigation. After the hearing, Webb was approached by Flight Lieutenant Miller, Lewis' best friend, with an unusual request. Miller explained that both he and Lewis had gone to great pains to illustrate their log books with photographs and information from the Far East tour which they had served together. Miller now held his dead friend's log book and was concerned that it should reach Lewis' family in Canada intact. By some unofficial sleight of hand, Webb was able to arrange this by personal courier.

From then on, 83 GSU's flying activities at last began to wind down and thus the steady trickle of aircraft losses also diminished. Despite Tempest SN126 being badly damaged by fire when starting up on 19th June, thereafter 83 GSU did not lose any more aircraft during their stay at Dunsfold. Taking advantage of the reduced flying, the station headquarters also

---

*In 1976, the Air Historical Group undertook a dig at the site and uncovered many parts of Lewis' Typhoon which had been buried in the soft earth. The instument faces, controls and even the pilot's watch were turned up, but the most startling find was one of the aircraft's 20mm Hispano cannon. The discovery of a live shell in the breech meant that the find had to be handed over to the Surrey Constabulary. To the present day, engine and fuselage wreckage can still easily be found the site being identifiable by the shattered tree trunk hit by the Typhoon on impact.

†Frank Webb enlisted in the RAF in 1939 as groundcrew, awaiting remustering to aircrew. In 1944 he had received his wings and commission in Canada. He had then returned to England in December 1944 and arrived at Dunsfold early in 1945. Before moving on to operational flying, he had to have corrective lenses fitted to his goggles. This delayed his posting to an operational Typhoon squadron and he was still with 83 GSU at Dunsfold until he was repatriated to Canada in August 1945.

arranged in July for the re-surfacing of Dunsfold's runways, using a sand and tar mixture which was found to produce a surface which was harsh on tyres. One aircraft to discover this was Percival Proctor HM400, paying a visit from the RAF Film Unit at Slough. The light aeroplane swung on landing and was badly damaged in the resultant crash. The pilot, Warrant Officer Bennett, was happily unhurt.

During the same period, 83 GSU underwent a change of rôle. Back in May, the unit had already lost its Communications Flight when it had been sent to the continent to join 83 Group Communications Squadron. The remainder of the unit was now tasked with receiving disbanding squadrons from the continent. First back were 401, 402 and 403 Squadrons RCAF of 127 Wing from Fassberg and Rheine in Germany. Their disbandment had commenced on 26th June at these airfields, but was not completed until 11th August 1945, while in tented camp at Dunsfold. Their headquarters and ground staff moved in on 9th July, followed the next day by their aircraft, 52 Spitfire Mk XVIs. These examples were brought back after the Wing had been required to exchange and leave behind in Germany its usual Spitfire Mk XIV types. As quickly as possible, the Wing's Canadian personnel were posted out, either back home to Canada or to the Pacific theatre. Before their departure, they were treated to the spectacle of Mosquito DD788 from 13 OTU joining the Dunsfold circuit on the 12th July with one engine dramatically ablaze. Despite having to execute a hurried belly-landing, pilot Flight Lieutenant Steele was unhurt.

On 1st August 1945, Dunsfold was reorganized into Biggin Hill sector. 83 GSU was renamed 83 Group Disbandment Centre in recognition of its new task and the next users of the Centre's facilities proved to be Dunsfold's old friends of 39 (Recce) Wing RCAF with 400, 414 and 430 Squadrons RCAF from Luneburg. 430 was first to arrive with 18 Spitfire XIVs on 7th August, followed on the 12th by 414 with 16 Spitfire XIVs and 400 with 17 Spitfire XIs. On the 22nd and 25th, 59 Typhoons of 143 Wing (438, 439 and 440 Squadrons RCAF) flew in after disbanding at Flensburg in Germany. Once again a familiar face was present since Paul Bissky, now a Squadron Leader and commanding officer of 439, ended up at Dunsfold for a third time before returning to Canada.

Following the return of the Canadians, a month's respite came in unit movements. The war in the Far East theatre had finished with the surrender of the Japanese on 15th August 1945, and as a general sense of relief settled upon the world this was reflected in a further lessening of activity in the peaceful Surrey countryside. By the end of August, only Friston remained as a satellite of Dunsfold as both Gatwick and Lasham were promoted to the status of forward airfields in their own right in the Biggin Hill sector. At Dunsfold itself, flying visits in various communications aircraft became a popular pastime, albeit records show that an element of light-headedness also seems to have crept in to this form of flying. On 18th September, Auster NJ636 was forced down through lack of fuel while returning from a visit to Woodvale and on 3rd October Miles Master W9032 landed in similar circumstances in open land at Betchworth, returning from Catfoss in Yorkshire.

In late September, the aerodrome again began to fill with aircraft. On 28th September, 1945 Wing Commander R. H. Thomas took over as the commanding officer of 83 GDC to find his new unit handling more and more Typhoons. The day before, some 50 Typhoon Ibs of 121 Wing (175, 181 and 182 Squadrons) were returned from Schleswig, while the 28th also saw 122 Wing headquarters arrive for disbandment with 486 Squadron RNZAF and 174 and 184 Squadrons RAF. While 174 and 184 returned their Typhoons Ibs from Flensburg and Lubeck repectively, 486 had been equipped with Tempest V aircraft at Flensburg. This latter type of aircraft was to remain in Germany with the occupation forces so the New Zealanders ferried back more Spitfires XVIs surplus to requirements. The next day, although not a 83 Group unit, 16 Squadron likewise began to fly in for disbandment. While all ground personnel had already reached Dunsfold on the 22nd, only a total of five aircraft were brought in, these being a mixture of Spitfire XIs and XIXs from Celle, Germany. 122 Wing completed its disbandment by 11th October but 16 Squadron lingered on until 20th October.

There were some sad sights at Dunsfold as the Typhoon squadrons returned to disband. From being a front-line machine, the Typhoon suddenly found itself no longer needed in the peace-time RAF. Leading Aircraftsman Darnley, a fitter with 49 Maintenance Unit at Faygate in Sussex, was sent to Dunsfold to put into practice his specialist skill of loosening propellers from their bosses. At Dunsfold he found no less than 100 Typhoons neatly lined up awaiting his attention. Once tough masters of the air over the battlefields of Europe, the Typhoons were now redundant and destined for scrap. To Darnley it was just another job and he methodically went along the lines carrying out his task. Only some time later, after his return to Faygate, did word reach him that he had performed his job just a little too well. The personal Typhoon of the commanding officer of 83 GSU had been parked on the end of one of the lines of surplus machines. Darnley had also neatly removed the propeller of this aircraft.

From 24th to 26th October, 1945, 83 GDC moved to Lasham with orders themselves to disband and hand over their outstanding commitments to 84 GDC, already resident at Lasham. As 83 GDC's ground crews despaired of packing and labelling what were now largely unwanted spares, thousands of nuts and bolts, brass and aluminium, were quietly dumped in the canal behind their dispersals. No doubt there they remain to this day!

While the future of Dunsfold now looked uncertain, another temporary rôle had been found for the aerodrome. Since May and June of 1945, RAF units had been stationed in Norway following the German surrender and, in *Operation Apostle*, had been helping set up the post-war Royal Norwegian Air Force. When 6130 Servicing Echelon arrived at Dunsfold on 20th October, 1945, this heralded the return of units of 88 Group in Norway. While the majority of returning formations were ground crews (of 6129, 6331, 6332 and 6334 Servicing Echelons), 88 Group Headquarters and 88 Group Communications Squadron, 276 Squadron, 128, 129, 130 and 132 Wings and various Supply and Transport flights, Embarkation and Signals units etc. returned by Dakota throughout November and December, 276 Squadron also bringing back nine Walrus amphibious aircraft. These had been performing air-sea rescue duties off the Norwegian coast and flew back from Gardemoen via Ghent on

10th November, 1945, 276 Squadron disbanding at Dunsfold four days later.

Another of Dunsfold's most famous visitors flew in on 5th December, 1945 when Spitfire RK197 dropped in, flown by none other than Group Captain Douglas Bader. Bader, released only a few months previously from German captivity, was calling on the station commanding officer Jim Hallowes. Hallowes had served under Bader before the latter was shot down over northern France and the two veterans of the Battle of Britain displayed an impressive array of medal ribbons between them.

The last RAF squadron to be officially posted to Dunsfold arrived on 12th December, 1945 when 667 Squadron flew in under orders to disband. This was an anti-aircraft and fleet co-operation unit which had previously been based at Gosport in support of the Portsmouth defences. Its aircraft were a motley collection of 10 Vengeance TT IVs, 4 Oxford Is and 13 Spitfire LF XVIEs. Despite their orders to run the squadron down, enough flying was undertaken to require a court of enquiry following the forced landing of Oxford PH210 in bad weather at Shalford near Guildford on the 17th.

On 1st January, 1946, Dunsfold again briefly assumed the parenthood of Lasham until the 8th February when 49 Maintenance Unit took over the Hampshire airfield. On 15th February, 1946, a farewell party was organised in the Officers' Mess to mark what should have been the formal end to Dunsfold's status as an active airfield and the transfer of Friston and Wartling to Tangmere's parentage. In practice, life continued very much as normal for a while. It was not until the 22nd of the month that 88 Group finally disbanded, followed on 26th February by a seemingly reluctant 667 Squadron who had managed to take ten weeks over their disbandment. No station commanding officer remained as Wing Commander Hallowes was posted on the 27th to another station, but still RAF Dunsfold lingered on.

For the next few months, detailed records of the use of Dunsfold do not appear to have been kept, but it is known that on 14th February, 1946, the aerodrome reverted to a Care and Maintenance basis, parented by RAF Tangmere. As such, Dunsfold lost its independence as a Forward Airfield but nevertheless remained within Fighter Command's control, supposedly on a non-flying basis.

Contrary to this official status, RAF aircraft are known to have remained at Dunsfold until at least May 1946. Aerial photographs taken by the RAF on 1st May, 1946 clearly show at least 4 Liberators and what appear to be 2 Halifaxes, or their transport equivalent, Haltons. These aircraft were parked on dispersal points but were sited by the Compasses gate, on the opposite side of the aerodrome to the hangars and technical site.

This photographic evidence is backed up by three other sources. Firstly, the log book of a former ferry pilot records the delivery, from Dunsfold to Prestwick in Scotland, of Liberator TS527 in February 1946. While not in the RAF himself, the pilot noted that the flight was for 41 Group of Maintenance Command, RAF. This Group, with its headquarters at RAF Andover, was responsible for collecting, preparing and delivering aircraft to and from the various RAF Commands. Secondly, an article in the Surrey Advertiser newspaper in May 1946 described a court appearance by nine boys, aged 14 to 16. All were bound over to keep the peace after being found guilty of entering a Liberator at Dunsfold, stealing a number of firemen's axes from the aircraft and using them to break into a storeroom. Justice Wenham of Guildford County Magistrates Court concluded that there had been "a lapse in security by someone in uniform who ideally should be court-martialled". Finally, a tale persists that the gold of the Yugoslavian government was flown back to Yugoslavia from Dunsfold aboard a Halifax around this time.

It would therefore seem that Maintenance, and perhaps also Transport, Command continued to make use of the aerodrome in 1946, probably due to the amount of space available for parking aircraft and also due to Dunsfold's relative proximity to London.

This proximity to London also led to unusual visitors on 8th June, 1946, the occasion of the Victory Day fly-past over London. Among the units taking part, the RAF's 164 Squadron and Fleet Air Arm's 816 Squadron both encountered bad weather after their run over The Mall. Overcast skies, heavy rain and thunderstorms gave 164 and 816 little hope of returning home to Middle Wallop and Lee on Solent respectively. When Dunsfold was sighted in a gap in the murk therefore, both formations' leaders thankfully gave the order to land, hurrying down into the circuit before the weather closed in again. The crews of 164's nine Spitfire IXs and 816's nine Firefly aircraft followed local tradition by pouring into Mrs Kirby's Gibbs Hatch Family Restaurant just outside the aerodrome. As Dunsfold was now no longer host to flying crews, the brief flurry of activity was a return to former times for Mrs Kirby and her daughter, rushed off their feet to serve the hungry fliers. Touchingly, as her own tribute to the wartime contribution of these squadrons, Mrs Kirby refused to take any payment for her lunches. Both commanding officers, Squadron Leader Farnes DFM and Lieutenant Commander Crabb, later wrote to Mrs Kirby enclosing squadron photographs and expressing their thanks for her generosity. Reflecting on the traumas of the poor flying conditions, Lieutenant Commander Crabb commented that "In fact, the lunch was the only good thing about Victory Day as far as we were concerned."

On 2nd September, 1946, Dunsfold was transferred from 11 Group Fighter Command to 24 Group Technical Training Command, having been finally declared an inactive site in August. Ever since March 1944, Air Ministry officials had commenced visits to assess the aerodrome's potential for post-war use, and in July 1944 proposals had existed for Dunsfold to become a School of Aeronautical Science and Engineering after the war. This planned use seemed likely to be endorsed when in June 1946, the Air Ministry confirmed that Dunsfold would be required for long-term use in the post-war RAF. This confirmation was in reply to calls from Surrey County Council that the land be returned to agricultural use, calls that had commenced twelve months before.

Despite the aerodrome's transfer to Technical Training Command, there was no evidence to support the requirement for long-term RAF use. Already, an Air Ministry letter dated 9th August, 1946 had instructed the RAF to make many of Dunsfold's facilities available until further notice to the Ministry of Civil Aviation, for use by Skyways Limited.

The end of an era had arrived.

Chapter Twelve
Skyways

Skyways Limited was a company which had been taken over and re-vitalised in May 1946 by Brigadier General Critchley, (former Director General of BOAC), Sir Alan Cobham and Captain Ashley, with offices in Piccadilly. The company had an expanding fleet of York, Lancastrian, Dakota, Dove and Rapide aircraft, available for worldwide charter work. Operations with their first York had commenced in May with a contract to the Persian Gulf. Skyways had then been successful in persuading the Ministry of Civil Aviation that they were in need of their own maintenance base and it was in response to this need that the Air Ministry's letter arranged facilities at Dunsfold to be made available to Skyways, with effect from 10th August, 1946. Two T2 hangars, the main stores, main workshops, office block, WAAF dining room, WAAF institute, WAAF ablutions, ten huts, garages, latrines and access to the control tower were all stipulated.

As can be seen from this list, in addition to the technical site on the aerodrome, Skyways were also granted use of the WAAF dispersed site just over Stovolds Hill. This was not the only dispersed site to be occupied, as an issue of mounting concern was the arrival of squatters who had moved into the other disused accommodation areas. Throughout September, Hambledon Rural District Council debated the problem, bearing in mind the then current severe shortages of housing. In trying to decide whether the squatters should be evicted, the Council complained that there was still no governmental plan for the aerodrome and this highlighted the fact that the local authorities had not yet even been informed of the arrival of Skyways. It was not until 11th October that it was formally announced that Skyways had temporary loan of the airfield, for the maintenance of their aircraft under contract to BOAC and BEA. On the basis of existing planning, the Air Ministry maintained that the aerodrome would definitely be required long-term for flying use by the RAF, but an undertaking had been given that the site would not be used for industrial purposes, as was then feared by the local authority.

Notwithstanding the continuing bureaucratic tangle, Skyways quickly settled in to make full use of their new home. As Dunsfold did not have its own customs office, overseas flights were operated via either Heathrow or Northolt, also enabling the company to make use of the en-route facilities of BOAC and BEA respectively and all aircraft then returned for maintenance and crew changes to Dunsfold where full night landing facilities were available. During the evening of 8th December, 1946, one such routine maintenance call led to an unusual incident. When Lancastrian G-AHCA returned to Dunsfold, the pilot reported that the cockpit heater was not working. After the aircraft was put away in the hangar, a mechanic went to investigate the fault and in the semi-darkness turned on by mistake a fuel jettison cock which was lightly wired into the 'off' position. A stream of fuel from the jettison pipe became ignited, possibly via an electric stove, and although the fire was contained with the help of extinguishers, the aircraft was destroyed, only a month after it had been delivered to Dunsfold. The hangar itself escaped damage and only slight burns were suffered by two mechanics who helped fight the blaze.

The company's first anniversary of operations came on 29th May 1947, Skyways by then being the largest air charter company operating in Europe. The company's annual report listed a current fleet of a Skymaster, Yorks, Lancastrians, DC3s, a Dove and a Rapide. The Lancastrians were used for fast, heavy freight carrying, with the plan that they would eventually be relegated to training duties once other aircraft became available. The company's principal contract was still the transport of oil company staff to and from Basra in the Persian Gulf, while cargoes from France and Italy expanded operations in late spring and early summer. Under consideration was the creation of a Far East subsidiary company in order to capture world-wide markets. Maintenance agreements had been signed whereby Skyways undertook the servicing at Dunsfold of the York and Lancastrian aircraft of F.A.M.A., the Argentinian airline which operated into London from South America. A recently won contract also gave a year's work to Dunsfold in delivering over 100 refurbished Spitfire Vb and Hurricane IIc aircraft to the Portugese Air Force. For the ferrying of the

Skyways aircraft were all given names prefixed by Sky, here a stewardess poses beside 'Sky Courier'.

aircraft to Portugal, a number of former A.T.A. pilots were used, including the famous woman pilot Mary Guthrie, normally Chief Stewardess for Skyways. On 29th October, 1947, Mary was lucky to escape a crash-landing near Reading while testing Spitfire W3950. The wreckage of this aircraft was brought back and languished at Dunsfold for some time before eventually being scrapped. Another wreck from the same contract was the last of the Hurricane batch for Portugal. This aircraft stubbornly refused to start for its ferry flight and was eventually removed from the contract. It remained in a corner of the aerodrome for some thirty years, gradually being reduced to only its fuselage framework by souvenir hunters. The makers' plate was rescued and photographs taken just in time before the remains were finally disposed of in the mid-1970s.

Another Skyways woman employee was Jane Tierney, later to become a successful novelist. Although holding a private pilot's licence, Jane was unable to obtain flying work so, like Mary Guthrie, she too had joined the ranks of Skyway's stewardesses. She was already familiar with Dunsfold as her husband had served as a 180 Squadron pilot at Dunsfold during the war and Jane had visited him in his officers' quarters in Stovolds Hill

Farm. By a complete co-incidence, today's owner of Stovold's Hill Farm is Jane's nephew. On her first visit to him in the property, Jane was startled by a strong feeling of déjà vu before she realised the connection.

At Dunsfold, Skyways were renting a good sized airfield with sound runways, hangars, control tower and living sites. Since moving in, more of the former RAF accommodation sites had been taken over, so that it was possible to accommodate a large proportion of the company's ground staff at Dunsfold. Four of the sites were used by single men (the work attracted many from the Polish Resettlement Corps camp in nearby Witley), or men living apart from their families. A fifth site was let out as married quarters. A total of 1,300 company staff were based at Dunsfold, excluding aircrew who numbered approximately 350. Those who worked for Skyways during this era recall the good team spirit in the company, on the accommodation sites the cameraderie of wartime returned as evenings were spent listening to the nightingales and washing in the open air, watched by families of rabbits. Almost everyone could quote, and believed in, the company's unofficial motto which was 'There's a right way, a wrong way and a Skyways'.

The attraction of the work offered by Skyways did lead to some local difficulties. In the post-war rush to build additional council housing, Hambledon Rural District Council already found it difficult to attract labour to undertake the new building works. Demand for housing was then only increased by Skyways bringing many newcomers into the area who also joined the waiting list for council accommodation.

The increasing tempo of Skyways' operations was unfortunately matched by the numbers of complaints from local people throughout the summer and autumn of 1947. In particular, Cranleigh School and Cranleigh Village Hospital maintained that Skyways aircraft were low flying at night and keeping people awake. The following month, the local Alfold Parish Council again applied pressure regarding use of the aerodrome, following complaints of engine testing during the three shifts operated by Skyways on a twenty four hour, seven days a week basis. There were calls, too, for roads to be reinstated through the aerodrome's site, but the Air Ministry still maintained that Dunsfold would be reclaimed as an RAF station in future and thus refused to lift the road closures which had been effected under wartime defence regulations. In November 1947, the South-West Surrey Planning Committee resigned itself to the fact that the aerodrome was a permanent feature, but still strongly recommended that commercial enterprise should be removed from the site. The Chairman of the Committee was particularly unhappy about the nissen hut accommodation provided by the so-called Skyways Hostel, which he described as 'a sort of slum'.

On Sunday 29th November, 1947, the aerodrome unhappily suffered a fatal accident involving a young navigator employed by Skyways, 24 year old Hugh Smyth-Piggott. Resident in nearby Cranleigh, Smyth-Piggott maintained a small Auster light aircraft, G-AHAJ, for his own use at Dunsfold and on the Sunday morning had taken off for Bristol with plans to visit his father, Group Captain Smyth-Piggott. Due to poor weather, however, he had landed at White Waltham before returning to Dunsfold.

In the early afternoon, he had again set off from Dunsfold for a trip to Shoreham on the south coast. Returning in the late afternoon, the Auster was seen by an eye witness, circling at low level on the outskirts of Cranleigh within the circuit for Dunsfold. While estimated at an altitude of only 60 feet, the Auster was cruising in level flight when its engine was suddenly heard to stop. The aircraft came down in a nose dive close to the Fullers Earth works at Baynards, near Cranleigh, the engine burying itself in the soft ground so that the fuselage remained vertical. There was no fire, but the young pilot was dead on impact. The cause of the accident remained a mystery, particularly as there had been a large meadow nearby suitable for a crash landing and no reason could be found for the engine failure.

In February 1948 the local District Council heard that despite earlier Air Ministry guarantees regarding future RAF use, the aerodrome was to remain as an industrial concern for at least ten years more, Skyways being expected to stay for a further four to five years. Concern still remained on the part of the Council over the poor housing conditions at the aerodrome and recommendations were approved to investigate and alleviate the problems as soon as possible. On a more positive note, the Air Ministry announced in early April that it would re-open the short section of footpath which had been closed under Defence Regulations, thus reinstating a through route from Old Rickhurst to Tickners Heath. Local opponents to the aerodrome were only briefly mollified!

In May 1948 further work came the way of Skyways when BOAC chartered their Skymasters for more oil company traffic to and from the Persian Gulf. BOAC had recognised it was uneconomical for their own types of aircraft to fly these routes, but the charter with Skyways overcame this. At the same time, at the request of the British government, Skyways began operating Lancastrians from the South African Transvaal to Madagascar. Sadly, May also saw the first fatal accident for Skyways in two years of operations. On the 13th of the month, their Dove G-AJOU crashed near Privas, south-west of Valence, in France. Among the fatalities were Earl Fitzwilliam and Lady Hartington, whose bodies were later flown back to Dunsfold.

Skyways' big break for success then came from an escalation of the Cold War in Europe. Following the Soviet blockade of land routes into Berlin, first the military, and then civilian operators, were called upon to airlift supplies into the city. Commencing on 4th August, 1948, *Operation Plainfare*, the civil aircraft effort, quickly snowballed and Skyways were in from the start with three of their Yorks (G-ALBX, G-AHFI and G-AHLV) on charter. This steady source of income, with the prospect of more to come, augured well for the future of the company and it was therefore a blow to high morale among the workforce when tragedy struck in their midst at Dunsfold.

During the night shift of Sunday 5th September, 1948, an explosion occurred in one of the main hangars. Harold William Carter, aged thirty, was squeezed up in one of the engine nacelles of a Skymaster aircraft in order to clean out an oil tank. Instead of using paraffin as recommended for flushing out oil tanks, Carter was using petrol. A fitter, Cyril Allen, was helping Carter when suddenly a terrific explosion was heard and Carter fell out of the engine, covered in flames. Scrambling to his feet, the unfortunate young man ran out of the hangar and on to the

Inside a Skyways hangar at Dunsfold. Left is a DC-4 Skymaster (G-AJPM) and right is a DC-3. (Photo BAe. Dunsfold.)

airfield, pursued by Allen and other workmates. Carter was caught and knocked to the ground where his colleagues succeeded in putting out the flames with an extinguisher.

Badly burned, but conscious and in shock, Carter was rushed to the County Hospital in Guildford, where he was admitted at 4.20 a.m. still alert and anxious about his condition. Sadly, some five and a half hours later, Carter succumbed to the combination of gross shock and extensive burns. At the subsequent enquiry, the Coroner heard that it was frequent, albeit dangerous, practice to substitute petrol for paraffin when cleaning aircraft oil tanks. In Carter's case it was found that the naked flame of a lamp had combined with petrol to cause a fatal explosion.

November 1948 saw the hoped-for airlift expansion when two Lancastrian tankers (G-AHBT and G-AKMW) joined Skyways' effort to Berlin. Partly as a result of the increased use of these aircraft, the same month saw the demise of one of the company's oldest aircraft with the scrapping of Lancaster Mk 1 G-AKAB 'Sky Trainer' (former RAF PP739), which had fallen into a sorry state after cannibalisation for spares. On 16th December, 1948 a

York of Skyways captured the honour of making the 5,000th civil landing of the airlift in Berlin, but from then onwards the company's fortunes suffered a series of bloody blows. Firstly, on 4th February, 1949 Skymaster G-AJPL 'Sky Wisdom' crashed at Castel Benito aerodrome in Libya, en route from Nairobi to Heathrow. Losing both port engines due to fuel starvation, the aircraft hit trees as the pilot struggled to retain control. In the resultant crash landing, eight crew and all forty passengers survived, but pilot Captain R. W. G. Kitley of Godalming was killed. Next, the crucial airlift operations were tragically hit when, on 15th March 1949, the first civil aircraft accident of the airlift occurred. After completing 147 sorties, Skyways York G-AHFI stalled on final approach to Gatow, Berlin and spun into the ground. The crew of three were killed instantly.

In April, Skyways added three more Lancastrians (G-AKSO, G-AKFH and G-AKSN) to the Berlin run, but within a month the Soviet blockade was lifted and the civil operation began to wind down. Before the Skyways commitment ceased in July, two further accidents ate into the company's assets. On 19th June, 1949, York G-ALBX was written off following a crash-landing in a field at Neustadt shortly after take-off from Wunstorf. Exactly a week later, Lancastrian G-AKFH was likewise written off in a landing accident at Gatow due to undercarriage failure, the crew being lucky to escape the resultant fire with only minor burns. The price for the company had been high in terms of aircraft, but 23,000 tons of supplies had been delivered in 2,749 sorties, the second highest number of flights by a civilian operator.

While Skyways had been busy with this tremendous effort, local politicians continued to ignore the much needed employment prospects that the company brought to the area. In June 1949, Surrey County Council had voted to press the Ministry of Town and Country Planning for the latest position on finding an alternative site for Skyways. On the other hand, protest meetings, mostly of employees and their families, were held in Guildford, Godalming and Cranleigh to support Skyways' continued use of the aerodrome. The meetings agreed to approach Prime Minister Clement Atlee, who coincidentally had

Skyways' Lancastrian 'Sky Lane'.

inspected the construction of the aerodrome in 1942 as Minister for Dominion Affairs.

Despite this, the Ministry of Town and Country Planning promised Surrey County Council that every effort would be made to find an alternative aerodrome better suited to Skyways' operations. In November 1948, the same Ministry had reported that such an alternative site had been found at Stansted in Essex, but by June there had still been no move on the part of Skyways, Surrey County Council being informed that there were difficulties in providing adequate accommodation at Stansted. Both Surrey County Council and Hambledon Rural District Council were opposed to the existence of the aerodrome, pressured by influential local land owners who begrudged the aerodrome attracting their labourers away. Not least of the aerodrome's opponents was Sir John Jarvis, MP for Guildford, whose estate in Hascombe was close to the aerodrome. Among the Skyways workforce itself, however, there were strong feelings for the company to stay in the area. A telegram to the Prime Minister asked for a public enquiry into the proposed move, a move which would affect over 1,000 employees, 75% of whom were ex-servicemen. It was pointed out that Skyways was the largest privately owned charter company in the world, then paying out over £60,000 each month to its employees. At the very moment that Skyways needed to convince their doubters, disaster struck. With the Berlin airlift finished and the air charter industry not holding the same profits as before, Skyways announced on 8th July 1949 that their Dunsfold workforce would be cut from 1,050 to approximately 650, bringing widespread redundancies. The company preferred to try to conserve its aircraft fleet and shed staff in the hope that trade would pick up again, but losses in revenue and aircraft accidents left Skyways in a sorry state and the future looked bleak. In October 1949, the local Councils began to fall out over the aerodrome's future. The Ministry of Civil Aviation had again recently confirmed that Dunsfold was still earmarked for future RAF use, but, with an eye to employment prospects, Godalming Town Council passed a recommendation that Dunsfold remain a civil aerodrome, even if Skyways were to leave. The Surrey County Council sourly observed that Godalming's recommendation was based purely on local considerations and pledged it would in no way affect county planning decisions. Although Sir John Jarvis then retired as the local MP, his successor, Mr G. Nugent, was a poultry farmer in Dunsfold and no more inclined to support Skyways or the aerodrome at this point in time than his predecessor.

In March 1950, Surrey County Council reiterated its dissatisfaction over the delay in resiting Skyways from Dunsfold to Stansted, but the problems then appeared academic. In February the Skymasters and Dakotas had been put up for sale at Dunsfold as the company faced up to economic realities. In March, Skyways went into voluntary liquidation.

Although Skyways managed to re-form on a limited basis with a much reduced fleet and workforce, their days at Dunsfold were now all but finished. If the local landowners scented victory, however, they were mistaken for two reasons.

Firstly, since December 1949 a top secret USAF Fighter Reinforcement Scheme had been formulated for the United Kingdom. This was a scheme whereby airfields were earmarked to receive additional American escort and defence fighter squadrons at times of international tension.* Air Ministry files show that Dunsfold, along with Blackbushe, had already been secretly designated as a reserve airfield for the RAF's Fighter Command. These two sites, joined by Tarrant Rushton, were now assigned to the USAF scheme, Dunsfold being marked down to receive a security squadron of F-84 fighters.

Secondly, in December 1950, the Ministry of Supply added Dunsfold to an existing suggestion of Blackbushe as a site for the new home of Hawker Aircraft Limited, then based at Langley in Buckinghamshire. A grass aerodrome, Langley was becoming unsuitable due to the growth of air traffic from nearby Heathrow, while at the same time, Hawkers' new generation of jet aircraft needed better facilities. Both the Ministry of Civil Aviation and the Ministry of Town and Country Planning strongly opposed the suggestion of Dunsfold, but the influence of the Ministry of Supply nevertheless prevailed and by March 1951 Hawkers were informed that the offer of Blackbushe was withdrawn and only the option of Dunsfold remained.

Not surprisingly, Hawker Aircraft Limited jumped at the offer of Dunsfold with its hard, long runways suitable for jet operations. The company was therefore granted a long lease of the aerodrome and began an association with the aerodrome which remains to this day.

*In 1951, Dunsfold was still designated to receive one squadron of defence fighters under what was then re-termed the USAF Fighter Deployment in War plan. The aerodrome was in the second priority group for development, this involving the addition to each end of the main runway of an operational readiness platform, a minimum of 75 yards in length. These were added at Dunsfold soon after the arrival of Hawker Aircraft Limited.

Chapter Thirteen
Hawkers - From Propellers to Jets

The new generation of jet aircraft for which Hawkers needed Dunsfold was already rolling off the Kingston production line.

The first of these types, the Sea Hawk, had generated its first order for 35 F 1 examples from the Royal Navy. Test flying had commenced from Farnborough, where Hawkers had acquired a single hangar in order to use the hard runways but, with the acquisition of Dunsfold, Sea Hawks could now be transported the twenty or so miles from Kingston by road for final assembly and test flying. Experimental test flying work was also now to be based at Dunsfold in one of the T2 hangars and to this end three Sea Furies (VW560, TF902, VX283), two of the early N7/46 pre-Sea Hawk naval design (VP413, VP422) and the sole surviving P1052 research prototype (VX272) also came to Dunsfold.

Of equal interest was the small collection of aircraft which served as a reminder of Hawkers' proud heritage in flying. Oldest was the 1924 Hawker Cygnet G-ABMB, sole survivor of just two examples built and now in non-flying condition. Soon seen in the air over Dunsfold were the Hawker Hart, a 1930s biplane light bomber (G-ABMR/J9941), Hawker Tomtit (G-AFTA/K1786) and Hawker Hurricane (G-AMAU/PZ865). The latter was already a well known aircraft, having been the very last Hurricane built, a Mark IIC. Hawkers had decided to keep the Hurricane themselves and since then it had distinguished itself in many air races, normally flown by the Hawker test pilots, but also at one time by Group Captain Peter Townsend in the colours of HRH Princess Margaret. The Tomtit, also the last surviving example of its type, was likewise used for air racing and was originally owned by Hawker's Chief Test Pilot, Squadron Leader Neville Duke, before passing to the company. Other types were Avro Anson G-AHXK, used as an executive transport, two Dragon Rapide biplanes, G-AHGC and G-ACPP, and a Miles Whitney Straight pilots' runabout, G-AEUJ, thus presenting a fascinating mix of the old and the modern in the aircraft flying from Dunsfold.

Avro 707B demonstrated at Dunsfold. (Quadrant 261168.)

One of the very first uses of the aerodrome by Hawkers provided an even more dramatic spectacle. Before the arrival of any Sea Hawk aircraft, Hawkers took advantage of the relatively good security provided by Dunsfold to display to the aviation press the results of recent delta wing development work. Within the Hawker Siddeley group of companies, Avro Aircraft Ltd. had undertaken such development with the Avro 707 series of aircraft, the design of which subsequently led to the scaled-up Avro Vulcan. It was the second such machine, the 707B, which was brought down to Dunsfold in the early August of 1951 from the Avro factory at Woodvale in Lancashire. Sleek and angular, the revolutionary design was shown off to full advantage by Avro test pilot Roland Falk, demonstrating an impressive and ear-shattering aerobatic repertoire before landing with the help of a brake parachute* and thus using up only

*This advent of the brake parachute also had a connection with the aerodrome. G. Q. Parachute Co. Ltd., a Surrey based market leader in the field, were permitted to use Dunsfold for testing purposes, this leading to their development of the world's first retractable aircraft braking parachute. The tests involved a modified Napier Railton racing car which roared up and down the runway, normally only at weekends when there was no flying. Weekends were also taken advantage of by Tommy Sopwith and other drivers of the Ecurie Ecosse motor racing stable. They too used the aerodrome's perimeter circuit for practice until local opposition to the noise put a stop to their activities.

a third of Dunsfold's main runway. The press representatives were highly impressed, even if local landowners were not !

As the Avro departed, Hawkers' staff continued to arrive, many transferred from Langley in the move which had tentatively begun in July 1951. The wartime squadron flight offices of Primemeads Farm and Broadmeads Cottage were designated as pilots' accommodation, the former for Chief Test Pilot Squadron Leader Neville Duke, who moved in in January 1952 and the latter, some two years later, for Squadron Leader Frank Murphy, head of production test flying. Both distinguished former wartime fighter pilots, Duke and Murphy were now well known countrywide at a time when test pilots were frequently in the news. Duke in particular had become famous during the war, receiving numerous decorations and running up a tally of 28 enemy aircraft to his credit. While Duke was able to quickly settle in at Primemeads, Frank Murphy discovered, like many a serving RAF officer before him, the peculiar drawbacks to Broadmeads Cottage. Rapidly, plans were advanced to at last provide services again to the picturesque house.

The remainder of Hawkers' flying team at Dunsfold represented no less expertise than that of Duke and Murphy. As number two to Duke on test flying duties, Squadron Leader Bill Bedford was a former RAF pilot who had served in Burma, flying Hurricane and Thunderbolts before instructing at the Empire Test Pilots School where he received the Air Force Cross. Having joined Hawkers in 1951, Bedford was also a highly accomplished glider pilot, holding several height and distance records. Assisting Frank Murphy were Frank Bullen and Don Lucey. Lucey was an ex-Fleet Air Arm pilot while Bullen, who had joined the company in 1949, was formerly a test pilot at Blackburns after wartime RAF Fighter Command service on Spitfires and Mustangs. One last flyer not to be overlooked was Bertie Coopman, now employed by Hawkers as Dunsfold's Senior Traffic Control Officer. Coopman was a former RAF Squadron Leader who had earned his wings in the first RAF, as opposed to RFC, flying class of 1918. During the Second World War, he had been one of the first fighter controllers and it was as such that he had come to know Neville Duke. On leaving the RAF in 1951,

Duke had encouraged Coopman to join Hawkers at Dunsfold where he soon brought a strict standard of discipline and efficiency to the tower. None of the pilots, regardless of their seniority, dared to ignore Coopman's advice.

Meanwhile, other accommodation was slowly being emptied as efforts continued to rehouse those remaining in the nissen huts of the dispersed sites. For a while a skeleton staff of Skyways stayed on, while those Skyways aircraft which had been left behind were either sold or scrapped. At least one remaining Skymaster was sold to a Australian buyer, this being the aircraft damaged in the fatal fire accident of 5th September, 1948, while a York lingered on for some time, tucked away in the gun butts. Eight Lancastrians also remained until they were all scrapped between 1951 and 1952.

Thanks to the arrival of Hawkers, many personnel who faced redundancy from Skyways were able to continue at the aerodrome with the new company which had much brighter prospects for the future. In addition to the Sea Hawk order, Hawkers had also received a contract for 198 aircraft of their latest P1067 jet fighter design - the Hunter. Both Hunter and Sea Hawk were subject to the government's 'Super Priority' category of funding and supply, designed to speed up the supply of new designs which were considered vital to the RAF and Fleet Air Arm.

On 25th October, 1951 the first production Sea Hawk F 1, WF143, arrived at Dunsfold for assembly, joining the prototype P1067 Hunter WB188 which was undergoing its early trials after a first flight at Boscombe Down on 20th July, 1951. A further six flights had followed before the Hunter was moved to Dunsfold, from where a triumphant display was flown at the Farnborough Air Show in early September.

Sea Hawk WF143 had its maiden flight at the hands of Neville Duke on 14th November, 1951 and flying duties at the aerodrome were now split between the two teams of pilots and the two types of aircraft being developed. Hunter test flying was undertaken by the experimental team of Duke and Bedford, while Murphy was responsible for allocating production test flying amongst himself, Lucy and Bullen, both for the Sea Hawks at Dunsfold and for the export Sea Furies at Langley, the latter aerodrome still in use for the piston engined types. If necessary, pilots were shuttled to and from Langley in one of Dunsfold's Dragon Rapide aircraft.

Subsequently, Sea Hawk deliveries commenced directly to the Fleet Air Arm at RNAS Ford in Sussex which was only a few minutes flying time away but, despite this promising start at Dunsfold, Hawkers were faced with a dilemma. Clearly, Kingston and Dunsfold could not continue to produce Sea Hawks if they were also to build the Hunter in volume. Plans were therefore made to switch future Sea Hawk production from Kingston to Armstrong Whitworth Aircraft Limited at Coventry, another member company of the Hawker Siddeley group. It thus became known at Dunsfold that the 35 Sea Hawks would be the aerodrome's first and last production batch. Instead, Dunsfold's future was to be firmly cemented to the Hunter.

On 5th May, 1952 the second prototype Hunter WB195 flew from Dunsfold piloted by Neville Duke and on 24th June, 1952 Dunsfold entered the supersonic age when Duke exceeded Mach 1.0 in a dive from 30,000 feet in WB188. As a result of this success, the Hunter was flown supersonically at Farnborough that year, but at the show Duke had the sad task of displaying the aircraft immediately after seeing his friend, John Derry, plunge to his death in the crash of the de Havilland DH 110 prototype. Duke's display was no less polished or professional despite the tragedy, sonic bangs being heard by the public from the Hunter's dive which began directly over Dunsfold.

Another earlier airshow performance by WB188 at Brussels in July 1952 aroused a great deal of interest amongst Britain's NATO partners, in particular Holland and Belgium. These countries were eligible for 'off-shore' funding from the United States in order to manufacture a modern fighter design. Consequently, two USAF pilots, Colonel Johnson and Major Davis, visited Dunsfold to fly the two prototypes in October 1952. With their professional seal of approval on the type, the Belgian and Dutch governments took the decision to adopt the Hunter as their standard fighter. Negotiations commenced with Fokker of Holland and Avions Fairey and SABCA of Belgium, for the licenced production of Hunters in their respective countries.

218

Three of the first production batch of Sea Hawk F1s. (Hawker Aircraft Ltd. via P. Amos.)

The last of the initial three prototype Hunters, WB202, flew on 30th November 1952. This being the first example to be powered by a Sapphire engine, rather than the standard Avon, WB202 was in effect the prototype for the already planned F 2 version of the design. Despite the nosewheel remaining down, the first flight of some 22 minutes was safely completed.

January 1953 saw the final Sea Hawks of the first production batch arrive from Kingston, heralding the end of a largely successful first production batch. The programme had not been entirely uneventful however, Frank Murphy having to carry out a belly landing at Ford in WF159 following an engine fire on 19th December, 1952. By March 1953, the Fleet Air Arm's 806 Squadron was operational on the type and only a pair of trials aircraft now remained at Dunsfold until 1954. This tailing off of the Sea Hawk commitment was perfectly timed, as on 16th May, 1953 Frank Murphy took up the first production Hunter F 1 WT555. The three Hunter prototypes meanwhile still worked ceaselessly to overcome niggling problems with the design; canopy misting, engine surging, condensation problems and lack of endurance being some of the more important early defects. The first prototype, WB188, in particular bore the brunt of many modifications, not least of which was the installation of a specially designed Avon engine with a reheat facility, thus giving over a third more thrust. The aim of this engine change

219

WB202 the prototype Sapphire engined Hunter F2. (BAe H1087)

was to stage an imaginative publicity coup for the Hunter - the breaking of the World Absolute Air Speed Record.

At this point in time, the record stood at 715.75 mph, pushed there in a blaze of publicity by Lieutenant Colonel Barnes of the USAF flying a North American F-86D Sabre on 16th July, 1953. Hawkers saw no reason why their new aircraft could not better this and, in Neville Duke, they possessed a pilot who had already participated in the RAF team which broke the record in 1946. By the end of August 1953, Duke and WB188 were ready and flew from Dunsfold to RAF Tangmere on the Sussex coast, close to the three kilometre course just off-shore near Little-hampton. The aircraft presented an imposing sight with a new pointed nose fairing and bright red gloss finish overall. Now designated as the Hunter F 3, WB188 made several practice flights in the hands of Duke during the first week in September, the only mishap being a minor accident while taxiing which required swift repairs to the undercarriage doors. On 7th September, 1953 weather conditions were ideal and Duke put the sleek aircraft along the course at an average speed of 727.63

WB188, the Hunter F3 in which Neville Duke broke the world air speed record. (BAe via P. Amos.)

mph (Mach 0.92), thereby returning to Dunsfold in triumph as the new world record holder.

A light-hearted postscript to the achievement came with the celebrations held on the evening following WB188's return. Numerous 'surplus' marker flares were fired off on the aerodrome and due to the presence of low cloud, their glare was reflected for miles around. Local police stations were inundated with telephone calls from the public, logging a variety of sightings from UFOs to forest fires!

Despite the success, there was a disappointing sequel to Duke's efforts. The end of the Korean War in 1953 led the British government to once again cut back on defence expenditure. Hawkers were advised to cease development work on both the reheated engine and an increase in wing sweep-back for the Hunter. WB188 therefore quickly lost its raison d'être and was relegated to RAF use, first as a ground instruction airframe and later as a gate guardian. Fortunately the significance of the aeroplane was belatedly recognized and it was spruced up for storage at RAF Colerne before an eventual move into RAF Cosford's Aerospace Museum, where WB188 resides to this day.

Chapter Fourteen

Hunter Production

As the Hunter now entered full scale production, Hawkers began to change the landscape of the aerodrome's technical site. The two war-time T2 hangars were clearly inadequate as production facilities and therefore work had commenced in 1952 to build a large three bay hangar complex between the T2s and behind the control tower. By August 1953, two bays were completed and they began to house the Hunter line while concrete was poured for the final phase.

The modern facilities and latest jet designs also attracted an increasing number of VIP visitors. King Hussein and Prince Hassan of Jordan were both given Hunter flights and, from the British royal family, both Princess Margaret and the Duke of Edinburgh made tours. On the occasion of the latter's visit, Prince Phillip asked Frank Murphy if he had personally known an ejector seat to fail. As Murphy laughingly pointed out, if he had, he wouldn't now be talking to the Duke!

Late 1953 saw further additions to the fascinating collection of aircraft using Dunsfold. Hawkers themselves operated an RAF Sabre, XD981, for control assessment and comparison with the Hunter and another company now came to the aerodrome bringing more types. Airwork General Trading were a company with a number of facilities around Great Britain, involved in the overhaul and refurbishment of military aircraft. Their main overhaul base had for some years been at Gatwick but, as with Hawker's experience at Langley, the advent of jet aircraft presented problems. Gatwick at that time was still a relatively small airfield with grass runways and while these had been sufficient for Sea Hornet and Seafire overhaul contracts, hard runways would be needed for new contracts involving jet Sabres and Attackers. Only twenty miles away, Dunsfold was ideal. Hawkers were willing to accommodate them and Airwork's activities matched the Ministry stipulation that Dunsfold only be used for test flying purposes.

Thus, Airwork's flight test facility moved to the wartime dispersals and blister hangars on the southern edges of the aerodrome, using two Bessonneau hangars provided by the

Ministry and sited near to the engine test beds which Hawker also agreed they could use. While just one or two Sea Hornets and Seafires were still to be seen in late 1953, the bulk of Airwork's time at Dunsfold was taken up with the overhaul of Fleet Air Arm Supermarine Attackers and RAF and USAF North American F-86 Sabres. The Attacker contract continued until the April of 1956 and left its mark on Dunsfold in more ways than one. In contrast to Hawker's jet designs, the Attacker was fitted with a tailwheel rather than a nosewheel. This caused the jet pipe exhaust to be much nearer the ground and Hawkers soon had cause for complaint to Airwork when they noticed that the Attackers were managing to melt Dunsfold's hard surfaces, which were still largely covered in the wartime mixture of bitumen and wood chippings. The work on Sabres continued until mid-1958, the aircraft either being returned to the RAF, or passed to the USAF after overhaul and refurbishment.

Under Chief Test Pilot Joe Tysko, a distinguished wartime Polish pilot, Airwork had handled over 100 Sabres and 40 Attackers when they left Dunsfold in 1958, their remaining facilities at Gatwick also having to close due to redevelopment of that airfield as London's second airport.

With the production of Sea Hawks safely out of the way, Dunsfold was now able to concentrate on delivering the first Hunter production aircraft to the RAF. Despite the first flight of WT555 in May 1953, it was to be some fourteen months before the RAF could accept its first Hunter F 1. In September 1953, pilots of the RAF's Air Fighting Development Unit had visited Dunsfold to fly WT555, but their first impressions found the Hunter lacking in its use of wing flaps for airbrakes. Production aircraft began to stockpile at Dunsfold while trials continued to search for an answer. Only in June 1954 was limited release of the F 1 permitted to the RAF, an airbrake fitted under the rear fuselage having provided the solution.

The performance of the Hunter immediately proved impressive in service use, albeit with continuing problems due to short endurance and engine surging. Hawkers had some of the answers in a production batch of 45 Hunter F 2 aircraft, built by Armstrong Whitworth alongside the Sea Hawk at Coventry. The F 2 used the Rolls Royce Sapphire engine rather than the Avon and proved to be virtually free from engine surge while at the same time consuming less fuel. These improvements in reliability and fuel consumption had also led to the first confirmed export order for the Hunter, 120 aircraft for the Swedish Air Force. While the contract, agreed in June 1954, entailed Hawkers producing the majority of the aircraft from their Blackpool factory, the first 24 were built by Kingston and flown from Dunsfold. Consequently, a number of Swedish Air Force pilots visited Dunsfold throughout 1954 and 1955 in order to monitor progress and become familiar with the F 2, development and trials work on this variant being undertaken from Dunsfold and commencing on 3rd November, 1953 when WN888, first of the production machines, arrived.

An even better solution to the Hunter's problems came in the form of WT701, which flew for the first time from Dunsfold on 24th October, 1954. This was the first Hunter F 4 of an initial order for 85 from the RAF. With increased fuel capacity and a surge-free improved Avon engine, the F 4 finally proved that the old saying 'If it looks good, it is good' applied to the Hunter. Sadly, the F 4 also brought tragedy through the seventh aircraft, WT707. During a flight to test fuel systems on 25th January, 1955, this aircraft suffered an engine failure over Sussex. As he headed for a powerless landing at nearby Ford, pilot Frank Murphy reflected that this was now his fourth such incident, all in Hawker aircraft and, stretching co-incidence to its limits, all into Ford. The sequence had started during his distinguished wartime service with 486 Squadron RNZAF flying a Typhoon from Tangmere and had continued with a Sea Fury test flight out of Langley and the Sea Hawk incident of December 1952. Despite a fast touch down at 230 m.p.h. Murphy nevertheless succeeded in getting into the airfield, but a combination of excess speed and the wet grass on which he made his belly landing, sent the aircraft bucking and skidding out of control. Some fifteen bounces were counted before the Hunter overran the boundary fence and continued on into a caravan site where three people were killed and two injured. Murphy himself miraculously survived the aircraft's disintegration, but nevertheless spent three months in hospital with cracked vertebrae. His flying helmet, today on display in Tangmere Aviation Museum,

The remains of the cockpit from Frank Murphy's Hunter F 4, WT707, after the crash at Ford on January 25th, 1955.

was split open and showed the indentations of all the canopy's bolt ends. It nevertheless saved his life.

Despite this setback, the F 4 Hunter was released for RAF operations and issued to the 2nd Tactical Air Force in West Germany. Fittingly, one of the first two squadrons to receive this variant, in April 1955, was Dunsfold's old friend 98 Squadron, now a fighter squadron within the 2nd TAF. Even more appropriate was the fact that 98's commanding officer of the time was none other than Squadron Leader John Smith-Carington, last seen at Dunsfold as a Mitchell pilot on 98 Squadron in 1944. For Smith-Carington and his colleagues, the Hunter F 4 proved a delight, a real 'pilot's aeroplane'.

The improvements of the F 4 also benefitted the Swedish Air Force. The first batch of the F 2s already rolling off the production lines for the service were converted to F 4 standard and designated Mk 50, the first example flying from Dunsfold in June and being delivered on 26th August, 1955. Prior to this, Sweden also purchased Hunter F 4 WT770 from the RAF's first production batch in February 1955 for evaluation, this aircraft thereby earning the distinction of being the first of many export Hunters. Others followed in March, when Major Sonderman of the Royal Netherlands Air Force took delivery of the first F 4 'pattern' aircraft on the 3rd, while Mr Anderson, of Belgian manufacturers Avions Fairey, flew out a second example on the 16th.

Denmark, like Belgium and Holland, was another NATO member looking to standardise its fighter force, albeit without the ability or potential to build its own aircraft. Thus Denmark had ordered 30 F 4 (designated Mk 51) aircraft from Hawkers in mid-1954 and the first example flew from Dunsfold on 15th December, 1955. Several Danish Air Force pilots were sent to Dunsfold where a training school was now flourishing, joining a dozen or so pilots of the Peruvian Air Force already undergoing conversion onto the Hunter. Peru had asked Britain for the urgent supply of modern jet fighters and the British Government therefore agreed to release sixteen of the F 4s only recently delivered to the RAF. This commenced in November 1955, and delivery by sea of all sixteen, re-designated as Mk 52s, was completed in April 1956.

Despite this reduction in their numbers of F 4 Hunters, the RAF were not left wanting as Dunsfold now had an even better Hunter for the service -the F 6. When the Air Ministry had advised Hawkers to drop development work on the P1083 design with increased wing sweep, they had nevertheless suggested that the company should consolidate on the basic design and instead seek to introduce larger versions of the Avon engine. This advice was followed by Hawkers and as early as 23rd January, 1954 the prototype F 6, with a more powerful Avon engine, was flown at Dunsfold by Neville Duke. This of course was some six months before even the F 1 entered RAF service yet, like its predecessors, the F 6 needed time to throw off engine surge difficulties as well as a new problem of 'pitch-down', both problems occuring during gun firing. Only when the Kingston factory finished the F 4 line in late 1955 was the F 6 ready to commence production. At Dunsfold, the test flying and deliveries of Swedish and Danish Air Force Hunters were completed, while development test flying was now concentrated on the two seat training variant of the Hunter, the T 7. The prototype of this

P1101 design, XJ615, was first flown on 8th July, 1955 by Neville Duke.

Just a month later, Neville Duke was to suffer an accident which eventually spelled the end of his test flying days for Hawkers. In August 1955, Duke took off from Dunsfold in Hunter WT562 to carry out gun firing trials. Off Littlehampton the engine failed and, like Murphy, Duke managed to make it back to Ford, thus saving the aircraft and consequently winning a Queen's Commendation for his efforts. After an engine change, an undaunted Duke collected the Hunter to fly back to Dunsfold from Ford. Shortly after take-off, when at only 1,000 feet, the Hunter lost practically all power. Thinking quickly, Duke turned for an emergency landing at nearby RAF Thorney Island. With insufficient speed he could not manoeuvre to line up on the runway and instead put down on the grass at over 200 m.p.h. As the aircraft bounced violently, Duke raised the undercarriage, but could not prevent the Hunter from careering on over the perimeter and crashing into a depression beyond. Emerging with spinal injuries which were to keep him from test flying for many months, Duke was later to realise that the number of the Hunter, 562, added up to 13 - just as that of his Tomahawk AN337, in which he had survived a desert crash during the war.

1956 saw a number of changes to the flying personnel at the aerodrome. To date, experimental test flying had been led by Neville Duke as Chief Test Pilot (CTP), assisted by his deputy Bill Bedford. On production test flying, Frank Murphy had led the original team of himself, Frank Bullen and Don Lucey, which had later been enlarged by David Lockspeiser, Hugh Merewether and Duncan Simpson in order to cope with the demands of the Hunter programme. Following his back injury, however, Duke discovered that pain occurred when 'G' forces were encountered. Therefore, in October 1956, he handed over to Bill Bedford as Chief Test Pilot to lead experimental flying, assisted by Hugh Merewether who moved over from production test flying. Frank Murphy was also to be replaced by Frank Bullen as head of production flying when Murphy moved into the Hawker sales team.

Broadmeads Cottage was left empty when Murphy moved to nearby Guildford in 1956, but when Neville Duke likewise left

Primemeads Farm, the old property continued as a pilot's residence since Bill Bedford then moved in. Promotion to CTP was not Bedford's only success that year. Building on the 1953 world air speed record success, Hawkers entered the Daily Mail London to Paris Air Race. While diplomacy required that the RAF's own Hunter entrant should not be beaten, Bedford, in a Dunsfold Hunter, managed to come second by the acceptable margin of thirty seconds! Free from any service opposition, Bedford also succeeded in establishing a new speed record for London to Rome return in a Hunter, also in 1956.

Although Dunsfold's Swedish, Danish and Peruvian orders were now completed, there was to be no lull in export potential for the Hunter. In April 1956, an Indian Air Force mission had visited Dunsfold and expressed great interest in the F 6 and the new two seater, raising high hopes of a future order. On the home front, the outlook was bleaker when 1957 brought worrying news for the Dunsfold workforce.

The White Paper announced by Defence Minister Duncan Sandys painted a bleak picture for the future of Hawkers. This notorious report predicted that manned military aircraft would no longer be needed in a future dominated by missiles. The English Electric Lightning, then still under development, would be the last manned fighter needed by the RAF. The Paper also meant the cancellation of the order for the last 100 Hunter F 6s for the RAF, a decision which sent a chill through the Dunsfold workers. Fortunately, they did not have to worry for long.

Taking advantage of the cancelled RAF order, the Indian Air Force contracted in July 1956 to purchase 160 Hunters in F 6 form and to be designated the Mk 56. The first 48 aircraft were examples withdrawn from RAF service and refurbished to India's standard. Several Indian Air Force officers joined the production test flying team at Dunsfold to help clear the aircraft for acceptance as soon as possible, returning to India by way of the initial delivery flights of the new aircraft. These flights commenced on 25th October, 1957 when Hugh Merewether in BA205 and Flying Officer Karnik in BA206 left Dunsfold for the sub-continent. Thenceforth, deliveries continued at a rapid pace and frequent visitors to Dunsfold were Canberras of the Indian Air Force which would regularly fly in a pilot to undertake a

Hunter delivery flight. This also appeared to entail a little unofficial shopping. It was reported that the delivery van from Debenhams department store in Guildford had been seen unloading at Dunsfold, directly into a Canberra's bomb bay. On another occasion, reminiscent of the wartime incident involving Curly Motheral of 180 Squadron, (see Chapter 10), even a motorbike was taken back to India in a Canberra's bomb bay. It was also alleged that gun ports of Hunters were occasionally jammed full of plastic containers holding beer!

There was now no looking back for Dunsfold, despite the British government's short-sightedness over the RAF's future requirements. The airfield buzzed with activity as Hunters of all types continued to roll off the assembly lines. Another six former RAF F 6 Hunters were supplied to Iraq in 1957, followed later by a further ten. From an original RAF order for fifty five two seater T 7s, ten aircraft were converted to have airfield arrester hooks and thus became T 8s for the Royal Navy, all the RAF and RN two seaters being delivered from the latter half of 1957 through to early 1959.

The beginning of a long association between Switzerland and Dunsfold began on 3rd April, 1958 with the delivery of the first of one hundred Hunter Mk 56s for the Swiss Air Force, the type having succeeded against competition from the American Sabre and British Gnat. Through U.S. funding, Jordan's Air Force also received six former RAF F 6 aircraft from 1958 to 1959, and the Lebanese Air Force benefitted likewise.

In Britain it was now recognised that the days of the Hunter as an interceptor were numbered and development work at Dunsfold shrewdly concentrated on the development of the F 6 for both ground attack and photo reconnaissance work. This brought about the FGA 9 and FR 10 respectively for the RAF and involved Dunsfold in the conversion of F 6 aircraft from 1958 through to the mid-1960s.

Another Hawker design had reappeared at Dunsfold in 1957 when the company decided that considerable overseas interest still existed in their Sea Fury aircraft, then being phased out of Royal Navy service. Consequently, a large number of surplus F 10, FB 11 and T 20 variants were bought back from the Fleet Air Arm and flown into both Dunsfold and Hawkers' facility at

Blackpool. While orders from Cuba and Burma, for 21 and 17 aircraft respectively, accounted for many of the Blackpool examples, those at Dunsfold continued to languish on the old wartime dispersal areas in the north eastern corner of the aerodrome. It transpired there had been over-optimism on the part of the sales team. Dunsfold did, however, play a part in the delivery of the Cuban order. Pilot Don Lucey and technical expert Len Hearsey were sent from Dunsfold to Havana to represent the company. Arriving just in time to be caught in the middle of Castro's revolution, both were fortunate to flee the country at the last moment by ship, using false identities.

Chapter Fifteen
Vertical Take-off

The advent of the 1960s brought the contrast of the arrival of Hawker's latest design alongside one of their oldest. On 8th February, 1960 the latter arrived at Dunsfold in the shape of Sopwith Triplane N5912 by road, for restoration to museum display standards. At the other end of the scale, while export sales of the Hunter went from strength to strength, another Hawker design was taking shape which was to catapult Dunsfold to the forefront of aeronautical development throughout the world.

Designated P1127, the revolutionary design aimed to produce a vertical take-off and landing military jet aircraft. While other companies and other designs, notably in the United States, had toyed with the principle of VTOL, none had proved successful enough to merit production. In Great Britain, however, Rolls Royce had already undertaken a great deal of experimental work on a vectored thrust engine that was to be named the Pegasus, the concept of vectored thrust involving four swivelling nozzles from the engine. These were able to direct thrust from the conventional rearwards direction to a downwards direction, thus allowing the aircraft vertical movement. They also, to a lesser degree, enabled thrust to be directed forwards, permitting backwards movement of the aircraft. It was around this engine that Hawkers designed the P1127 and, in the spring of 1960, work began on the construction of a gridded pit, close to the end of Dunsfold's main runway. The pit was planned to vent away the downward thrust which would come from the new aircraft during hover trials and, in addition to this, an engine running pen was similarly modified, with below surface ducts necessary to channel away exhaust emissions.

The Air Ministry had ordered two prototypes of the P1127 from Kingston and on 15th July, 1960 XP831, the first prototype, arrived by road. Official roll-out of the assembled aircraft took place on 31st August, 1960 and engine tests were then run throughout September and the first half of October. In one of these tests, the all important prototype was almost lost when a fuel leak led to a fire in the confined space of one of the

231

engine running pens. Thereafter, all engine tests were performed out on the airfield where faster access to any problems was guaranteed.

By the latter half of October, the P1127 was cleared for its historic first flight - but what of the pilot? Chief Test Pilot Bill Bedford had just managed to break a leg in a car accident in Germany, shortly after flying a Hunter demonstration. His ankle was therefore still in plaster when the P1127 was finally ready for its first flight, but Bedford was not to be deterred. The aviation authorities' medical board eventually gave Bedford a clearance unique in the annals of aviation medicine: 'Fit, civil test pilot, tethered hovering only'. On 21st October, 1960 Bill Bedford lifted XP831 into the air for the first time to a tethered height of twelve inches. Besides his plaster cast, Hawker's Chief Test Pilot was also distinguished by another peculiarity. The Pegasus engine originally had such limited power that weight considerations were crucial. The conscientious Bedford could therefore be seen wearing plimsolls rather than his standard heavy flying boots. This 'soft shoe' approach was not inappropriate for such a revolutionary new aircraft. Matching Bedford's medical improvement, the flight envelope was only carefully and slowly extended, untethered flight not being permitted until November 1960 and the first transition from vertical to horizontal flight only followed in September 1961. Bill Bedford graphically described this sensation as similar to 'a brick sliding across ice'.

Early problems and shortcomings were inevitable and numerous in such a remarkable new design. In particular the inflatable edges to the prototype's engine intakes 'flapped like a spaniel's ears' according to Bedford, while more difficulties were encountered with the P1127's unusual outrigger wheels. Advice had already been proffered on the latter from an unexpected source - 'you mark my words, you'll have trouble with those things' had been the comment from the employee who pushed the tea trolley in the experimental hangar. As the man had shrewdly noted, his trolley had similar wheels to the outriggers and wheel shimmy badly affected the trolley's stability. Just as he had prophesied, the P1127 suffered similarly.

XP831, the prototype P1127, undergoing tethered hovering trials in October, 1960. (BAe. 302/60)

Yet another era in Dunsfold's history had begun on 20th February, 1961 with the arrival of the Folland Aircraft Company, bringing with it the Hunter's trainer rival, the Gnat T 1. Follands had previously operated from Chilbolton aerodrome in Hampshire but, on joining the Hawker Siddeley Group, it had been decided that rationalisation could lead to the disposal of Chilbolton. On their first day at Dunsfold, Folland flew in an interesting variety of aircraft, XM691, XM692 and XM696 being Gnat T 1 trainers and closely followed by XK741, the sole Gnat F 1 fighter variant to come to Dunsfold. The latter had only attracted export orders rather than any interest from the British Government but fortunately the T 1 trainer version had been selected by the RAF. The arrival of the Gnats was in turn followed by two Meteor T7s, WA690 and WF877, which had been highly modified to test Folland's own ejector seat design. The pre-Gnat Folland Midge design also came to Dunsfold, but in a non-flying condition.

Four days later Gnat T 1 XM694 arrived, joined by XM697 and XM698 and the pre-production aircraft XM704 to XM709. Most of these aircraft made their first flights from Chilbolton before landing at Dunsfold. It was not to be until 25th June, 1962 that the first Gnat assembled at Dunsfold, XP500, made its first flight, this and future airframes being delivered by road to

Folland Gnat XM693 at Dunsfold in September 1961. (BAe.)

Dunsfold from the Hamble parent factory, with just the wing tips removed. All Gnat test flying at Dunsfold was undertaken by a team led by Folland's Chief Test Pilot, Squadron Leader Ted Tennant.

As the Gnats settled in to their new home, test flying continued on the P1127. While a test flying programme is designed to test most elements of an aircraft's abilities and equipment, one fitting which hopefully remains untried is the ejector seat. On 14th December, 1961 however, the P1127's Martin Baker seat was tested in a drama involving XP836, the second prototype, during a low level high speed run over the Wiltshire countryside. Pilot Bill Bedford recalls that the first hint of trouble came from an abrupt lateral rocking motion accompanied by a roaring noise and rapid deceleration.

"I immediately called up the Naval Air Station at Yeovilton to make an emergency conventional landing. On final approach, however, the aircraft progressively rolled to the left and, even with course stick and rudder movements, I couldn't hold it. I decided I would have to build up more speed to regain control and I therefore fed on the power. That was it! At only 200 feet and 200 m.p.h. the aircraft went, not so much quickly but rather in a very determined manner and I knew the sands of time were running out.

"In those days there was no rocket ejector seat, just the ordinary cartridge seat and I knew it was going to be marginal. I was not sure if I was going to make it but the words of the seat's designer, the great Sir James Martin himself, went through my mind. We had discussed how

234

Three P1127 prototypes (L-R XP831, XP976, XP980) in 1963. (BAe. P1127 109/63.)

best to get out of a VTOL aircraft if the engine failed in a hover. The advice of Sir James had been "Bill, if you are ever short of time, use the handle between your legs." So, adrenalin pumping, I grabbed the handle and shot through the canopy. There was a big tug as the parachute deployed and as I looked down at my feet I hit the ground. The aeroplane hit a barn nearby and blew up.

"The whole business had been quite a surprise, such was the rapid deterioration from a moderate emergency to a dire disaster. I picked up my stop watch which was still ticking and walked around feeling rather relieved and happy to be alive. Very soon a Royal Navy helicopter arrived and I was hauled aboard. I remember being impressed by the thick blue carpet in the helicopter and worrying about the effect on it of my muddy flying boots.

"Back at Yeovilton I had a quick check-up in the sick quarters and then made a 'phone call to Dunsfold to explain about the crash. A brandy and ginger, followed by lunch, completed my day out before I was returned to Dunsfold by the Royal Navy."

Two days later the cause of the crash was explained when a farmer found one of the fibreglass rotating nozzles which had come off at high speed. The design of the nozzles was subsequently changed to stainless steel.

A return to RAF squadron use came briefly in the late summer of 1961 when on 30th August, 92 Squadron was deployed to Dunsfold for a week with fifteen Hunter F 6s and two T 7s for the Farnborough Air Show. The service pilots were fascinated to obtain a first-hand view of progress on the P1127, but there was clearly still a great deal of development work to be done. On 30th October, 1962 however, problems again hit the P1127 programme when the third prototype, XP972, suffered an engine bay fire while flying from Dunsfold. Despite poor weather conditions of cloud and rain, pilot Hugh Merewether elected not to eject and managed to find and reach RAF Tangmere, where he succeeded in landing without power on the grass. Although the aircraft was ultimately scrapped, Merewether deserved the highest praise for preserving the engine for examination and identification of the problem. His bravery was later recognized by the award of an OBE.

On a more positive note, the same day as Merewether's crash saw the arrival at Dunsfold of a Belgian licence-built Hunter, bought back by Hawker Siddeley Aviation Limited (as Hawkers had now been re-titled) after completing its useful life in the Belgian Air Force. This heralded a new chapter in the history of the Hunter since, although export demand for the type still remained high, the Kingston production lines were now dedicated to the P1127. The option left was for Hawker Siddeley to buy back, for refurbishment, both overseas licence-built examples and those aircraft already supplied directly from Dunsfold. The viability of this was proved when it was discovered that of the first batch of F 6 aircraft phased out by the Belgian Air Force in 1962, many had only flown around 300 hours. From late 1962 to 1966, no less than 96 ex-Belgian Air Force Hunters were bought and flown in to Dunsfold by the aerodrome's test pilots, with all traces of previous ownership removed.

Other Hunters were traced and obtained from a variety of unlikely sources. One such source was an Air Training Corps unit in Birmingham which had enthusiastically painted its Hunter in a garish bright green and brown camouflage scheme, the whole being liberally coated with bird droppings from storage outdoors. Despite its sorry state, the Hunter was returned to Dunsfold for refurbishment and sold several months later in pristine condition to the Swiss Air Force.

Hawkers had also repurchased 45 Hunter F 4s from the RAF, but soon appreciated that, unlike the F 6, the earlier F 4 did not possess the stronger wings needed for carrying external stores. While some examples were converted to GA 11 standard for the

Royal Navy, many remained on Dunsfold's dispersals. Among the F 4s were to be seen a number of machines in the markings of 98 Squadron and thus once again the squadron's colours were seen at Dunsfold as they had last been in 1944 on the aerodrome's Mitchell bombers. By 1966, all but one of the surplus F 4s had met its end at the hands of the scrapman.

1962 saw the commencement of deliveries of Dunsfold's Gnat T 1s to the RAF, the first being on 2nd February, 1962 and flown by Dick Whittington. Heavy snow falls soon after meant that Dunsfold was temporarily closed and Gnat delivery flights to the RAF were consequently halted. Eager to maintain the delivery programme, the RAF hit upon the idea of trailering the aircraft to Gatwick Airport, which was still open, in order to fly them out. No sooner had the first RAF team arrived at Dunsfold and loaded up their trailer when a sudden thaw cleared the runway and negated all their hard work.

Pilots of the Royal Rhodesian Air Force were to be found at Dunsfold in December 1962 to fly out the first two of an order for twelve Hunter FGA 9s, all former RAF F 6s. Another overseas departure, in May 1963, was the company's celebrated demonstrator, Hunter T 66A G-APUX which left Dunsfold on loan to the Iraqi Air Force, pending delivery of Iraq's own Mk 69s.

G-APUX later went on to perform a similar temporary service for both the Jordanian and Lebanese Air Forces before returning to Dunsfold. It was then again converted, this time to T 77 standard and, as J-718, was delivered to the Chilean Air Force in August 1967. If this sequence of service life were not enough, it should be noted that G-APUX was originally an amalgam of no less than three different Hunters, one two seater and two single seaters. By the end of its career this aircraft, in various parts and guises, had flown in six air forces.

In February 1963, came the first landing of a jet VTOL aircraft aboard an aircraft carrier when on the 8th, Bill Bedford flew XP831 from Dunsfold to HMS Ark Royal in the English Channel. The Royal Navy were not entirely welcoming as they wanted to keep their large aircraft carriers and the P1127 was seen as a threat to this aim. Following the trials however, the Flag Officer (Aircraft Carriers) admitted that he had been most impressed by the demonstration and, even more so, by the complete absence of fright on the part of the spectators. Normally, said the Admiral, new aircraft came aboard bigger, heavier and faster, yet the P1127 was the complete opposite to this trend. As the commanding officer of the Ark Royal's air component remarked, "You have proved that it is far better to stop and land rather than land and try to stop." Twenty five years later, Bill Bedford was delighted to re-enact that landing when, on 8th February, 1988 he was flown in a Royal Navy two seater Sea Harrier to the latest HMS Ark Royal. He maintained that the experience had made him feel twenty five years younger and asked to be put down for the fiftieth anniversary by which time he will be ninety years old.

The same day as Bedford's historic carrier trials, Dunsfold delivered to the RAE at Farnborough another new Hunter variant, the sole Mk 12. This was a two seater conversion from an F 6 and was to act as a trainer for the TSR 2 aircraft, incorporating a Ferranti head up display and a large vertical camera mounted in the nose. The aircraft was painted in an attractive green and white colour scheme and served all its active life at Farnborough until destroyed in an accident there in 1982.

A somewhat unexpected final bonus came the way of Dunsfold's neglected Sea Furies when an order was placed by a German company requiring target towing aircraft. Eventually a total of six TT 20s and one FB 11 were refurbished and supplied, all being delivered from Dunsfold to Cologne between March and September 1963. Despite this order no others were forthcoming and, of the surplus numbers left on the aerodrome, only a few more were to escape the scrap man. Those that did were sixteen FB 11s and two T 20s which were delivered by road to the Dutch Air Force at Deelen in Holland between February and June 1964. These were to take the place of twenty-two Dutch Hunters which Hawker Siddeley had discovered were about to be condemned to runway fire fighting exercises at Deelen. Taking their place, the Sea Furies soon came to a fiery end, but the Hunters were flown to Dunsfold by the Dutch Air Force between February and April 1964 for refurbishment and a second life. In early 1965 four more Hunter T 7s were returned from Holland.

For the Sea Furies left behind at Dunsfold their end came when Coley's Scrap Metal Company was invited on to the aerodrome to take apart and remove the remaining airframes. Along with the Sea Furies, Gloster Javelin XH760, which had also somehow found its way to Dunsfold's dump, was likewise removed.

One other Sea Fury was fortunate enough to escape both the one way trip to Holland and the scrap man's intentions. It had been noted that FB 11 TF956, the very first production FB 11, was languishing amongst the unwanted airframes. Further investigation revealed a distinguished flying record, since TF956 had seen action during the Korean War aboard HMS Theseus. With 807 Squadron for over 200 hours of operational sorties, it had twice been hit by enemy flak in April 1951, and still carried the scars of repairs on its rear fuselage. When the Hawker historic fleet was donated to the RAF in late 1971, the Sea Fury was initially included, but clandestine negotiations ensured that TF956, 80% restored, was spirited away to eager Royal Navy hands at Yeovilton. Admiral Fell subsequently asked Dunsfold's then Chief Test Pilot, Duncan Simpson, down to Yeovilton to perform the restored aircraft's first flight on 20th January, 1972. For many years TF956 provided pleasure at hundreds of air shows throughout the country as part of the Fleet Air Arm's historic aircraft flight. Sadly, in 1990 the aircraft was lost when, following an air display, its undercarriage failed to lower for landing and its pilot was forced to bale out and ditch the aircraft in the sea.

The Paris Air Show of 1963 was to have been an opportune moment for Dunsfold to display the P1127 against the French Dassault Balzac design which was shaping up to be the main competitor to Hawker's aircraft. The French aircraft, using the lift jet principle rather than vectored thrust, was reliant upon a sturdy concrete platform built especially for the purpose in front of the crowds. The P1127 had no such need and its display, flown by Bill Bedford on 16th June, was to amplify this by a final landing on the grass close to the concrete platform. After the Balzac had gone through its paces, Bedford put the P1127 through an outstanding display before transitioning to a straightforward low hover before landing. Suddenly, the aircraft lost thrust due to a nozzle malfunction. There was no option but to carry out an immediate belly landing, first hitting the concrete platform before landing heavily on the grass in front of the startled spectators. Perhaps not surprisingly, the French took little further interest in the P1127.

On 7th March, 1964 a modified and improved version of the P1127, the Kestrel FGA 1, made its maiden flight from Dunsfold. This was the first of an order for nine such aircraft, funded by Great Britain, West Germany and the U.S.A. Under this arrangement, a Tripartite Squadron was formed to evaluate the type with British, German and American service personnel. Conversions for the pilots began at Dunsfold in early 1965, where four representatives of the RAF were joined by two pilots of the US Army, one from the US Navy, one from the US Air Force and two officers of the German Luftwaffe. In the latter contingent was Colonel Gerhard Barkhorn who had finished the Second World War as the Luftwaffe's second highest scoring fighter pilot with a remarkable total of 301 enemy aircraft destroyed.

After the Tripartite Squadron had formed and converted to the Kestrel at Dunsfold, it then moved to begin its evaluation operations at RAF West Raynham. Thus, while the Kestrel now led the way as the P1127 family's latest off-spring, none of the nine examples produced remained at Dunsfold and it was therefore the surviving P1127 prototypes which bore the modifications and improvements necessary to continue refining the design. On 19th March, 1965 XP984, the sixth and final prototype P1127, had to force land at RAF Thorney Island while on a test flight from Dunsfold. Although damaged, the aircraft was repaired and continued its test flying career until destroyed on landing at RAE Bedford in 1975.

The last Gnat to be delivered to the RAF, XS111, left Dunsfold on 14th May, 1965 going directly to the famous Red Arrows aerobatic display team which had flown Gnats since the team's creation in 1964. XS111 marked the end of the Gnat era in one respect as, gleaming in its bright red finish, it made a last low pass over Dunsfold's runway before setting course for RAF Fairford. In another respect, Dunsfold continued its association

The Tripartite Evaluation Squadron with a Kestrel. Colonel Barkhorn is standing second from the right. (BAe. P38/65.)

with the type as the RAF's T 1s periodically returned for modifications and overhauls.

After the completion of Gnat deliveries to the RAF, one trials aircraft, XM697, remained at Dunsfold. This languished at the back of a hangar before eventually being donated to 1349 Woking Squadron of the Air Training Corps where it was painted in Red Arrows colours and kept for many years. In recent times the aircraft has been sold on and is expected to be restored by a private owner to flying condition. One final unofficial legacy of the Folland move to Dunsfold was the aerodrome's connection with Donald Campbell's fatal attempt on the world water speed record. His Bluebird boat was powered by an Orpheus engine which had already been donated by Dunsfold from a Gnat. When Campbell experienced hydraulic pump problems, Dunsfold again quickly stepped in by providing the expertise to solve the difficulties, but it was on his very next attempt that Campbell was killed on Lake Coniston in 1967.

In mid 1965, the decision had been taken to replace the company's two Dragon Rapide aircraft with a single DH Dove,

G-ASMG. Rapide G-ACPP had already been sold in 1961 to Canada, but Dunsfold's complement of the type had been restored to two when G-AHAG was transferred from Brough in 1965. By October of the same year, the wings of both G-AHGC and G-AHAG had been removed and placed on the bonfire ready for 5th November when a prospective buyer telephoned from Cornwall.* For only £200 G-AHGC was salvaged and left the aerodrome in the spring of 1966 to serve the Land's End to Scilly Isles passenger route for several years. Even the picked over remains of G-AHAG were subsequently saved for restoration.

Following the important Kestrel tripartite trials, the first of six pre-production P1127 (RAF) aircraft, XV276, flew on 31st August, 1966. While very similar in appearance to the Kestrel and the original P1127, this variant was in fact 90% redesigned and powered by an uprated Pegasus engine. In recognition of the differences, yet another name was announced, a name which was to become known world-wide - the Harrier.

The six pre-production Harrier GR 1 aircraft were retained by Hawker Siddeley for extensive trials work at Dunsfold, paving the way for a production order for sixty aircraft which was duly confirmed by the British Government in early 1967.

With the immediate future of the Harrier now secure, Bill Bedford stepped down from test flying after a remarkable period as Chief Test Pilot. While he too joined the Hawker Siddeley sales team, his CTP duties were assumed by Hugh Merewether. From December and throughout 1968, Dunsfold concentrated on clearance trials for RAF operations, testing the Harrier's ability to carry additional fuel tanks, bombs and rockets. At the same time, demonstrations were flown for anyone thought to be a potential customer, a Harrier already having been flown from Dunsfold for trials aboard the Italian Navy's carrier, the Andrea Doria, in October 1967. A steady stream of foreign pilots, impatient for the Harrier to visit their countries, also made their way to Dunsfold, eager to test the revolutionary new design.

---

*Another 'plucked' fuselage to be found on the aerodrome from the latter half of the 1960s onwards was Avro Ashton Mk II WB491. One of only six Ashtons built, the type was a conversion of the Avro Tudor airliner and was used as a research aircraft, fitted with Nene turbojets. WB491 had ended its research days at RAE Farnborough before being purchased by Surrey Constabulary and sited at Dunsfold for incident practice, on one of the wartime dispersal points within the perimeter track.

Most prominent of these came from a country which had not even been targetted by the Hawker Siddeley sales team - the U.S.A.

In September 1968, staff in the company's chalet at the Farnborough Air Show were startled when a General and two Colonels of the United States Marine Corps walked in and announced, "We want to fly the Harrier." Within a fortnight Colonels Miller and Baker were at Dunsfold to do just that and returned home full of praise and keen to order the aircraft. In a country traditionally loathe to purchase weaponry from overseas, the Marines would clearly have to battle with their government for the Harrier.

1969 began with an influx of the blue of RAF uniforms when in January the pilot instructors and groundcrew of the RAF's newly formed Harrier Conversion Unit arrived. Their job was to learn how to deal with their new aircraft, now rolling off Dunsfold's final assembly lines and scheduled to begin deliveries to 1 Squadron at Wittering on 18th April. Of the first production batch, the sixth example, XV743, was fated not to survive the short wait for delivery. Just five weeks after its first flight, the Harrier was being used on 27th January, 1969 by Major C. R. 'Chuck' Rosburg, a highly experienced pilot who had been evaluating the Harrier for the US Air Force. Rosburg's final flight began with a vertical take off from the small pad sited in the copse within Dunsfold's perimeter track. He was accelerating into his transition to horizontal flight when the aircraft began to sideslip, inducing what is technically known as 'momentum yaw'. While the dangers of this had already been experienced and identified, it was later suggested that Rosburg, taking off into the sun, may have been unable to see the small vane ahead of his windscreen which was designed to indicate the on-set of yaw. Whatever the reason, the Harrier entered an uncontrolled roll still at low level and Rosburg elected to eject. Tragically, the aircraft's wings were at almost 90° to the ground and the rocket seat therefore blasted the pilot out sideways, slamming him into the runway while the Harrier crashed into the ground a short distance away. Terribly injured, Rosburg was rushed to hospital in Guildford, but died shortly after arrival.

XW174, the prototype two seat Harrier which crashed near Stonehenge on June 4th, 1969. (BAe. 109549)

Within six months, Dunsfold's Chief Test Pilot Duncan Simpson was lucky to escape with his life after ejecting from another Harrier. On 22nd April, 1969 the maiden flight of XW174, the first two seater T 2 training variant of the Harrier, had taken place. On 4th June Simpson was flying this aircraft from Dunsfold when the aircraft's fuel system failed at low level over Salisbury Plain. Efforts to relight the engine were futile and, although Simpson immediately performed a 180° turn back towards Boscombe Down, he realised that a Harrier full of fuel made a very poor glider. Aiming to preserve the aircraft as much as possible, Simpson lowered the undercarriage and flaps while trimming the Harrier to attempt a glide landing into fields near Stonehenge. At only 500 feet he then ejected, but in doing so Simpson suffered severe spinal injuries which included a broken neck. Miraculously his nervous system was unharmed and he subsequently recovered to return to test flying. While XW174 was completely written off, enough wreckage was preserved in order to indicate that a blocked fuel control unit had caused the problem.

Chapter Sixteen

Enter the Hawk, Exit the Hunter

The new decade did not begin auspiciously for Dunsfold when problems continued to plague the Harrier T 2. On 11th July 1970, in an incident similar to Duncan Simpson's of April, 1969 Barrie Tonkinson suffered another fuel system failure, this time in XW264 during a Saturday morning test flight from Dunsfold. Despite his lack of power, Tonkinson managed to reach Boscombe Down aerodrome, but knew that emergency facilities were not available at the weekend. With no other options, he successfully made a fast glide approach and put down on the grass at 170 knots. As soon as his injuries allowed, Tonkinson then climbed from the cockpit and distanced himself as fast as possible from the aircraft which caught fire and burned out.

On a more positive note, 20th November, 1970 brought the maiden flight of the AV-8A (Harrier Mk 50) ordered by the United States Marine Corps, and the formal handover of the first aircraft came in a ceremony at Dunsfold on 6th January, 1971. The official photographs of the occasion are fondly recalled by aerodrome employees for two reasons. Firstly, a large pin-up poster had escaped the notice of the public relations staff and managed to find its way into the background of the shots of the Hawker Siddeley and Marine Corps top brass. Secondly, and also in the background of the photographs, was a large wooden sign, hanging from the ceiling and proclaimimg MAKE *EVERY* WEEK *YOUR* SAFETY WEEK. While the sentiment was valid, it could be seen that the sign was hanging somewhat precariously. Shortly after the ceremony the sign allegedly fell and slightly injured an electrician!

Thanks to the AV-8A order, Dunsfold hosted more exotic aircraft, starting on the dull grey winter's morning of 23rd January, 1971 when the massive silver bulk of a USAF C-133 Cargomaster turboprop transport swept into Dunsfold's circuit and landed to collect the USMC's first Harrier (serial number 1583840) for delivery to the USA. In addition to Cargomasters, giant C-141 Starlifter jets were also used to pick up AV-8As from Dunsfold.

On 16th September, 1971 another new variant to fly was the sole Harrier Mk 52 two seat company demonstrator with the civil registration G-VTOL. For many years G-VTOL was to be known for its superb demonstrations of the Harrier's capabilities, but its initiation to the work was not a happy one when, in late 1971 during a Middle East tour, it was involved in another set-back to the Harrier's export hopes. Just as P1127 XP831 had embarrassingly crashed at the 1963 Paris Air Show, so now did G-VTOL. While hovering in a display close to the residence of the ruler of Abu Dhabi, the Dunsfold test pilot lost his horizon against the sand and landed heavily, denting the aircraft's nose and buckling the undercarriage.*

A combination of limited resources and restricted hangar space led, in late 1971, to Hawker Siddeley regretfully deciding that they could no longer maintain their small group of historic aircraft at Dunsfold. Consequently, the Hurricane went in flying condition to the RAF's Battle of Britain Memorial Flight while the Hart and Cygnet found a good home at the RAF Museum, Hendon. As already recounted, last minute subterfuge ensured that the Sea Fury restoration project went home to the Fleet Air Arm at Yeovilton. Before the final break-up of the collection, commemorative photographs of the Hurricane, Hart and Cygnet were taken along with Hawker Siddeley's latest product, a Harrier GR 1. In arranging the aircraft in various poses on the grass at Dunsfold, a crane was used to carefully lift and move the aircraft to and fro. As this was being done with the Harrier, a delivery van drove onto the perimeter track and braked to an abrupt halt as the driver took in the scene before him on the airfield. After watching the Harrier swaying gently in its harness for a minute or so, the van driver leaned from his cab and a derisive Cockney accent was heard to shout "Wot you doin' there Guv'nor, teachin' it to fly?"

Another unorthodox Harrier flight involved demonstrator G-VTOL which took off from Dunsfold on 7th February, 1973 loaded into a Canadair CL-44-0 Guppy cargo aircraft, for a tour

---

*G-VTOL was also later involved in another incident of misjudgement when it ran off the end of Dunsfold's runway 26 on landing. Using 150 tons of rubble, a road had to be built over soft ground at the end of the runway to enable a crane to retrieve the aircraft from the edge of the perimeter woods.

A Harrier GR3 of 20 Squadron.

of South America. Flown by pilots John Farley and Don Riches, G-VTOL's main rôle was to star in the International Aerospace Show at São Paulo in Brazil, but the trip also took in a total of five countries before a return to Dunsfold in mid March.

In 1973, Dunsfold began to receive back RAF Harrier GR 1s for conversion to GR 3 standard, work which cosmetically ruined what grace the Harrier possessed by adding an elongated snout type nose. While undoubtedly ugly, this extension housed a Ferranti laser rangefinder which considerably enhanced the aircraft's ground attack capabilities. In addition to the conversion programme, the RAF also ordered twelve new single seat and four two seat aircraft to the improved standard, the two seaters being designated the T 4 and having the same nose extension.

The aerodrome lost one of its hardest worked aircraft on 10th April, 1973 when the first Harrier, XV276, crashed on approach to Dunsfold during an evaluation flight by a pilot of the Swiss Air Force. While throttling back, Major Stauffer had inadvertantly closed down the engine and, at low level, did not have the time to restart it. Ejecting safely, Stauffer was relieved to watch the Harrier crash into open land at Collins Farm near Cranleigh without damage to life or property, albeit he came close to landing amongst the burning wreckage.

A verse and memorial, penned by former Chief Test Pilot Bill Bedford, reveals that a neighbour of his had a strange premonition about the accident and contacted him about it shortly before the demise of XV276.*

Further heartening indications of a secure future for work at the aerodrome had been evident from early 1972 when an ancient lorry began a series of trials which involved it trundling up and down Dunsfold's runway. On the back of the lorry was a wooden cockpit mock-up of Kingston's latest HS 1182 aircraft, a design which had first appeared on the drawing board in late 1968 and was aimed at replacing the Gnat, Jet Provost and Hunter as the RAF's jet trainer. The wooden mock-up trials went a long way to perfecting an acceptable cockpit layout, concentrating in particular on what would be the instructor's view from the rear seat. In March 1972, the RAF had confirmed their interest in the type and ordered 176 aircraft, to be assembled and test flown from Dunsfold in the same manner as the Harrier.

The roll out ceremony of the new design, now christened the Hawk, took place on 12th August, 1974 and on 21st August prototype XX154 took to the air for the first time in the capable hands of Chief Test Pilot Duncan Simpson. With an eye on appearing at the important Farnborough Air Show in just a couple of weeks time, the first flight took place despite problems with the Hawk's nosewheel which refused to castor properly. Unable to manoeuvre itself on the ground, the aircraft therefore had to be towed out and lined up for take off on the runway. The flight was a great success although on landing the nosewheel steering problem still remained and the Hawk had to be towed off the runway.

Another maiden flight, of the first two seat TAV-8A Harrier for the US Marine Corps, took place on 16th July, 1975, eight such aircraft being delivered from October 1975 to 1976. The aerodrome was now buzzing again at full capacity as Hawks, Harriers and Hunters jostled for space in the crowded hangars. Out on the airfield's flight line an impressive variety of national

*See Appendix C.

Roll-out day for the Hawk, seen with the aircraft it was destined to replace; Hunter, Jet Provost and Gnat. (BAe.742496.)

colours could also be seen on the aircraft undergoing test flying: a Hunter for Kenya, a Hawk for the RAF, a Harrier for the US Marines. A less easily identified service was also beginning to receive a batch of Harriers which carried no national markings on their test flights out of Dunsfold. These aircraft represented the long sought after second export order for the Harrier, dating from 1973 when the Spanish Navy confirmed it would be placing an initial order for six single seat and two two seat aircraft. Due to the British government's sensitivity over arms sales to Franco's Spain, this order had to be placed, and delivery effected, via the USA. Known in Spain as the Matador, the first Harrier AV-8S flew on 18th September, 1975 and all aircraft were subsequently shipped to the USA still without displaying Spanish markings, before being then delivered on to Spain aboard the Spanish aircraft carrier Dédalo.

Foreign pilots thus continued to beat a path to Dunsfold, now also keen to look not just at the Harrier but also at the new Hawk trainer which, as a much simpler design, held greater interest for smaller, budget conscious, air forces. While another

A Matador (Harrier AV-S) for the Spanish Navy. (BAe. 802926)

accident might have therefore been understandable in the hands of an inexperienced pilot trying a new design of aircraft, it was all the more unexpected when the next tragedy at Dunsfold involved a tried and tested aircraft, flown by one of Britain's most able pilots.

The incident came on 20th November, 1975 on the occasion of the visit to Dunsfold by a Chinese government trade delegation. While principally concerned with Hawker Siddeley's Civil Aircraft Division at Hatfield (the Chinese were already purchasers of Hatfield's Trident airliner) the delegation had also expressed a desire to see the Harrier, notwithstanding continued reluctance by the British government to approve sales to China.

The delegation was flown down to Dunsfold by Hatfield's Chief Test Pilot, the distinguished wartime night fighter ace Group Captain John 'Catseyes' Cunningham. The trip was made in one of the company's latest HS 125 executive jets, G-BCUX. Also on board were second pilot David Wingate and Hatfield's Sales Director, J. A. Johnstone.

Some twenty minutes after completion of an afternoon Harrier flight demonstration, the HS 125 was boarded for the return

The foam covered remains of the HS 125. (Surrey Advertiser.)

journey to Hatfield, and Cunningham took off into an overcast sky from runway 07 as dusk fell, shortly after four o'clock. As soon as the aircraft was airborne, Cunningham raised the undercarriage but, as he then looked ahead, his line of vision was obscured by a flock of plover birds struggling to wheel out of the line of the climbing jet. Hits were felt and immediately both engines lost power, no response coming from the throttles.

In an instant, Cunningham assessed his options, gauging that he was still only half way along the runway and fifty to a hundred feet up. Quickly he lowered the aircraft's nose to maintain flying speed and ordered Wingate to lower the undercarriage, calling that he would be taking the aircraft back onto the ground. To Cunningham, it looked as if touch-down could still be made on the end of the runway before overshooting into the fields beyond.

Exactly as the experienced pilot had estimated, the HS 125 touched down smoothly on the last of the tarmac before bumping on across the fields. Smashing its way through a hedge and ditch, the aircraft lost its undercarriage just before bursting through another hedge to belly slide across the A281 Horsham to

Guildford road, eventually shuddering to a halt in the field beyond the road. Immediately, Johnstone opened the cabin door and ushered the uninjured Chinese out of the aircraft. As soon as they were clear, Cunningham urged his second pilot to follow, aware of fire gaining a hold further back in the fuselage. It was only when he himself made to leave the aircraft that Cunningham discovered he could not stand. Crawling to the exit door, he was helped to his feet and led away by Wingate, the aircraft now being well alight from fuel leaking from the damaged wing. Seconds later, the aerodrome's fire crews arrived on the scene having followed the path of the aircraft across the fields and the fire was extinguished before it took a complete hold of the broken aircraft. As the firemen battled, a passing student stopped his car and photographed the dramatic scene, Alastair Martin-Bird marvelling that the crew and passengers had emerged virtually unscathed. That they did so was due in no small part to the skill and swift thinking of John Cunningham, skill which could be traced by the dead straight trail of the aircraft's passage over the rough fields. At the Surrey County Hospital in Guildford, the test pilot was found to have suffered two crushed spinal vertebrae but he made a good recovery and returned to flying in February 1976.

Sadly, there was to be a tragic postscript to the incident. Although not initially realised, the emergency services inspecting the wreckage discovered parts of a motor vehicle. By a fatal trick of timing, there had been only one vehicle on the long straight stretch of the A281 road crossed by the jet and it had been directly underneath when the HS 125 lost its undercarriage and crashed down onto its belly. None of those on board the aircraft had therefore been aware of a car being beneath them. The car had been on its way back from picking up five girls from school and, by another bizarre twist of fate, the car's woman driver was the wife of one of Dunsfold's pilots, Leslie 'Dick' Whittington, a colleague of John Cunningham. Of the five girls, two were daughters of the Dunsfold pilot. None of the car's occupants had stood a chance of survival.

A second demonstrator joined Harrier G-VTOL in May 1976 when the Dunsfold assembly line's seventh Hawk airframe was designated the first Mk 50 series aircraft and was retained by the company. It received the dual identification of military serial ZA101 and civil registration G-HAWK, and took to the air for the first time on the 17th, before joining the vigorous trials and marketing campaign to secure further orders for the type. Disappointing failures to date in the market place had begun in 1974, when a Belgian Air Force requirement had been met by the French Alpha Jet. Further disappointment followed when the Royal Australian Air Force decided not to go ahead with an order and possible share in Hawk construction, choosing instead to extend the life of its existing Italian MB 326 jet trainers. In early 1975, the Argentinian Navy was the next service to express interest in the Hawk as a Skyhawk replacement, but Hawker Siddeley, in view of the small scale of the potential order, would not commit themselves to the extensive modifications which would have enabled the Hawk to operate from the Argentinians' aircraft carrier. In view of later events in the Falklands campaign of 1982, it is interesting to consider how Argentinian Dunsfold-built Hawks would have fared in combat against the Royal Navy's Dunsfold-built Sea Harriers.

The painting of G-HAWK in a desert camouflage scheme indicated where sales were most anticipated, but when the first all-important export order came, it was from the relatively unexpected customer of Finland, who ordered fifty Mk 51 aircraft in September 1977. This has since been followed by Hawk deliveries from Dunsfold to the air forces of Kenya (Mk 51), Indonesia (Mk 53), Zimbabwe (Mk 60, the Dubai (Mk 61), Abu Dhabi (Mk 63), Kuwait (Mk 64), Saudi Arabia (Mk 65) and Switzerland (Mk 66). The Mk 62 variant was omitted from the sequence due to an order from Venezuela being cancelled following the 1982 Falklands conflict.

While the Hawk went from strength to strength, 1976 also saw the last refurbished Hunter roll off the Dunsfold assembly line. This was an FGA 70A single seater for the Lebanese Air Force, the last of an order for six single seaters and three T 66C trainers. The completion of the order came none too soon as, in return for relatively modest orders, Hunter refurbishment had been taking up valuable space needed for both Harrier and Hawk production. Indeed, fine weather permitting, work had continued on some Hunters out of doors in front of the

G-Hawk (ZA101) on the Australian tour.

production hangars, immediately adjacent to the open-topped water storage tanks of the aerodrome's fire service. This practice almost led to a drowning on one occasion when a fitter, working on the fin of a Hunter, stepped back off the wrong side of the tailplane on which he had been standing. The last sight of the man had been a clenched fist still holding aloft a spanner as he disappeared beneath the surface of one of the static water tanks. Fortunately, several colleagues were quickly on hand to haul the spluttering non-swimmer from the water.

Although 1980 was to see the conversion at BAe Brough of three Hunters to T 8M standard as part of the Sea Harrier development programme,* the Hunter now all but disappeared from Dunsfold's skies after almost 25 years of constant production or refurbishment. It had seen service in both the RAF and Fleet Air Arm, while overseas sales and production took it to the air forces of Sweden, Denmark, Peru, Holland, Belgium, India, Switzerland, Iraq, Lebanon, Rhodesia, Kuwait, Jordan, Saudi Arabia, Singapore, Abu Dhabi, Qatar, Kenya, Oman,

---

*Of the three T 8M Hunters, XL602 was based at Dunsfold where it remains on test flying duties into the 1990s.

Chief Test Pilot John Farley

Somalia and Chile. Though the Hunter ceased flying at Dunsfold, there were still numerous examples of the type to be found on the aerodrome, these being re-purchased ex-Danish Air Force Mk 51 Hunters, now surplus to requirements, which lingered on for a few years more in corners of the aerodrome until claimed by collectors, museums or the scrapman.

Two contrasting types to leave Dunsfold for sunnier climes in early 1978 were Hawk demonstrator G-HAWK and Tiger Moth G-ANRF. The Hawk was departing for a month's promotional tour of eight countries in the Middle East, while the Tiger Moth took off on 7th February, 1978 for a flight to Darwin in Australia. Piloted by Flight Lieutenant David Cyster, an instructor at RAF Valley, G-ANRF was re-enacting the pioneer flight of Bert Hinkler from England to Australia exactly 50 years before.

More work for the aerodrome was secured in 1978 when the RAF ordered a further 24 Harrier GR 3s and four T 4s to be delivered between 1980 and 1983, and the year also saw the emergence of yet another variant in the Harrier dynasty when John Farley, who had now succeeded Duncan Simpson as Chief

Test Pilot, took up the first Sea Harrier FRS Mk 1 aircraft, XZ450, on 20th August. Designed as a fleet defence fighter for the Royal Navy, the Sea Harrier stemmed from a 1971 requirement which had resulted in an initial order for 34 aircraft being placed in 1975. XZ450 was the first example of this order, deliveries commencing in June 1979 with XZ451.

A mysterious tragedy touched Dunsfold when, on 25th April, 1979, the body of Water Board official Mr John George was found hidden in a copse near the aerodrome. Mr George had been shot to death at close range. A huge manhunt throughout south east England eventually spread across the Channel, first to Guernsey and then to Brittany in France where two young English brothers, John Nicholas Gerald Richards and Jason Neil Andrew Richards were arrested by French police. It was not until 22nd August that Surrey police secured the brothers' extradition and a team, led by Detective Chief Superintendent Don Underwood, brought the pair back by chartered aircraft for questioning at the murder hunt's headquarters in Godalming. As the nearest aerodrome to both the scene of the crime and Goldalming police station, Dunsfold therefore saw the arrival of the chartered Cessna 404 from France. Amid tight security, the aircraft swung onto the perimeter track and then turned to halt alongside trees from which police vehicles emerged. The Richards brothers were led in handcuffs to a police van, which moved off in convoy. Instead of being taken out of either of the two main exits, they were whisked away out of the Honeymeads Gate, thus avoiding waiting pressmen.

While the two were subsequently found guilty at the Old Bailey of murder, neither of the brothers revealed the full circumstances of the crime. The most likely theory centered on the suggestion that Mr George, a keen bird watcher, had stumbled upon the pair with the proceeds of two recent armed robberies.

On 17th July, 1979 Dunsfold was involved in a drama for which it had long been designated. Thanks to its long runway and relative proximity, the aerodrome carries the designation of 'Emergency Reserve Airfield' in support of Gatwick Airport, particularly important as Gatwick has only one runway and thus any emergency carries the likelihood of bringing the airport to a standstill.

On this Tuesday evening, local people were first alerted to the situation when, sirens wailing, no less than 25 ambulances screamed through quiet villages to converge on the aerodrome. At Dunsfold a sombre scene greeted them. At one end of the aerodrome fire crews were already tackling a huge blaze where two aircraft had apparently collided. Gradually the details were reported. A British Airways Tristar wide-bodied passenger jet, crippled by engine problems, had headed for Dunsfold instead of risking a landing at crowded Gatwick. On touch-down at 7.46 p.m. the giant jet had veered off the runway and collided with one of Dunsfold's redundant Hunters, the resultant fire sending a huge column of black smoke high into the still evening air. Twisted metal and bodies were strewn across the runway and grass, at least 250 dead being reported.

The injured were ferried in the ambulance fleet to the Surrey County Hospital at Guildford, and later to overflow wards at Godalming Ambulance Station. For those passengers beyond medical help, Guildford Council's Woking Road Depot was hurriedly converted into a make shift mortuary. The Surrey Constabulary incident headquarters, staffed by officers drafted in from all over the County, began to deal with a barrage of enquiries from distraught relatives and friends.

Fortunately, this was *Operation Anvil*, Surrey Constabulary's disaster exercise based on Dunsfold's emergency airfield rôle. John Cunningham's HS 125 crash of November 1975 had emphasised the need for future planning and overall the exercise was considered a great success. So efficient indeed was the response of the emergency services, that a real life casualty at the Surrey County Hospital, nursing a broken arm, was swept up with the Red Cross 'volunteered injured'. Before the mistake was realised the woman concerned had even had her broken arm photographed for the record by the police photographer!

Chapter Seventeen
To The Present

The turn of the decade saw Dunsfold buzzing with activity, even to the extent that a Hunter was again to be seen flying when Brough-produced T 8M XL612 arrived. In addition to RAF and Royal Navy Harrier and Sea Harrier production, the Spanish government had ordered a second batch of Matadors (Harrier AV-8S) and, freed from the political sensitivity of the first order, Spanish Navy pilots now ferried the aircraft, already painted in Spanish national markings, directly to Spain from Dunsfold. Deliveries of the Hawk to the RAF, which had begun in November 1976, now reached the Red Arrows aerobatic flying display team which converted from its Dunsfold supplied Gnats to Dunsfold supplied Hawks in the winter season of 1979/1980, thereby maintaining the strong links between the aerodrome and the world famous team.* On the Hawk export front, the first Mk 52 for Kenya, serial number 1001, had flown in December 1979 and was delivered in April 1980. Indonesia's first Mk 53, LL 5301, flew on 6th June, 1980 and Finland's first Mk 51, HW-302, likewise took to the air on 16th October, 1980 deliveries of the two orders beginning in September and December respectively of the same year.

While sales of the Hawk were now approaching respectability, the BAe† marketing teams were still struggling against formidable competition, particularly from the Alpha Jet. In Egypt in 1977, and again in Morrocco in 1978, the French design had beaten the Hawk for vital orders and thus, when at the end of May 1981, Dunsfold's Hawk demonstrator left for yet another overseas tour, determination ran high that this time second place was not good enough. The challenge was formidable.

Reverting to its military identity of ZA101, G-HAWK was leaving for a tour of the USA in a bid to win a contract to provide the US Navy with a replacement for its ageing TC-2 and

---

*These links have led on occasions to the Red Arrows using Dunsfold as a base for displays in the south east, for example during the two day Biggin Hill International Air Fair.

†Hawker Siddeley Aviation Ltd. had by now been incorporated into British Aerospace (BAe).

Sea Harrier FRS 1, XZ450, on its maiden flight August 20th, 1978. This aircraft was shot down over the Falklands on May 4th, 1982. (BAe.782970)

TA-4J jet training aircraft. Optimistically painted in a new US Navy style colour scheme, the Hawk carried out a 30 day tour with great success, backed by a sales pitch which included the startling statistic that, by choosing the Hawk, the US Navy could save 50 million gallons of fuel - enough to supply 200 of its F-18 Hornet fleet fighters for a year.

On 19 November, 1981 the US Government formally announced that the Hawk had triumphed over its rivals, the Alpha Jet and the Italian MB 339. Designated the T-45 Goshawk, all aircraft are assembled in the USA by British Aerospace's partner in the bid, McDonnell Douglas, and therefore no airframes pass through Dunsfold, albeit the aerodrome was still to retain an interest in product support.

The first flight of Zimbabwe's Mk 60 Hawk on 1st April, 1982 was the last vestige of normality for a number of weeks at Dunsfold when suddenly the crisis arose which was to deliver ultimate proof of the Harrier's effectiveness - the Argentinian invasion of the Falkland Islands. Air cover for Britain's naval task force was to be provided by the Fleet Air Arm's Sea Harriers, while the RAF were to contribute GR 3 aircraft for ground attack and reconnaisance operations. Early in the month, Dunsfold therefore found itself on a war footing.

The aerodrome's first contribution was to give up those trials aircraft based at Dunsfold which were officially owned by the Ministry of Defence. Sea Harrier XZ450 was the first to go on 3rd April when it was transferred to 800 Squadron at Yeovilton. Two days later, it was this aircraft which sat proudly at the head of HMS Hermes' ski jump when the aircraft carrier sailed from Portsmouth. On 4th May, 1982, during a bombing run on Goose Green airfield, XZ450 was hit by Argentinian anti-aircraft fire and crashed, killing its naval pilot, Lieutenant Scott.

A second trials aircraft, XZ438, was delivered on 19th April to 899 Squadron, the Sea Harrier Handling Unit, also at Yeovilton. Although it did not travel south with the task force, this aircraft too came to grief. On 17th May, it was engaged in fuel carrying trials when it crashed on take-off from Yeovilton's ski jump. While the pilot ejected safely, the aircraft was a total write-off.

Dunsfold's third contribution enjoyed greater success. Sea Harrier ZA194 was still undergoing assembly when the conflict escalated and its build programme was subsequently rushed forwards by two months, enabling it to make its maiden flight at Dunsfold on 23rd April. By 18th May, ZA194 was aboard HMS Hermes in the South Atlantic, having caught up with the carrier via Yeovilton, the Gambia, Ascencion Island and a temporary stay aboard the ill-fated Atlantic Conveyor, later to be sunk by an Argentine Exocet missile. By then the Sea Harrier was operating with 800 Squadron aboard Hermes. On 23rd May, 1982 and just one month after its first flight, ZA194, flown by Lieutenant Hale, shot down an Argentinian Air Force Dagger over Pebble Island.

RAF GR 3 ground attack aircraft were also expected to assist with combat patrols. Rapid trials work within a matter of days at Dunsfold brought about a fitting which enabled the GR 3 to carry Sidewinder air-to-air missiles like its Sea Harrier cousins. The latter were so successful in their fighter patrols that this largely left the RAF's contingent to concentrate on ground strikes against Argentinian positions. By the end of the campaign, over 2000 combat sorties had been flown by 28 Sea Harriers and ten Harrier GR 3 aircraft, all built and test flown

The first Indian Sea Harrier FRS 51, IN601. (BAe.D809111)

at Dunsfold. Six Sea Harriers and four GR 3s were lost through accidents and ground fire, but in air combat at least 28 Argentinian aircraft were shot down by Harriers for no loss. The British government was quick to appreciate how crucial the Harrier had been in the success of the task force and immediately ordered another fourteen Sea Harriers at the conclusion of the conflict.*

Assistance of a more human nature was given when Sea Harrier test pilot Taylor Scott volunteered his considerable experience and skills to the Royal Navy who were facing a shortage of Sea Harrier pilots as well as aircraft. Scott subsequently joined 899 Squadron at Yeovilton as a weapons instructor before transferring to the newly formed 809 Squadron on 1st June, 1982 as senior pilot. With 809, Taylor Scott sailed aboard the new carrier HMS Illustrious for the South Atlantic, but the conflict was over before Illustrious was called upon and Scott was demobbed in September to return to Dunsfold.

*A final direct reminder of the Falklands conflict came in March 1983 when XZ989, a RAF Harrier GR 3, was returned to Dunsfold from the Falklands via RAF Wittering for repair assessment. This aircraft had been badly damaged while landing at San Carlos on 8th June, 1982. The damage incurred was such that Dunsfold deemed the aircraft fit only for ground instructional duties and XZ989 was eventually returned to the RAF.

After the frenetic work of April and May, Dunsfold returned to normality secure in the knowledge that, once again, its product had been proved a world-beater. No-one was perhaps more pleased than the Indian Navy. Having ordered 18 single seat FRS 51 and two T 60 two seater Sea Harriers in 1979, the Falklands experience vindicated their choice just a couple of months before the maiden flight, on 6th August, 1982, of IN601, the first FRS 51.

Yet another maiden flight, of the Hawk Mk 61 variant for Dubai, took place on 11th November, 1982, this being the first of a total of 24 aircraft for the United Arab Emirates, eight Mk 61s for Dubai and 16 Mk 63s for Abu Dhabi. Soon afterwards, RAF Hawk T 1s also began to reappear in strength.

This came about in 1983 when a programme commenced for the conversion of 88 of the RAF's Hawks, plus the Red Arrows' aircraft, to T 1A standard with the ability to carry Sidewinder air-to-air missiles. Returning to Dunsfold at the rate of 25 a year, the Hawks' new capability was to enable them to operate as a second line of defence for UK installations in time of war.

A visually startling concept was demonstrated for the first time at the aerodrome on 26th April, 1983 when the 'Skyhook' system was proved viable in conjunction with Harrier aircraft. Enthusiastically promoted by Dunsfold test pilot Heinz Frick, and developed by BAe in conjunction with Dowty Boulton Paul, 'Skyhook' is a large crane-like structure with which it would be possible to equip relatively small ships such as frigates or even merchant ships. For take-off, the aircraft is swung outboard on the crane, the pilot starts up the aircraft and selects hovering power. The crane's lock-on head then automatically dis-engages and leaves the aircraft in free flight. On recovery, the aircraft manoeuvres close to the head and an optical system guides the aircraft onto the docking pads. If only refuelling is required, this can be done immediately without even shutting the aircraft down. As yet, the concept has still to be fully tried onboard ship, but as a replacement for the current complement of just one helicopter, one or more Sea Harriers would represent an enormous leap forward for a frigate's weaponry, with vast improvements in both attack and defence capabilities. If used aboard merchant vessels, then a level of airborne protection

G-VTOL demonstrates the 'Sky Hook' in 1983. (BAe. 852721)

would be achieved not seen since the valiant CAM ship Hurricanes of the Second World War.

From the mid 1970s, both the US Marine Corps and the RAF had expressed interest in an advanced Harrier II design, principally with the aim of obtaining better performance and range, coupled with improved avionics and greater weapon carrying ability. While much of the development was US-led, a Memorandum of Understanding agreed to share the construction of components between Britain and the USA, each aircraft being in effect a dual nationality composite airframe, with either BAe in Britain or McDonnell Douglas in the USA responsible for their own country's final assembly and test flying programmes. Designated the AV-8B in the USA, the Harrier II for the RAF became the GR 5 variant and the first example, ZD318, lifted off from Dunsfold on its maiden flight on 30th April, 1985. Flying the new aircraft was Chief Test Pilot Mike Snelling who had succeeded Andy Jones.

Again, with the GR 5's future secured by RAF requirements, and another order from the Royal Navy for a further 25 new Sea Harriers in the summer of 1985, Dunsfold was assured of work for several years to come. The Royal Navy had also succeeded in obtaining governmental approval for a Sea Harrier mid life up-date programme, aimed at producing an FRS 2 variant for the 1990s and clearly Dunsfold would be responsible for the type. Export Hawks continued to roll off the assembly lines, with Kuwait's Mk 64 flying for the first time on 4th September, 1985. Now also close to fruition was the first prototype of yet another Hawk variant, the single seat 200 series. Without any service requirement from either the RAF or Royal Navy, the Hawk 200 was a company-financed private venture launched in 1983 by BAe with an eye to overseas sales. In September 1984 a full-scale replica had been displayed at the Farnborough Air Show with a stated aim to have a prototype flying in 30 months time, ready to show at Farnborough in 1976.

Eleven days ahead of schedule, the prototype Hawk 200 ZG200 flew from Dunsfold on 19th May, 1986 and was soon launched into a demanding test programme aimed at a Farnborough appearance in September. While great hopes were held for ZG200, the aircraft was involved in another of the aerodrome's tragedies on 2nd July, 1986.

Scheduled for the next day was a press preview of the new prototype and, in preparation for this and the forthcoming Farnborough Air Show, 47 year old Deputy Chief Test Pilot Jim Hawkins had planned a punishing schedule of manoeuvres. Locals had already noticed the intense flying activity and on the aerodrome itself those outside the hangars watched the agile aircraft plunge about the sky. Suddenly, at the top of a zoom climb from 200 feet to 3,000 feet, the Hawk tumbled back down in a attitude which alarmed those watching. Anxiously they watched for Hawkins to recover but the tree line of the aerodrome's eastern boundary was passed and the Hawk did not reappear. Instead, a sickening thud told of the aircraft's fate and, when crash crews rushed out of the Compasses' Gate, within a few yards they discovered blazing wreckage scattered across the Alfold to Dunsfold road. The Hawk had just missed this leafy country lane in a nose dive into an adjoining field, smashing a five feet deep crater into the clay surface. Hawkins, who had joined the Dunsfold team in 1973 on leaving the RAF, died instantly. The subsequent investigation could find no fault

Above, Hawk 200 ZG200 on its maiden flight, May 19th, 1986.

Right, all that remained of ZG200 after the crash on July 2nd, 1986.

with the aircraft and could only conclude that the pilot had become disorientated. While the loss of a sole prototype was a severe blow to British Aerospace, former Dunsfold test pilot Frank Bullen voiced the real loss. In a quote to the local press, Bullen observed that, "time and money will undoubtedly produce a second prototype......but today the life of a talented and brave test pilot came to an end." As Bullen had observed, a second prototype Hawk 200 was duly produced and ZH200 first flew on 24th April, 1987.

Dunsfold again made national headlines in tragic circumstances on 22nd October, 1987. This was over the so-called 'Marie Celeste' mystery when Harrier GR 5 ZD325 took off from the aerodrome for a routine test flight in the hands of BAe test pilot Taylor Scott. Scott had been a Sea Vixen and Phantom pilot in the Royal Navy before receiving a posting as Naval Liaison Officer at Dunsfold in 1977, playing an important part in the team responsible for introducing the Sea Harrier into the Royal Navy. He subsequently left the Navy with the rank of Lieutenant Commander to join British Aerospace's test flying team at Dunsfold. As already detailed, he had briefly rejoined the Navy from June to September 1982, charged with working up an additional Sea Harrier squadron at the time of the Falklands conflict. Only recently, on 1st October, 1987, Scott had been promoted to become Deputy Chief Test Pilot at Dunsfold, the position having not been filled since the loss of Jim Hawkins the previous year.

The aircraft was the sixth production GR 5 and had taken off from Dunsfold at 16.59 hours climbing to the west as planned. The test flight was the aircraft manufacturer's final check before handover to the RAF the next day and was principally concerned with a test of the oxygen system. At 17.06 hours, Scott checked in with London Military Radar (LMR) as he levelled out at 30,000 feet. There was no further radio contact until, at 17.33 hours, LMR attempted to contact Scott, but could not raise a response either directly or when attempting relays by other aircraft. Eventually a westbound C-5 Galaxy of the USAF was vectored to an intercept some 140 nautical miles west of Eire. Its crew reported the Harrier as pilotless and remained in visual range, taking still and video photographs. At 19.03 hours, ZD325 went into a descending spiral when it ran out of fuel and disappeared into the sea 500 nautical miles west of the southern tip of Eire. Throughout, there had been no emergency call from the doomed aircraft.

Scott's body, still wearing a badly damaged parachute, was found 24 hours after the accident in a field near Winterbourne Stoke, Wiltshire. The aircraft's dinghy pack and fragments of canopy were also found some distance from the pilot's body.

The inquest, which was not conducted until April 1988, could only record an open verdict on Scott's death since the actual cause of the accident could not be determined beyond doubt. It was generally accepted, however, that the most likely explanation involved a cockpit wander lamp jamming and activating the ejector seat's override system. This could have released the

The pilotless Harrier ZD325. Photographed from a C-5 on October 22nd, 1987. (Cpt. J Brunz)

pilot's seat harness and would then have fired the parachute deployment rocket of the Martin Baker Mk 12H ejector seat through the canopy, thus dragging the pilot out with terrible force. Martin Baker took immediate design steps to prevent any possible reoccurrance of this theory. Coroner John Elgar paid tribute to Scott as a brave, dedicated and skilled test pilot, concluding, "We in this country are very considerably in his debt."

In November 1987, Dunsfold's Hawk demonstrator ZA101 showed a new shape when it took to the air again after conversion to a series 100 aircraft. With a distinctive elongated nose, the series 100 benefits from an up-rated engine and improved avionics and navigation package. This includes a Forward Looking Infra Red system (FLIR) with pilot's passive Night Vision Goggles, for night navigation and target identification, and a laser rangefinder. This two-seat attack version of the Hawk had in fact been foreseen as early as 1981 when Venezuela had signed a contract for a mix of Mk 62 trainers and an enhanced ground attack variant - subsequently to become the Hawk 100. However, the events of 1982 in the South Atlantic had led to the order quietly being cancelled and the series 100 project had therefore languished for a number of years.

The advent of 1988 found Dunsfold bursting at the seams with aircraft as Harriers had to be stock-piled pending the outcome of investigations into Taylor Scott's accident. Consequently, planning permission was obtained for the erection of two temporary Rubb hangars which were sited on the disused short runway, close to the present control tower. Harriers were thus stored until the all-clear was received to resume deliveries to the RAF.

By this time, the gestation period of the GR 5 had lengthened considerably. After a maiden flight in April 1985, the first handover, of ZD324, had taken place on 1st July, 1987 but full service release was delayed to November 1987 following technical problems with the inertial navigation system. Even the freak hurricane of 15/16th October, 1987 had hit the programme when hangars suffered roof damage and two Harriers were slightly damaged by falling debris. The investigation into Scott's accident then further held up the initial order for 62 aircraft and it was not to be until February 1988 that test flying was allowed to recommence. Only in March 1988 did 223 OCU commence training sorties from RAF Wittering.

Sea Harrier FRS 2 ZA195 made its initial flight from Dunsfold on 19th September, 1988, this being the first development aircraft in a programme to up-rate the Royal Navy's FRS 1 aircraft and provide a fleet air defence fighter into the 1990s and beyond. With experience gained from the Falklands campaign, BAe had been working on the design since 1983 when a contract was signed for a feasibility study into such a programme. Two existing Sea Harrier FRS 1 airframes were initially converted to FRS 2 standard, along with a BAe 125-600B executive jet, ZF130, which was turned into a flying test bed for the new fighter's avionics which include the Ferranti Blue Vixen fire control radar. ZF130, with its distinctively reshaped nose, is based at Dunsfold and began test flying in mid 1988.

A chapter of Dunsfold's history closed when, on 30th September, 1988, single seat Hawk 200 ZH200 and two seat Hawk 100 ZA101 left Dunsfold for a 13,000 mile ferry trip to Australia for that country's bicentennial celebrations. After a number of displays there, the tour then took in the Phillippines, Indonesia, Brunei, Singapore, Malaysia and Thailand. While the trip was a great success and underlined the Hawk's fine serviceability record, the return of the two aircraft was not to Dunsfold. Instead it was to Warton in Lancashire for it was here that the Hawk production and development line was now moved, leaving only the first Mk 66 example of a 1987 order for the Swiss Air Force to be completed at Dunsfold.

The Hawk's move from Dunsfold was part of a rationalisation programme which followed on from BAe's 1986 £5 billion Al-Yamamah defence support contract with Saudi Arabia. As part of this contract, the Saudis had ordered thirty Hawk Mk 65 trainers, the type's maiden flight having been on 11th August, 1987 and the first four aircraft were handed over in a ceremony at Dunsfold in October 1987. Subsequently, a further order was placed by Saudi Arabia in August 1988 for an undisclosed number of Hawk aircraft. While exact details of the contract were not initially made public, it was nevertheless confirmed that the order would include the single seat 200 series Hawk, so providing BAe with the important first customer for the type. Thus, with Saudi orders for both single and two seat Hawks now confirmed and linked to the supply of BAe's Tornado aircraft from Warton, Dunsfold relinquished the Hawk to concentrate on the new generation of Harriers. When the first Swiss Air Force Hawk Mk 66 flew from Dunsfold in April 1989, this was the last Hawk to undertake its maiden flight at the aerodrome, the remaining nineteen examples of the Swiss order being designated for final assembly at Emmen in Switzerland.

Fuelled by the departure of the Hawks, rumours had grown in October 1988 that Dunsfold was to be sold as an airfreight only airport to complement Gatwick. Denying the speculation, BAe pointed out that they had just invested in the building of a new design and avionics block at the aerodrome and had also transferred work there from their recently closed Weybridge site. While there are few long-term certainties in the aircraft manufacturing industry, BAe pledged Dunsfold's security at least until the mid 1990s.

Another reason for the rumours lay perhaps with the new activity to be seen which commenced on 27th November, 1988 when a BAe 748 twin turboprop landed. Instead of taxiing to the BAe factory complex, the aircraft made its way along the perimeter track to the opposite side of the airfield and the new hangar facility of the DH Group Ltd., a company specialising in the design and installation of avionics systems for civil aircraft. Having obtained a lease from a local landowner on one side of the boundary fence and from BAe on the other, the company had replaced the last remaining war-time blister hangar with their

269

own modern structure. They had also reinstated a taxiway back to the perimeter track, reviving echoes of the past and the war-time Mitchells of the Royal Dutch Naval Air Service which were based in this corner of the aerodrome.

The new hangar is designed to accommodate aircraft up to the size of a BAe 146 airliner, but to date has more usually held three or four BAe 125 executive jets or Bell Jetranger helicopters undergoing installation and modification work. Other more exotic temporary visitors have been historic aircraft requiring specialist restoration or avionics work, including a Pembroke, Spitfire and Sea Vixens.

As deliveries of state of the art Harrier GR 5 aircraft continued, yesterday's front-line early model Harriers became today's museum pieces. Already, a USMC AV-8A had been shipped back from the USA for display at Yeovilton's Fleet Air Arm Museum and as GR 5s took over at RAF Wittering, a GR 3 was relegated to gate guardian duties there. For the RAF's other GR 3s there seemed little hope of a future until a report in the influential 'Flight International' magazine in February 1989. The article gave brief hope that Dunsfold might to be about to embark on a Harrier refurbishment programme similar to that which had led to so many overseas Hunter sales in the 1960s and 1970s. The idea was strengthened when Prime Minister Margaret Thatcher personally took a hand in trying to sell refurbished ex-RAF Harrier GR 3s to Zimbabwe, already an operator of Hawks. Disappointingly, the plans did not bear fruit, perhaps not surprisingly when one considers the high technology and specialist nature of the Harrier, compared to a relatively simple design such as the Hawk or earlier Hunter.

Another Harrier went to a museum when the aerodrome said goodbye to one of its old workhorses in April 1989. Veteran company demonstrator, two-seat Harrier T 52 G-VTOL, was retired to the growing Brooklands Museum at Weybridge where it joined a former Danish Air Force Hunter F 51, also donated by Dunsfold via the Brooklands Technical College. While concentrating on Weybridge's own rich heritage, the Brooklands Museum nevertheless now offers the nearest to a Dunsfold museum that one can expect.

Charles Church's Spitfire, G-MKVC, at Dunsfold only hours before the crash in which Mr Church was killed. (Author.)

A regular feature of aerodrome life not so far mentioned is the annual air show, now termed the Families' Day and held each summer since the early 1970s for both Dunsfold and Kingston employees, their families and friends. Of the aircraft to fly in for the 1989 show on 1st July, one was to suffer a tragic end before the day was out.

Spitfire G-MKVC had recently been completely rebuilt by property developer Charles Church at his Hampshire airfield and workshops. At Dunsfold, it had been displayed by one of Church's pilots before returning in the late afternoon to its home airfield at Popham. As the early evening was still fine, Church himself then almost immediately took the Spitfire up again. A few minutes later a 'Mayday' call was heard following engine failure and the Spitfire crashed short of an attempted glide approach to Blackbushe aerodrome. The aircraft was completely destroyed and Church died instantly.

When the Surrey Constabulary began to show interest in the aerodrome in mid-1989, it was to bring about an interesting if brief addition to the aerodrome's flying operations. From

September to November of that year, an Aerospatiale AS 355 Twin Squirrel helicopter, G-SASU, was based at Dunsfold for an evaluation trial by the county police force. Despite the force's desire to take advantage of such a resource on a permanent basis, lack of funding has so far precluded any further operations.

And so to the present day and what do the 1990s hold for the aerodrome? Despite numerous rumours in recent years of imminent closure, Dunsfold is safe to at least celebrate its 50th anniversary in 1992 but a major variable in the equation of Dunsfold's future concerns defence contracts in the light of the new world climate of détente.

So far, such contracts still form the solid base of work at the aerodrome, the RAF having announced a further order for 34 Harrier GR 5s in June 1988, bringing the total order to date to 96 aircraft, valued in excess of £350 million. Two thirds of the way through deliveries of the RAF's order for their first batch of 62 such aircraft, the Kingston and Dunsfold production and assembly lines incorporated minor changes to produce the GR 5a, essentially a mid-way stage towards the already planned night attack version of the Harrier, the GR 7. Eventually, all GR 5 aircraft will receive a retro-fit to GR 7 standard, thus permitting operations in fine night conditions and during poor day time weather. The first aircraft to be delivered already conforming to full GR 7 standard left Dunsfold in 1990.

In March 1990, the RAF also ordered 14 Harrier T 10 two seaters in order to train Harrier GR 7 pilots in the night attack rôle, the new aircraft being replacements for the first generation Harrier T 4 aircraft used by the RAF's 233 OCU at Wittering. Also in 1990, the Royal Navy ordered ten new build Sea Harrier FRS 2 aircraft to supplement their converted FRS 1 airframes.

In the future, however, orders for military aircraft are likely to be cut back in the context of a splintered Warsaw Pact and new alliances between the superpowers. The RAF has already revealed plans to close two of its airfields in Germany, traditionally the Harrier's NATO 'front-line' and, recognizing a shrinking military market, British Aerospace announced a decision in December 1990 to close Dunsfold's parent factory at Kingston by the end of 1992. In the short term Dunsfold benefits as it has taken over the Harrier production line, receiving the jigs for GR7 and US AV-8B construction in June 1991. It is now becoming responsible for aircraft construction, rather than just assembly. Beyond 1995, however, the order books look depressingly bare. New use of the airfield at Farnborough by British Aerospace also brought further uncertainty as it was indicated that BAe's naval aircraft development could be centered there.

Any future alternative development of the aerodrome will always face the constraints of planning permission. In terms of aviation, this only specifies test flying and places severe restrictions on any activity outside of normal Monday to Friday working hours. In particular, these restrictions presently preclude use of the aerodrome for general light aviation, a situation well illustrated by the inability of even the Dunsfold Flying Club to use Dunsfold's facilities. The club exists for British Aerospace employees, but can only use Dunsfold on a very limited basis. In addition to attending the annual Families' Day, the Club hosts a small scale fly-in at Dunsfold each September. Otherwise it operates from Goodwood aerodrome near the south coast, using two Grumman AA-5 Traveller light aircraft, G-BBBI and G-MALC.

If aviation does not continue at Dunsfold then there is little likelihood of any other form of development being approved as the site is subject to 'Green Belt' restrictions. Instead, like many another aerodrome thrown up under war-time emergency regulations, Dunsfold would again face great pressure to return to agricultural use. Only time will tell.

Chapter Eighteen

Dunsfold's Moles

No history of the aerodrome would be complete without mention of the aerodrome's subterranean activities.

These are the duties of the Royal Observer Corps (ROC) who, unbeknown to many, maintain an underground monitoring post within the boundaries of Dunsfold aerodrome. From the surface little can be seen of the post other than a small concrete block, a slit trench and three monitoring devices. Within the concrete, however, lies the entrance shaft down to a specially equipped underground room.

Dunsfold's post was built around 1960 following a decision in 1955 by the ROC to switch to the new rôle of reporting radioactive fallout. Prior to 1955, the ROC had, since 1925, been an organisation responsible for reporting air raids, its maximum strength of 32,000 Observers having been reached during the Second World War. With the change in emphasis, a major rebuilding programme was undertaken from 1956 to 1966 in order to provide underground monitoring posts and protected headquarters. It was therefore within this period that the existing post on Cranleigh Common was closed and the new one built at Dunsfold, then still owned by the Air Ministry. Despite the change in ownership of the aerodrome, the ROC operates as before, thanks to British Aerospace's willingness to act as host and provide classroom facilities on the aerodrome for training purposes.

The possible crisis for which the post exists is the explosion of a nuclear weapon. The Observers work in an environment which gives complete protection from radiation and by means of 'bomb power' and 'ground zero' indicators, they would be the first to report any nuclear explosion. From their survey meters, the post's crew would then register the arrival of fallout and the amount of radiation in the area, reporting every five minutes to group headquarters in Horsham. By historical coincidence this is 2 Group, recalling the days of the RAF's 2 Group Mitchells based at Dunsfold in 1943 and 1944. From Horsham, the information is passed to the scientists of the United Kingdom Warning and Monitoring Organisation who predict strength and movement of fallout and alert the nation accordingly. The post itself also holds maroons and hand operated sirens, effective for a three mile radius, to warn the local population. Rations and support systems are designed to enable the crew to stay below for at least twenty one days, by which time any local fallout is expected to have dissipated.

One evening a week, a shift of three volunteer Observers reports for duty and descends the vertical ladder to No. 25 Monitoring Post, one of a series of 870 around the UK. In the months of dark evenings the walk from the aerodrome's perimeter track to the post's entrance is a feat in itself, often only possible with the help of a flashlight in the inky blackness. Once below however, the post's own batteries light up a room no larger than a modest lounge yet equipped with two bunk beds and an array of monitoring and communications equipment. Off to one side, an annexe reveals a small toilet, only to be used when the post is manned on a twenty-four hour basis at times of crisis. No doubt the facility is all the more crucial at such times.

During normal peacetime, the weekly post attendance involves training, practice in monitoring and the reporting of weather conditions (the latter to be used in order to predict the movement of fallout). ROC membership is voluntary and largely unpaid, other than expenses for meetings, exercises and travel. Nevertheless, a dedicated group of men and women continue to willingly give up their free time for the weekly shift plus an annual camp at an RAF station. This dedication is all the more important in areas such as south west Surrey, where a considerable percentage of the population travels into London to work. Such commuters have little time or opportunity to then give of their time in the evening.

The defence cuts of 1991 also brought the end in sight for the ROC. Thus, soon, the post at Dunsfold is likely to be left unmanned and another chapter in the aerodrome's history will close.

Chapter Nineteen

Reminders of the Past

The present day Dunsfold aerodrome of some 500 acres represents a relatively small and compact site, particularly so for modern jet aircraft operations. It is also much reduced in size from its wartime state, due to three periods of contraction.

The first came soon after the RAF's departure, when the dispersed accommodation sites to the north of the airfield reverted to civilian use. While Skyways used many nissen hut sites for staff lodgings, this was always seen as being inadequate and temporary, local pressure being firmly behind removing the buildings which attracted squatters. Thus it was that by the time Hawkers moved in, the hutted accommodation was marked for demolition. This subsequently took place on all sites, but one surviving structure was the squash court on the main communal number 2 site. This was retained and maintained by Hawkers for the recreational use of their staff and continued to serve this purpose until modern replacement courts were erected on the airfield itself in the 1980s. Today, the building remains in a sadly dilapidated state, hidden among the trees close to the aerodrome's water tower. The tower was itself the war-time original until the late 1980s when a replacement structure was built on the same spot. The only other remains on the communal site are the concrete bases of all the other buildings and the communal air raid shelters, largely intact. The fire service's reserve water storage tanks can just be spotted in the dense undergrowth, now dry and housing two old derelict vehicles.

Action to combat the post-war squatter problem came too late to prevent a semi-permanent presence being established and while all structures were eventually taken down, site number 8 attracted a gypsy encampment which survives to this day. The mobile homes use the original war-time roads and hut bases, ordered to such an extent that there is really little physical difference from the former nissen hut lay-out.

As with the main communal site, site numbers 4, 5, 6 and 7 were replanted with trees, appropriately so as they had originally been cleared within wooded areas, with the aim of helping to provide concealment from the air. On these sites, only the trackways, paths, shelters and hut bases remain and they are dark and dismal places, thanks to the density of the tree growth. Is it purely coincidence that one of the darkest and most overgrown sites is that where murderer Neville Heath had his quarters? Certainly, the trackway leading into the woods to this spot has an eerie quality of its own when seen at night from the Cranleigh to Godalming road, any moonlight giving a ghostly refection to the pale concrete surface. Least remains of site 3 where even the trackway and building bases were taken up to return the site to agriculture.

Of the other sites, the sick quarters location at site number 9 still displays its own small water tower and shelter, while the site of the W.T. station atop Stovolds Hill can be identified by a surviving hut. The administrative number 1 site still displays the solid angular bulk of its headquarters block, along with the airfield's control tower this must have been the most substantial structure built. The block is now used by a farmer as a sheep pen. Perhaps best preserved is the aerodrome's sewage works site number 10 which does not appear to have altered at all since its construction. When examined in 1988, an overturned sign was found to be the original Air Ministry notice forbidding entry.

On the opposite side of the aerodrome, a second contraction came in the mid-1960s when a number of dispersal areas were ripped up in order to return more land to farming. At Tickner Farm, (formerly Brickyard Farm), a cluster of war-time hutting still serves for general storage purposes, albeit the structures have been added to and were moved from other sites to their present resting place. It was in this corner of the aerodrome too that the last blister hangar remained until 1988. When a civil avionics company leased the land in 1988, however, the blister had to go to make way for a new hangar and the huts too appear to have now outlived their usefulness. On the rise only a few yards away the remains of one of the four Bofors gun sites can be seen, the crew hut, shelter, toilet and gun-post all surviving but in various states of dereliction. An almost identical site, but with the crew hut still in use by a farmer, still stands by Lakers Green, not far from the Compasses Gate. A little further to the east of the Tickner Farm Bofors site, a public footpath passes by a dense clump of brambles which hides the top of the underground battle headquarters, access still being possible via a ladder to the dank and semi-flooded interior. Throughout this corner of the former aerodrome, small shelters and huts are to be discovered in the hedgerows and trees of farmers' fields, often displaying evidence of use as 'dens' by small boys of the locality. It should be noted, however, that while public footpaths lead through or past the communal, W.T., underground battle headquarters and sick quarters sites, all other areas are on private property and would-be explorers should first obtain the landowners' permission. Shooting parties add to the potential hazards!

On the airfield itself, the march of time and technological progress gradually eats away at the reminders of the aerodrome's origins. Until British Aerospace succeeded in purchasing the freehold of the aerodrome in 1980, little improvement was possible under the terms of the government's lease. It is nethertheless a sad fact of life that for the aerodrome to survive, its facilities have to keep pace with the demands of commercial success. It is no use trying to attract high calibre staff if their workplace is to be a barely improved 1940s nissen hut and so the 1980s have seen a programme of modernisation which has led to the demolition of many war-time buildings. This said, today's visitor to Dunsfold can still see a great deal of evidence of the aerodrome's history.

From the main gate, the road dropping down to the perimeter track is the old A281 Guildford to Horsham route which used to extend across the airfield site to what is now the Compasses gate. Turning left and proceeding clockwise around the perimeter track, the gun butts are still to be found on the left before crossing the main runway and the first of the disused runways can be seen branching off from the active one. Next come the concrete tracks leading into what were the bomb storage bays, followed closely by the first of the dispersal sites where 180 Squadron's Mitchells once stood. Little of this has changed, although the blister hangars have gone, and it is possible to spot shelters and small arms ammunition stores beyond the modern squash court block. The long low buildings which were once 180's radar and radio workshops are now the home of the aerodrome's Sports and Social Club. Close by is the distinctive shape of Primemeads Farm, often to be spotted in the background of photographs of the aerodrome. It lies beside the road from the perimeter track to the Compasses gate and as such is the other end of the former route of the A281. Primemeads, a fine 17th century building, was for many years the designated home of the aerodrome's Chief Test Pilots of the 1950s and 1960s before it passed first to the aerodrome manager and then to its present occupant, the Secretary of the Sports and Social Club.

Past the Compasses gate and more dispersals are clustered alongside the Wey and Arun canal, extending past the threshold of the other disused runway. From here, the Dutchmen of 320 Squadron fought their war, although the second complex of their dispersals has now given way to the new hangar development of the DH Group by Tickner Farm and one is more likely to see a BAe 125 executive jet parked here today, a pale shadow of the purposeful Mustangs, Mitchells, Typhoons, Tempests and Spitfires which once graced the site.

Continuing, the radar and radio huts of 98 Squadron remain, as does Broadmead Cottage, 98's former flight offices where Wing Commander Paul once finalised the details of the squadron's D-Day operations and from where Wing Commander George Hamer led the harrowing Arnhem raids. Today, after many years abuse as a practice base for the aerodrome's fire service, this historic and once fine old cottage is in a dangerous condition and its future looks bleak. Alongside the house, another road leads to the former Broadmeads gate, now closed except for use in emergencies and on air show days. By the gate, one of the two original fuel farms built by the Canadians still fed the bowsers servicing the aerodrome's Harriers until redevelopment in 1991.

Rounding the southern extremity of the perimeter track, the other end of the main runway is crossed and the present day flight line is then found on the right on a resurfaced portion of the eastern end of the disused short runway, leading to the modern control tower in the centre of the airfield. The engine test bays on the left also use war-time hardstandings, close by the Honey Mead gate.

On completing a tour of the perimeter track one finally reaches the main technical site where now only very few nissen and maycrete structures are still to be found, now mostly used only for storage purposes. Of the two T2 hangars, one remains largely in its original form, albeit extended, while the other has been replaced by a more modern structure, but in the same general style. While British Aerospace's three-bay production hangars now crowd the space between the T2 sites, room has still been left for the war-time control tower, also extended and now used as pilots' offices. Still standing in front of the old tower is the commemorative plinth recording the construction of the aerodrome, maintained by British Aerospace. Unfortunately, the plinth is very much on the 'active' side of the aerodrome which itself is governed by the Official Secrets Act. Public access to the memorial is therefore not possible.

Chapter Twenty
We Shall Return

The latter half of the 1980s has seen an upsurge in the activities of the associations formed for wartime comrades in arms. Men and women who were in their early twenties during the war have all now reached retirement age and with the consequent increase in their leisure time, these veterans are now seeking to renew old friendships and revive memories from those testing years. Plans have also turned to revisiting airfields, where such remain, and here the Dunsfold men have always been given a warm welcome by British Aerospace. As present aerodrome manager, Roy Britain, explains. "This is our way of saying we haven't forgotten what the services did during the war, and we thank them for it."

First off the mark had been the well organised Dutch 320 Squadron Association, led by Hans van der Kop who had been Commander Burgerhout's navigator at Dunsfold in 1944. Post war, van der Kop had remained in the Royal Dutch Naval Air Service and had qualified as a pilot. Eventually he went on to command 320 Squadron in the 1960's, overseeing their conversion to Lockheed Neptune aircraft for maritime reconnaissance duties. Hans van der Kop had already produced a highly readable account of his wartime adventures,* in which he detailed his operations from Dunsfold.

On 9th July, 1987, as leader of the 320 Squadron Association, van der Kop led a group back to Dunsfold in style, thanks to the generosity of Admiral Sir Raymond Lygo, then Chief Executive of British Aerospace. Lygo, another former naval flyer, had known van der Kop for some years and provided a BAe 146 airliner to ferry the Dutch in from Valkenburg in Holland. In addition to touring the aerodrome, the Association also attended a special service in their honour at Dunsfold Church where they presented a commemorative plaque and their squadron colours to the Vicar, the Reverend Bryan Paradise.

Next to visit was a small group of six of the Canadian sappers who had built the aerodrome. While touring England on holiday, they called at the aerodrome gates in September 1987 and were permitted onto the airfield to inspect the commemorative plinth,

*See 'The Flying Dutchman', published by Patrick Stephens Ltd. 1985.

Members of 320 Sqn. RDNAS Association return to Dunsfold in July 1987. Hans van der Kop is on the extreme left. (BAe.)

still standing, which records their efforts in 1942, forty-five years earlier.

The next year, on 26th June, 1988, former RAF personnel returned for a reunion with the 137/139 Wings All Ranks Association.

Made up predominantly of the Mitchell ground crews of 98 and 180 Squadrons, a pre-meeting was held at their favourite 'watering-hole' at the nearby 'Leathern Bottle' pub, before continuing on to the aerodrome. A coach tour round the old wartime dispersals provoked many a memory, the only difficulty being in persuading the veterans back on to the coach for the next stage of the tour. Close to the old 98 Squadron dispersals lay the wreckage of Mitchell B-Beer, only recently recovered from its 1944 resting place. Excitement reached a peak as the former crews scrambled among the sharp edged debris, several eye witnesses to the tragic crash being present.

Former Leading Aircraftsman Reg Day's account of the visit, printed in the Association's newsletter, gives an idea of the emotions felt.

September 1987. Former Canadian Sappers Roy Soldiuk, Bun Hudgson, Sven Edbom, James Gilchrist, Jack Gray and Cal Haywood return. (BAe.)

Home at Last

This was the big one. The Mitchell men were home again, back to the airfield where we grew up, in many senses of the word.

For me, a double occasion, as only a week previous I had been given a name, address and 'phone number of ex-LAC Fred Halsey, with whom I had served on 'A' Flight, 98 Sqdn. We met up at Cardington in April 1942 and stayed with 'A' Flight through all the moves until July 1946.

The information had come via Paul McCue, the Dunsfold historian, from correspondence with Wg. Cdr. Paul, a previous C.O. of 98 Sqdn. Anyhow, I decided to try the number given. When the 'phone was answered I just stated his number, name and rank. There was a stutter, stammer, gasp and momentary silence; eventually a "Yes". I would have loved to have been at the other end of the line at that instant. I then realised it was indeed Fred, told him who I was and then we were away for about half an hour or so. Towards the end of our natter I told him of our Association and that we were going back 'home' for a reunion, gave him all the gen. and Bill's address and hoped to see him if he decided to come along.

The journey from Guildford was a bit nostalgic picking out the odd bit that jogged a memory or two and as the journey got longer, wondering how the heck we used to cycle this bit in all winds and weathers at least once a week (must have been worth it!).

The Leathern Bottle Pub seemed to be having a reunion of its own when we arrived there. Lots of faces known to one another and lots of introductions - even local people wanting to know what we were all about.

After grabbing a pint, I started to look around and spotted Fred Halsey through the window. He hadn't changed a bit to me, although he said he didn't recognise who I was at first (even I don't recognise myself now). We had time for a few stories before being mustered into a convey to get to Dunsfold. Shades of 314 Supply and Transport Column off to Old Sarum. Funny thing was that the car I came in was driven by Jock Adams, who was the Despatch rider of 314 STC, on that journey in 1944 - I dared him take the lead just in case we landed up at Tilbury!

On the road up to the camp I was trying to place where the barrier used to be and the entrance to the communal site, which went off to the right up that lane somewhere. Going through the main gate, my only thought was the pain in my arm, for this was where the Station's Sick Quarters used to be and where the jabs were punched in regularly. I couldn't say that anything was as I remembered it, even the old control tower seemed to be crowded over.

The coach run round the peritrack was the high point. As we left the main building area, the old familiar picture opened out. 180 and 320 dispersals, the Compasses Road, then the old radar/radio hut still looking the same.

I wasn't quite prepared to see what had been placed on the side of the hut. Although I knew that some remains had been found, I never expected to be able to see, let alone touch them. That heap of scrap metal I knew immediately had to be our old B-Beer of A Flight which landed with a 500lb bomb hung up. On touch down it dropped off, blowing the kite to pieces and killing the crew and Flight Sergeant Tubby Jones who was over by the hangers. That was September 8th, 1944 and I remembered the crew. My idea of sifting over the remains was to try to find a bit of the number. I did succeed in finding the bottom of the red B of the nose panel. It was a very funny feeling for Fred and I to think that we must have sat in, and worked on, that same aircraft all those years ago.

We were now on home ground - 98's dispersals. There was our headquarters, 'Rose Cottage', still standing, although not quite as I remembered it as it was overgrown and the dispersals for A Flights' Mitchells were long gone. I hope that it is left as a memorial. Some of those present may have puzzled why I ran off after 'Rose Cottage'. No, I wasn't going for a call of nature, I had noticed something on the other side of the peritrack. Still there as I remembered, 'my' dispersal, where D-Dog and I spent 1943/44 together. I half expected to find her there waiting to be D.I.'ed and run up.

It was a wonderful day and over much too soon. Wherever the next reunion may be and whatever we may do, it can never be the same as the time that the Mitchell men came home to Dunsfold.

Accompanying the Association's members was also Derek Porter, who had lived near to the aerodrome during the war and witnessed much of the drama of those years. Derek had also been privileged to attend the aerodrome's official opening as his father had been the Air Ministry's clerk of works on the site. Taking up the exact same position where he had stood in front of the control tower 46 years before, he thought of the many incidents which the aerodrome had indelibly stamped in his memory (see Chapters 4, 7 and 11).

On 8th November, 1988, 320 Squadron again returned to Dunsfold, but this time in modern form. At midday, a Beech Super King Air of the Royal Dutch Navy dropped out of an overcast sky, bringing five officers and two ensigns of the present day 320 Squadron, keen to see both the Harrier and their squadron's former base.

The author, Paul McCue, had been invited along to give a brief history of the aerodrome and in particular 320 Squadron's part in it, while Bill Bedford, former Chief Test Pilot, returned to give his highly entertaining account of Harrier development and test flying. Over lunch, which preceded a tour of the production hangers, it emerged that one of the senior pilots present (320 currently fly Lockheed P-3 Orion aircraft), had joined the squadron when Hans van der Kop was still commanding officer, thus just maintaining a link back to the wartime days of 320 Squadron at Dunsfold.

Exactly three weeks later, Dunsfold was again busy playing host. 37 members and wives of the Medium Bomber Association toured the airfield and Harrier production lines, among the former aircrew being many of Dunsfold's well-known Mitchell pilots such as Squadron Leader Leven and no less than two squadron commanders, Wing Commander John Castle of 180 and Wing Commander George Hamer of 98.

In 1989 came the turn of the Mustang men. The 39 (Recce.) Wing RCAF Association organised a grand tour to mark the 45th anniversary of their move to the continent. First stop on 3rd June before crossing to France, Belgium and Holland, was Dunsfold. No less than 96 veterans and their wives attended a church service at Dunsfold, donating a commemorative altar frontal to Reverend Bryan Paradise. On arrival at the aerodrome, they were greeted by the sight of the Canadian flag, raised by their hosts British Aerospace and joining the Association's own RCAF flag which travelled with the Canadians. One proud former airman was looking forward to having his photograph taken alongside the plinth recording the aerodrome's opening in 1942. As Russ Bone stood smartly to attention for the photographer he recounted how, all those years ago, he had been in the RCAF honour guard when the plinth was unveiled by General McNaughton.

To complete the visits, 5th June, 1990 saw 49 members and wives of the Canadian branch of the Medium Bomber Association call at the aerodrome, as part of their own European tour. Led by Dr. Hank Hastings, former 98 Squadron navigator to Joe Knowlton's crew, the group included many of the Canadian aircrew who have featured in previous chapters, including Frank Morgan (who had already made one return visit to Dunsfold), late of Major Gronmark's 180 Squadron crew and Lorne MacFarlane, also of 180 Squadron. No less than three former pilots had taken part in the same operation and witnessed the tragic crash of 'B-Beer' in September 1944.

With this last Canadian visit, representatives of all of today's existing associations have returned to their war-time haunt to pay their respects.

Nearly half a century seperates these two photographs. Above, 'Grumpy' 'B' of 98 Squadron receives its 101st operation symbol. FL176 went on to complete 125 bombing sorties, the 2 Group record, which is why the Mitchell at the IWM collection at Duxford is painted as 'Grumpy'. In April 1990, former 139 Wing groundcrew paid 'Grumpy' a visit, below.

Chapter Twenty-one

In Memoriam

Throughout its existence, Dunsfold's flying operations have inevitably led to loss of life, aviation holding its fair share of risk, even in peace-time. During the war years these losses were considerable as the aerodrome's squadrons continued to take the fight to the enemy.

For those who died, either on the aerodrome or in the vicinity, there was the option of either a home town burial (if this were in the British Isles) or interment in the Brookwood Military Cemetery, only some 14 miles away. For Commonwealth and other crews from overseas, Brookwood was normally the only option. Very occasionally, as already detailed in the preceeding chapters, burials took place in nearby villages where a local link existed.

For many aircrew however, the end came either over enemy territory or the channel and in many such cases, no trace has ever been found of the missing fliers. For these men with no known resting place, the Air Forces Memorial exists at Runnymeade in Surrey and lists over 20,000 RAF and Commonwealth air forces airmen missing in action. Amongst these are recorded those who took off from Dunsfold, never to be heard of again.

Only one last act of remembrance is now awaited, in time for 1992 when the aerodrome will celebrate its 50th birthday. In contrast to many other historic aerodromes, Dunsfold still has no memorial of its own to the sacrifices made by its flyers. To right this wrong, a Dunsfold Memorial Fund is already in existence and in the not too distant future some form of tangible memorial, sited for access by the public, will record the aerodrome's still little known contribution to the aviation history of this country.

RCAF/RAF DUNSFOLD 1942-1946
FLYING UNITS:

400 Squadron RCAF (Mustangs) (Mosquitos)
Dec.'42 (det. flight), Feb. '43 - July '43, Dec. '43 - Feb. '44 (det. flight, Mosquitos)
414 Squadron RCAF (Mustangs)
Dec. '42 - April '43, June '43 - July '43
430 Squadron RCAF (Tomahawks, Mustangs)
Jan. '43 - July '43
231 Squadron RAF (Mustangs)
July '43
180 Squadron RAF (Mitchells)
Aug. '43 - Oct. '44
98 Squadron RAF (Mitchells)
Aug. '43 - Oct. '44
320 Squadron RDNAS (Mitchells)
Feb. '44 - Oct. '44
83 GSU / 83 GDC RAF (Typhoons, Tempests, Spitfires)
Jan. '45 (Flying Training Wing), Feb. '45 - Oct. '45
667 Squadron RAF (Oxfords)
Dec. '45 Feb. '46

STATION COMMANDERS
5.12.42 - 31.12.42 Wing Commander R. F. Begg (RCAF).
1.1.43 - 18.1.43 Wing Commander E. H. G. Moncrieff AFC (RCAF).
19.1.43 - 10.11.43 Wing Commander H. J. Burden DSO DFC (RCAF).
11.11.43 - 21.11.43 Group Captain L. W. Cannon (RAF).
22.11.43 - 30.6.44 Group Captain L. Dunlap CBE (RCAF).
1.7.44 - 1.9.44 Squadron Leader J. J. Secter (RAF).
2.9.44 - 5.2.45 Squadron Leader A. G. Sudworth (RAF).
6.2.45 - 28.5.45 Squadron Leader G. Hampson (RAF).
7.6.45 - 27.6.46 Wing Commander H. J. L. Hallowes DFC DFM (RAF).

Appendix B

Ditching report of aircraft 'H' FR180 18th March, 1944

Captain: Sgt H. J. Ot
Navv/B: Sgt. H. F. Gans
WOP/AG: Cpl. I. Posthumus
AG: Sgt. J. J. C. Lub

Captain's Report

I was flying aircraft 'H' in position 5 of the leading box. After releasing my bombs I executed a left turn with the formation. Just as I started to weave with the box I received hits in my port engine and belly turret, slightly wounding my WOP/AG. This was at 13.02 hrs. Immediately afterwards the starboard engine and wing were hit and my navigator was slightly wounded. By this time the port engine was on fire and I observed pieces, approximately six inches long, flying off it. The hydraulic system was punctured and with the aircraft in the condition I have described, I was forced to fall out of formation. I feathered the port engine and by this means extinguished the fire. I could scarsely keep the aircraft under control as it was shuddering so badly. The ailerons and rudder were unserviceable and the elevator was only movable through 5°. There was a square hole of about eighteen inches in the floor on the starboard side of the bomb aimer's compartment and the perspex was completely smashed. All my instruments were also unserviceable. I then told the WOP/AG and AG to stand by to bale out. Very shortly afterwards, when still trying to make for the Channel, the starboard engine spluttered, picked up, and then went dead. To maintain height was impossible. At this time we were at approximately 8,000 feet and still above the French mainland. I decided to try and ditch the aircraft and informed my crew of this decision with which they were in full agreement. During this time I was waiting for another aircraft to cease calling 'Mayday' and I was losing height rapidly. The coast was crossed at approximately 3,000 feet with the aircraft still falling fast. I succeeded then in calling 'Mayday' once at approximately 1,000 feet. After this I jettisoned the escape hatch and tried to lower my flaps, which I found to be totally inserviceable. Immediately following this the aircraft hit the water at a speed of 160-170 mph at 13.10 hrs. By exerting all my strength at the last moment I managed to pull up the nose of the aircraft so that we hit the water with the bomb door part of the fuselage. The aircraft bounced twice off the water before finally settling with the escape hatch level with the surface.

As a result of the first bounce my navigator and I received severe knocks on our foreheads, although I was still strapped in. The navigator, in a very dazed condition, was first out of the aircraft. I followed him and found the WOP/AG already in the water. He reported that the AG could not get out. At the same time I noticed that the navigator was unable to release the dinghy so I went down to get it ordering him to help the other gunner. However, the latter had released himself by this time. After inflating the dinghy I returned to the cockpit for the emergency kit but the cockpit was completely submerged. I went back to the dinghy, stood off about 20 yards from the aircraft and picked up the WOP/AG. The navigator stood dazed on the wing of the sinking aircraft but jumped at the last moment. I pulled him aboard and then the AG. The time the aircraft was afloat after touching down was approximately two minutes. It then sank, starboard wing first. After my crew was in the dinghy I bandaged the leg of my WOP/AG and the wrist of my navigator. About ten minutes later we were spotted by two Spitfires which stayed with us for thirty minutes. Forty five minutes later six other Spitfires found our dinghy and stayed with us until we were picked up by a Sea Otter at 15.15 hrs. The Sea Otter could not take off with us and set off to taxi back. At 19.30 hrs. an Air Sea Rescue launch took us aboard and landed us at Dover at 21.00 hrs.

(Signed)

H. J. Ot

Ditching Report of Aircraft 'M' FR177 18th March, 1944

Captain: F/L H. J. Voorspuy
Nav/B: Sgt. J. Vink
WOP/AG: K. van Nouhuis
AG: Cpl. N. Engelsma

Captain's Report:

I was flying No 4 in the leading box of six aircraft. After having attacked one of the *Noball* targets we were on our way out, height 1,000 feet, when we received two close bursts of heavy flak, the first one near the nose, the second one under the starboard engine. Our position at that moment was two miles south-west of Abbeville. The RPM of the starboard engine went up to 2,700. I closed my throttle and pitch immediately and tried to feather the engine, but that proved to be impossible. I lost a lot of oil. The engine kept going for another three minutes when my oil pressure dropped to 0. I switched everything off then, the engine kept on making approximately 1,500 RPM. After the hit my wheels came down and flaps went down about 25°. I was still flying at 1,000 feet and started losing height at 200 feet per minute - IAS 145. I called 'MAYDAY' one minute after the hit and was told by the controller to steer 320°. After my starboard engine was completely unserviceable I started losing height at 400 feet per minute - IAS 130. We crossed the French coast at position 2 miles south of Cayeux, height 5,700 feet. When I crossed the coast I received a tremendous amount of light flak but no hits were observed. (After I had fallen out of the box at 11,000 feet I had, for approximately one minute, heavy inaccurate flak). I kept on transmitting over the VHF on Channel B and was again told to steer 320°. When I was down to 600 feet I gave a transmission and told the controller that I was going to ditch. I turned into wind then but when I was about 30° off the wind direction I saw I was flying along the swell. I stopped turning then and landed the aircraft on the water at 98 MPH IAS.

The tail hit the water first and the aircraft broke off near the tailplane. When the aircraft was lying on the water the nose went down and the tail came out of the water at an angle of approximately 30°. My navigator had opened the hatch at 100 feet. When the aircraft came to rest my navigator pulled the inside handle for the dinghy release. I got out of the aircraft immediately and climbed on the wing. The dinghy had not come out so I got it out and opened the bottle after which the dinghy inflated. I heared my WOP/AG shout for help so got into the dinghy and went to the tail where I saw him hanging onto the aircraft with the complaint that he had cramp. I got him in the dinghy easily. My navigator dived for the emergency packets and dinghies. By that time the navigator's compartment was full with water coming in through the nose and upper hatch. He threw one dinghy and parachute bag out but these were lost. He got out of the aircraft again and jumped from the wing into the water and swam to the dinghy where I helped him in. My air gunner was lying in the water near the starboard wing tip. He had taken his boots off as soon as he got into the water, but was unable to inflate his Mae West. However, he was able to float out and after some rowing trouble with the dinghy we got him in with some difficulty. As soon as I had got my WOP/AG into the dinghy I saw two Spitfires overhead. The aircraft floated for five minutes after which it went slowly down. The Spitfires stayed with us all the time and we were picked up by a Walrus of the Air Sea Rescue Service after sixty-five minutes. Time of ditching: 13.14 hrs.

Position of Ditching: 50°21' north - 00° 45' east.

Note:

After I was hit my WOP/AG got in the under turret and switched the IFF on emergency. My AG got the camera out of the mounting and closed the camera hatch. He had no time to throw the camera behind the armour plate door, with the result that it was lying loose in the aircraft and nearly hit my WOP/AG in the landing! Pretty dangerous!

I as well like to point out that we all have the greatest admiration of the efficiency and helpfulness of the Air Sea Rescue Service.

(Signed)

H. J. Voorspuy

An Ode to the First Harrier

By A. W. (Bill) Bedford

Chief Test pilot HSA Dunsfold 1956-1967

Here lieth the body of Hawker Harrier XV**276**
Who first 'lifted off' from Dunsfold on August 1966,
Seven years she proudly bore the brunt
of much of the exacting development,
Her latter years with Pegasus Eleven
Put out to hay as prelude to Heaven.

*

On 9th April '73, neighbour Susan rang excitedly,
"You may think I'm a nut but I've had a dream;
A Harrier will crash it would certainly seem;
Issue an edict now for thorough inspection
to try and reverse my serious reflection.
Two premonitions I had in years gone by
and both came true - I do not lie.
In '53 it was a disaster to my boyfriend,
Ten years later the Paris crash was almost your end."

*

Susan dear, your premonition much respected
But rest assured our planes are well inspected,
Will pass your word to the engineers
But they will say, "Have no fears".

*

The following day the premonition came true
And a Harrier crashed out of the blue.
Swiss test pilot Stauffer ejected without a flaw
to become, Martin Baker ejector number three thousand,
Four hundred and sixty four!

*

To he, as pilot of this aircraft on its maiden flight,
The tangled wreckage was indeed a sorry sight,
Like a broken body with limbs torn off,
All scattered and battered and dead,
Like the loss of an old friend;
Leaving one's heart sad and heavy like lead;
Quiet for ever, that exciting personality,
In Colling's Farm, buried for eternity,
Once vibrant with sparkling performance and technology,
But now a useless scrap hunk of metalogy.

*

With the pathetic crumpled tail end, silhouetted
against the setting sun,
It looked like a tombstone of a man
whose days are done.

*

Thursday April 11th telephone rings....
"This is Dunsfold **276**!!, Susan Fairclough speaking;
Bill, I'm sorry to hear that my premonition came true."

Index of Military Personnel

Index of Civilians

Other titles from
Air Research Publications

The Whitley Boys
4 Group bomber operations 1939-1940.
A graffic and detailed account of offensive operations in the first
year of WWII as experienced by a Whitley gunner. Includes
detailed descriptions of raids and complete loss / casualty list.
224 pages ISBN 1 871187 11 7 Price £11.95

Blitzed! The Battle of France May-June 1940
The struggle to halt the German invasion of Europe. Includes
RAF and Luftwaffe loss listings.
256 pages ISBN 1 871187 07 9 Price £15.95

Battle over the Third Reich
A photograghic account of the battle for air supremacy over
Germany as seen by the Luftwaffe.
184 pages ISBN 1 871187 10 9 Price £17.95

The Me262 Combat Diary
The most detailed combat history of the German jet fighter ever
published. Includes extensive appendices and tables.
256 pages ISBN 1 871187 08 7 Price £15.95

Spitfire Squadron
No. 19 Squadron at war 1939-1941
Including a reprint of the classic book 'Spitfire!'
192 pages ISBN 1 871187 09 5 Price £14.95

Hurricane Squadron
No. 87 Squadron at war 1939-1941
An extensively illustrated history of the squadron.
48 pages ISBN 1 871187 00 1 Price £5.95